AS I WALKED

One Man's Quest for Sexual and Spiritual Identity

The almighty Hand can never be clearly seen while any human help is sought for or is in sight. We must turn absolutely away from all else if we are to turn fully unto the living God.

George Muller

To [illegible]
God bless you
"As you walk"
Geoff - MR P.

I lift up my eyes to the mountains — where does my help come from?
My help comes from the Lord, the Maker of heaven and earth.

Psalm 121:1-2 NIV

PUBLISHED BY
OUR WRITTEN LIVES, LLC

Our Written Lives provides publishing services to authors in various educational, religious, and human service organizations.
For information, visit www.OurWrittenLives.com.

Library of Congress Cataloging-in-Publication Data
Van Heerden, Juliet

As I Walked: One Man's Quest for Sexual and Spiritual Identity
Library of Congress Control Number: 2021901024
ISBN: 978-1-942923-46-6 (paperback)

All pen and ink art is Geoff Pennock's original work.

Cover Design by Robert Mason

Interior Design by Our Written Lives, LLC

Author Photo by HerculesImages.com

DEDICATION

To the grace and glory of God, who makes the impossible possible. Also, to my beautiful, precious wife and dearest friend whose spirituality and encouragement helped to save me from eternal death.

Love, Mr. P

To Jesus, the Author and Finisher of my faith. And to My Honey, who coached and prayed this project through and fended for himself when I went into "writing mode."

Juliet

In memory of our dear friend, Walter, for loving like Jesus and never being afraid of inviting sinners to sit around his table.

PREFACE

Nobody tells you how to get out of the maze, yet they condemn you for being stuck in the maze. Jesus comes to show you the way out. Sometimes He speaks directly, sometimes in a dream, or through a passage of scripture. Sometimes He will send another human who has been there—someone who memorized every twisted turn of the maze along their own broken way to victory. You know there is hope when that courageous someone takes you by the hand and walks with you out of your valley and into the light. In this book, that courageous person is Mr. P (with a little help from his wife, her daughter, and their son-in-law).

We call them "The P's," my sister and I, partly because they were found between "O" and "Q" in the days of phone books, but mostly because they are two "peas" in a pod. They are in love and inseparable—even after 29 years of marriage. My long-ago journal starts their story this way:

1990

They ***love*** *each other?*

Our eyes lock across the plank table in a cozy Amish restaurant, four brows forming question marks as Sis and I scrutinize our soon-to-be stepfather, Geoff Pennock, or Mr. P as our mother fondly calls him.

How or when *this* transpired, my undergrad brain cannot grasp. I knew they'd been corresponding, but how could a few foreign-postmarked letters totally transform our existence?

Now, here he is in the flesh—good-looking in a European-sort-of-way, wrapping our mother in love so thick there is barely room for four of us in the wooden booth. I feel a little nauseated, a little curious, and a little envious.

Who doesn't want their mom to be happy? But whose mom falls in love with a Brit who lives in Switzerland? Who is this guy anyway?

1991

They love each other.

With trembling hands, I light white candles in an ancient alpine church. Mother's shoulders peek from the sleeves of her pale blue dress, her honey eyes dancing at him as they stand facing the preacher. They say their vows. They sing together. They kiss—for a long time. Sis and I watch it all with wonder. On this day, our mother becomes "Mrs. P."

1992

He loves her. He'll be lost without her.

I plead with God as Mr. P's cries echo off the mountain pass.

"Aiuto! Aiuto! Help me!" he screams.

Paralyzed, I lay pinned to the asphalt, my pelvis severely fractured. Smoke escapes our overturned car where Mother's seatbelt holds her hostage.

September 17, 1992 is my family's landmark date. That day both broke us and made us. We have our own dating system for historical family events. Everything takes place B.A. (Before the

Accident) or A.A. (After the Accident). The accident changed us all, especially The P's.

I'm Juliet, daughter of Mrs. P. She's also known as Mom, by my sister Annie and me, or as Susan, by the rest of her world. It's difficult to remember when she wasn't a "P."

Although he is not my father, Geoff Pennock's love for my mother through their nearly thirty years together has profoundly impacted my life, reshaping my view of men and marriage. Everyone has a spiritual journey. Some are destined to be shared. Mr. P's story, a modern Jacob-wrestles-with-the-angel tale deserves an audience. Though he, like Jacob, still walks with a limp, Mr. P did not let go of God until he received his blessing. Her name is Susan.

May God bless you, P's, for humbly allowing me into your sacred space. Vulnerability is not for the faint of heart. Thank you for sacrificing your privacy on the altar of Revelation 12:11. I am so very proud of you both for allowing faith to be your victory.

JULIET VAN HEERDEN

CONTENTS

Ticino, Switzerland

Chapter 1

THE ACCIDENT

Only those who have hurt much can love much.
Mother Teresa of Calcutta

One person's memoir cannot be written in isolation when we live our lives in community. It is the summer of 2019. After years of praying about this book, I am finally crafting it with The P's. I'm visiting their cozy two-story New England-style cottage. Mom and I sip lavender tea from mismatched mugs at their round wooden table and rehash "The Accident." Mr. P sits quietly in his wingback chair, feet elevated on a leather Moroccan pouf. Like JFK's assassination or 9/11, we each have our own memories, our own versions of 9/17/92.

"I grabbed my favorite worship book to read in the car," Mom begins. "I remember whispering goodbye to your sister. Annie was exhausted after Venice."

I've heard my mother tell this part before. I can almost repeat it word for word.

"We dragged your luggage into the apartment elevator. At the bottom, we stepped out into crisp September morning air. I anticipated autumn foliage on the way to Zürich airport," she continues.

"I remember how heavy my suitcase was," I blurt. "That thing could have killed someone."

"It was such a lovely holiday," Mom reminisces. "Hiking the Alps, relaxing on the French Riviera, swimming in the Mediterranean, shopping for handmade treasures in quaint villages." She sips her tea, holding it in her mouth for a moment. "Remember our picnic in the Valle Verzasca? The river so clear and cold?"

"One of my favorite days, for sure. Those two weeks blurred by. I wasn't ready to return to America."

"You were tired that morning," Mom says. "That's why you laid down on the back seat to rest."

"I felt yucky before we even started the three-and-a-half-hour trip. Food poisoning and the previous day's forever-train ride from Venice nearly did me in. What do you remember about the actual impact of the accident, Mom?"

"I remember praying silently before beginning to read aloud. Immediately, I felt something bump the back of our car. I glanced up to see us to see us careening toward a huge metal guardrail."

"That's when you screamed, 'Jesus, no!' in that voice that makes the hair on my arms stand up."

"The car began spinning. That is the last thing I remember." My sixty-nine-year-old mother's high blonde ponytail swishes side-to-side as if to shake the thought away.

"What about you, Mr. P?" I ask. "What do *you* recall? I've never heard your version. I just remember you screaming, 'Aiuto! Aiuuuuuto!' after I woke up on the highway."

Mr. P sets his Yorkshire Dales mug on the floor. Thirty seconds pass before he speaks. Then his words flow, punctuated by Italian-style hand gestures.

"A vehicle came from the on-ramp and hit my Renault on the back-left bumper. We crashed into the guardrail. Instantly, I felt as if I were inside a tumble dryer. My head kept banging Susan's as our hatchback turned over and over and over. It landed on the highway upside down, then slid several feet with your mother's head dragging on the tarmac. Everything eventually stopped moving."

He turns toward me. "That's when I realized you had been thrown out the back with the luggage. Somehow, I managed to get my door open. *My* only visible injury was a scratch on my knee, but the thought of my wife being dead scarred me for life."

Even now, twenty-eight years later, his light blue eyes fill with tears as he verbalizes his worst fear. "I could not get a pulse as she slumped there, hanging upside down, her body trapped by the seat belt— her head and arm outside the car, bleeding."

I reach for Mom's hand across the table as Mr. P clears his throat and continues. "My head was dizzy, and I felt nearly out of my mind with shock. After waiting until I was fifty years old for God to heal my tortured brain and give me a wife, I could not fathom how a funeral for my *Principessa* fit into His plan."

Mr. P shakes his head, sitting silently for a moment. His next words shock me as he raises both hands in a rude gesture reenacting his response that day, "I stood in the middle of the highway, shrieking unprintable profanities at the sky."

"If my precious wife was dead, I didn't care *what* I said to God. My heavenly Friend has forgiven my blasphemy, but He and I spent years working through my anger at Him for allowing that tragedy."

At seventy-eight years old, Mr. P's memory remains sharp, even after several mini strokes in recent years. He leans forward in his chair. "I screamed for help in Italian, 'Aiuto!' No one came. Half a dozen cars stopped, but no one got out. Probably because our car was smoking. That's when the towering man appeared. He understood everything. *And* he had a knife.

"'I will cut your wife free,' the stranger spoke with urgency. 'We must move them because the car is going to blow up.'

"Do you remember any of this?" Mr. P's eyes catch mine.

I shake my head.

"He severed the seat belt strap and gently pulled Susan from the car. Together we moved you both to the edge of the road. 'Your mother is dead.' I remember saying those words as I held your legs while he lifted your torso. We carefully carried you, but you cried out in pain. The moment we laid you down, the Renault was instantly engulfed in flames. When I turned to thank our helper, he had vanished.

"As a nurse, I knew I should do something, but I just stood there, covered with blood from my wife's dripping head. I thought I'd gone through hell before, but those moments on the highway were worse than any despair I had ever experienced. Had I lost my beautiful bride just one year after our fairytale wedding?"

My mother scoots her chair away from the table and goes to Mr. P. Cradling him against her dress, she rubs the top of his graying head.

"Peedy . . ." Mom's bottom lip pooches out as she affectionately says his nickname. "I wasn't dead. I opened my eyes to see smoke billowing from the car and felt an overwhelming urge to scream. A gentle quiet voice said to my mind, 'Keep talking to Jesus. Stay still. Breathe slowly.' I felt the contrast between cold pavement against my body, and warm liquid flowing from my head down my neck."

She turns toward me. "That's when you asked, 'Mom, *are* you dead?' I was wondering the same about you, JuJu. Even though you said you were okay, I sensed otherwise and began taking slow, deep breaths to stay calm. I worried about you because of your previous accident. Had it only been a year since your awful fall from that barn?"

I nod, silently observing The Ps—listening, trying to remove myself from the painful word picture they are painting. But I am there, lying on the cold, damp asphalt with my mother. Wondering why my legs won't move. Remembering the scarlet scar down the length of my back. Praying my newly healed spine is not re-damaged. The scene is surreal.

Mrs. P returns to the table and pours warmth into my half-empty cup from the spout of her china teapot as my lips form words around my memories. "Suddenly, there was a deafening explosion as the car blew up, literally melting the asphalt on the road. The noise and flames were terrifying. I remember reaching for your hand, Mom, and holding it as the ashes rained on our faces."

"I felt so relieved when the ambulance arrived," Mr. P interjects. "I had worked in hospitals for years, but the scene before me was like a nightmare movie. My poor American princess—lying there on the pavement, having her lovely locks chopped off as the medics prepared to suture her head closed on the spot. I was too nervous to imagine the injuries you both had sustained, yet thankful your faces were undamaged. It was all too much."

"I could feel them cutting chunks of my hair, and sensed they were stitching my head," says my meticulous mother. "Imagine how traumatic it was for me, a lifelong hairdresser, to watch strangers toss bloody blonde wads of my hair onto the pavement." She makes three flicking motions with her wrist as she says, "bloody blond locks," then reaches up to fluff her ponytail.

I inhale the calming scent of lavender from my mug and exhale the words, "I remember Mr. P walking around in circles, waving his arms like a lunatic."

"The ambulance sped us to Bellinzona hospital," Mom continues. "The emergency room staff was memorably kind. After a series of x-rays, you and I were once again placed side-by-side on stretchers and transported to the larger hospital in Lugano. We were given a sixth-floor room on the same ward where Geoff had worked for 12 years! My poor husband would be our nurse, but first he needed to rest. He was totally losing his mind, babbling three languages in bits and pieces and pacing back and forth between our beds when your sister arrived."

"It's true!" Mr. P agrees emphatically. When Annie finally got to Ospedale Civico, I *was* in a state—covered in blood, speaking an incoherent mixture of Italian, French, and English. My colleagues gave me a Valium and put me in a bed, too."

I text my sister to ask what she recalls. Her response makes me queasy.

Sis texts the gory details in spurts. *They gave me a trash bag with your and Mom's clothes. They had cut the clothes off of you. Everything was soaked in blood. Your white canvas shoes were filled with congealed blood. You were wearing a white graphic tee and white jeans. They were covered in blood and other horrific stains, shredded by the asphalt.*

Silence for a moment, then *ding*—another text.

Mom's favorite sweater had been cut off of her and was soaked in blood. Mom's shoes were filled with blood. They gave me your luggage to bring home. I don't remember any other details. I just remember the trauma in the trash bag.

"No wonder you were out of your mind, Mr. P," I say after reading Annie's texts aloud. "That sounds like a lot of blood."

"I'm going out to water the garden," he abruptly announces. "All this talk about the accident has nearly done me 'ead in," he says in his Yorkshire accent. "I think we're done with Chapter 1."

"We are not done," I whisper to Mom as he closes the door.

"Well, I think *he's* done. It's hard for him to think about. That day altered everything in our marriage. We can keep talking if you like."

"Yes, please. I want to understand what things were like for you. I've always known how that day changed me and my life, but because we lived on different continents for so many years afterward, I wasn't able to observe your reality up close. Were you also angry with God?" I ask.

"I still don't understand why God allowed this to happen," my mother sighs as she re-straightens the neat piles of letters and photos covering her table. "I've been in more than ten car accidents in my life, always as a passenger. This one left me in a terrible condition.

"My head was beaten severely because the seat belt became loose upon impact. My frontal lobe received the first impact from the dashboard. Because of the resulting traumatic brain injury, or TBI as they call it, I *couldn't* feel angry with God, even if I wanted to. I couldn't feel anything. For years. My emotions totally flatlined."

"You were definitely different from the spirited mom I grew up with. That's for sure."

"The vibrant, funny, artsy and curious person I was no longer existed after the accident," Mom agrees. "I didn't even know myself. I couldn't relate to anyone on an emotional level. That was especially hard on our new marriage.

"The day after the accident, Mr. P read Psalm 50 verse 15 to me as we waited for you to come back from the surgery for your broken pelvis.

Call upon Me in the day of trouble;
I will deliver you, and you shall glorify Me.

Psalm 50:15 NKJV

"That became my wish—to glorify the God who preserved my life. Like two people drowning in the sea, Mr. P and I clung to Jesus together, our Life Preserver. I may have lost my emotions, but I did not lose my faith. Jesus was and still is my Priest, my Advocate, my Brother in heavenly places and my Best Friend."

"I'm so sorry, Mother. I cannot imagine what it was like for the two of you. All I could think about back then was myself. I had my own anger with God for allowing me to be injured so many times and to break my poor pelvis again!"

I stand up and move to the sofa. "It's a bit chilly this evening."

"We were quite the pair," Mom says as she covers my legs with a fuzzy throw. "I will never forget you with that very strange metal contraption screwed into your hips and sticking out in front of you like a towel bar."

"And I will never forget you silently shaking and puking for days in your hospital bed just a few feet from me. I felt so helpless as I lay on my back with that scaffolding holding my pelvis together. Helpless and afraid for you. I couldn't understand why you didn't talk."

"It *was* scary." Mom grabs a bag of Giant Peruvian Inca Corn, one of our favorite Trader Joe's treats, and starts to munch. "The doctors discovered a blood clot on my brain, as well as a skull fracture and major concussion. That's why I couldn't stop vomiting. May I read to you from one of my old journals? I found it when I was gathering photos and letters to help you write this book."

"Sure, but you'll need to hand me those corn nuts so you can read," I joke, holding out my hand.

"You can have them. I just needed a little snack." Mom hands me the bag and picks up her journal. "I wrote this quite a while after the accident. When Mr. P was working, I spent many hours alone in our apartment, going through medical reports, writing notes, trying to understand myself."

I try not to crunch my corn too loud as Mom begins to read. The first entry is about my sister.

> *Annie visited day after day, waiting for me to speak. I remember her sweet voice and gentle hands washing the blood out of my hair several days after the accident. She told me all that dried blood had turned my hair orange, making it a sticky mess. My Annie has been a comfort and friend to us here.*
>
> *Many days are a blur. Annie also came to the hospital and put curlers in my hair in an effort to help me look human. I had pieces chopped to the scalp on one side and longer pieces on the other side. She says my mind was so confused I asked, "Why did they cut my hair in this style?"*

"For as long as I can remember, you've been all about the hair! I've never seen you look so awful in all my life," I comment. "It was garish."

Mom nods in agreement, "I wish bad hair was the worst thing that happened to me." She continues reading.

> *As doctors came in and out giving reports, I began to comprehend my condition. My spine was fractured at T11 and T12, so I was fitted with a back brace. I had an open skull fracture over the frontal lobe, contusions, and a blood clot in the right part of my brain.*
>
> *My right elbow was pulverized, requiring surgery. And my wrist was also fractured. My right hand was black and blue, swollen to the point of not being functional. The muscles in my hand were damaged, stiff, and extremely sore.*

Mom stops reading and stares at me. I set down the bag of corn.

"I don't know if you realized how bad my head injury was when we were in the hospital. You were highly medicated and strangely silent yourself. My TBI caused seizures that made me vomit for days. One in particular was so severe, I could only pray for God to take me. The seizure lasted for hours, with my legs beating against each other uncontrollably. My knees throbbed the next day."

"Really? I didn't know that, Mother. I've never heard this story before."

"I seriously thought I would die. So did Mr. P. He slept on a small cot between our beds that entire night. Because of the blood clot in my brain, doctors had ordered no drugs. My husband's experience as a registered nurse made it impossible for him to passively watch my indescribable suffering. He made an unprecedented decision to break off the corner of a narcotic. As soon as he gave it to me, I calmed down and went to sleep.

"For years, deep within my head was extreme pressure and pain. The word headache is an understatement for what I experienced. Along with the pain, I had rocking sensations, ringing in my ears, swishing sensations! It was awful!"

Mom reads again from her journal.

My diagnosis included 'epileptic crisis with probable attacks on focus and concentration due to the commotion of the brain.' I was also left with something called 'positional vertigo.' The constant sensation in my head was like Jell-O rocking in a bowl. It is difficult to explain such misery.

Mr. P opens the back door. "Are you two still going?" he asks on his way to the kitchen for a drink of water.

"Yes. Mom is telling me about her seizures."

"Oh, dear!" he exclaims. "That was horrible and scary. I can't bear to think about it!"

I hear his footsteps tromping upstairs toward their bedroom. Mom lowers her voice saying, "Later, I had one of those epileptic spells in my bathtub at home. I went completely under the water! No one was there. It was terrifying. I could have drowned! Thankfully, it didn't last long. I had a firm grip on the side of the tub and pulled myself back up."

"Oh, Mother. I can't imagine . . ."

Mom continues reading.

Nine days after the accident doctors operated on my shattered right elbow. On the day of the operation, I was carefully draped so I couldn't see what they were doing. Anesthesia was not an option because of the clot in my brain. It was too risky. The nurse gave local anesthetic to numb my arm. I felt a bit woozy, but the pain was terrible. I could feel the cutting and the probing for what seemed like hours. After that, I cried a lot. My nerves were shot!

After surgery, my arm hung limp, like a doll arm, the elbow joint held together with wire in a figure eight shape. It remained frozen in one position for months. I was told it would never be 100% the same, but with physical therapy I should eventually regain normal movement.

Mom stops reading, "That was a lie," she says. "I was never again able to earn an income doing hair with my crooked little arm." Then, "I'm almost done. Just a bit more. You will remember this next part."

> *As we improved, sometimes Juliet and I walked the hospital halls together, pretending we were supermodels. Both of us walked a bit cockeyed. We would laugh at one another, then try again to walk normally.*

"I do remember that. I was on crutches and you tried to keep up, but you walked like a robot. Your arms and legs didn't work together."

"That's right," Mom says. "The first therapy I received took place in a large pool, the only place I could walk without excruciating pain; the only place I could move with any semblance of coordination."

"Those six weeks in the hospital felt like eternity," I say as Mr. P joins us.

"The days were very long," Mom agrees. "Broken up only by the kind visits of friends. Geoff, do you remember your former patient, Mrs. Hoffman?"

"I do. She brought my wife roses," Mr. P says as he places one cupped hand on each of my mother's porcelain cheeks in a small gesture of love before sitting again in his favorite chair.

"That's right," Mom recalls. "A bouquet of pink roses for me, and Lindt chocolates for JuJu. Those flowers gave me such joy. It was the kindness of people that helped us survive those long weeks in the hospital."

"That and the many, many boxes of Swiss chocolates they gave us," I tease. "That chocolate was the only perk of having a car accident in Switzerland!"

"Chocolate became my comfort food for years," Mom admits. "I could eat a whole box in one sitting."

"I also remember the day Laura and Dina came and massaged our legs," I recall.

"Yes! That was wonderful. My legs were like pincushions after all the steroid injections!" she exclaims.

"And Walter brought special food for us," I add. "A welcome change from those hospital trays."

"Remember the day Heinz, Connie, and Bronia came with all the children from our wedding?" Mr. P chimes in.

"The children were lovely," smiles Mom. "It's hard to believe they are all grown now." She pauses, glances out the window, then continues. "I especially remember the Sabbath our friend Noami came to visit. She was studying to be a pediatric surgeon. She told us of when she was a newborn, sent home from the hospital to die. Her mother asked the whole church to pray. Noami survived and committed her life to help heal children. Her miracle tale encouraged me. I believed God also allowed us to live for a purpose. After Noami's story, hope filled my heart that I would get well."

We sit in silence, each thinking our own thoughts. Then Mom picks up a piece of paper from one of the piles on the table. "I found a copy of the letter you helped me write to our family back in America," she says. "I think the last couple of paragraphs summarize our experience very well."

> *As I write this, we are still in the hospital. It has been five weeks. Now each day brings improvement. I praise God He saved our lives. We believe angels were working in our behalf on the day of our accident. God's love and Spirit have given us strength to bear the pain and suffering.*
>
> *Geoff has not only been a super husband, but a super nurse. The blessing of God's love has shone through him as he has taken care of both of us.*

> *I praise God for the letters, cards, and flowers, and especially the prayers of friends and family. They are what really brought us through this.*

"That all sounds very nice," Mr. P states. "But I was no hero. The truth is I *hated* seeing you like that. Hated knowing I came out with only a scratch and my wife was damaged beyond repair."

"There is always truth behind the scenes when we write letters to people we love," I reply. "What was your truth, Mrs. P?"

"Must you dig so deep?" she asks. "Sharing these things with the world feels invasive. It's our private life together."

"Yes, but in order to help the reader understand how this tragedy was a direct assault on Mr. P's transformed sexuality, we need to tell the truth about what the accident did to The P's as lovers."

I choose my words carefully because I know I am treading on sacred ground. I know how protective The P's are of their privacy and their marriage. It's a wonder they finally granted me permission to tell Mr. P's story. I've been begging them to allow me to do so for years. I don't want him to die without giving victims of sexual confusion, abuse, and molestation the gift of his powerful testimony.

"Okay," Mom concedes. "I'll read from my journal the bit I left out." She glances sideways at Mr. P. He nods his consent. She sighs and picks up her journal. Mrs. P's voice quivers slightly as she reads.

> *My kind, romantic husband became my caregiver. The incredible love life we experienced during our first year of marriage turned upside down. My physical pain, mental confusion, and lack of emotion due to brain damage left my new husband to cope with me in a professional way. He became my nurse rather than my lover.*

I will exalt you, Lord, for you lifted me out of the depths
and did not let my enemies gloat over me. Lord my God,
I called to you for help and you healed me.
You, Lord, brought me up from the realm of the dead;
you spared me from going down to the pit.

Psalm 30:1-3 NIV

Un tragico sorpasso

Sull'autostrada a Biasca si rovescia e brucia una Renault: due feriti, di cui uno grave

Top: Newspaper clipping of the accident

Bottom: Mr. P with the burned vehicle

Luccombe, Somerset

Chapter 2

LITTLE LAD

Why would we need to experience the
Comforter if our lives are already comfortable?
Francis Chan

Their bedroom is rouge. Rouge walls. Satin and velvet bedding. Rouge and gold drapes. Ornate gold Italian frames exhibit oil paintings and petite family photographs. My eyes devour every detail as Mr. P fiddles with the remote. The P's only television is in this tiny chamber, where the bed fills the room. We lie shoulder to shoulder with Mom in the middle. I rub my bare feet against the velvet as we wait for the DVD to load.

"You will love this!" Mom says. "It's Mr. P's English childhood."

"I used to read Raymond Briggs' children's books to my students." I reach into the bag of Skinny Pop between us. "Well, I couldn't really read *The Snowman* because it's a book with no words, but the kids loved it. *The Snowman* was always one of the first books the children chose from our classroom reading bins. I've never heard of this movie though.

"*Ethel & Earnest* is a true story." Mr. P announces as the soundtrack begins. "It portrays how we really lived during and after World War II."

Eighty-six minutes later, the Skinny Pop is gone. Paul McCartney sings, "In the Blink of an Eye," while the credits roll. Mr. P and I are wiping our eyes with the backs of our hands. Mrs. P uses a monogrammed handkerchief.

"Oh, I loved it, but I hate the ending!" I brush salt off of their velvet comforter. "Why do people have to die? They remind me of you P's. Don't you two leave me. You *must* live until Jesus comes back!"

"It really is fantastically done," Mom agrees. "I wish we could have known one another from the beginning like Earnest and Ethel." She reaches for Mr. P's hand.

"The bits about the war get me thinking," he says.

"Tell me." I prop myself up on pillows, click my blue gel pen and open the composition book I brought along just in case the movie jogged some memories.

Mr. P closes his eyes and speaks quietly, his British accent perhaps a bit more pronounced than usual. "When the boy Raymond must leave his parents and be evacuated to his aunts in Dorset because of the bombing in London, it reminds me of the evacuees *my* parents took in. Two little girls, maybe five or six-years-old came to live with us. They were my sisters before my sisters Jean and Jennifer were born. Loads of British opened their homes to children during the war.

"Recently, I read about Nicholas Winton. At age 94, he was knighted by Queen Elizabeth for rescuing hundreds of Jewish children. He brought them from Czechoslovakia into England and put them in people's homes. People were different then. They were not just thinking of themselves like they do now. I remember reading somewhere nearly one and a half million evacuees left London at the start of the war. They had to go somewhere, didn't they?"

"I don't remember this part from history class," I say. "World War II seems a lot more real tonight than it did in my textbook days. How long did those girls stay with your family?"

"I'm not sure, but it must have been until the end of the war, when I was about four.

"We lived in the West Riding of Yorkshire, in the north of England. My town, Dewsbury was in what they called the Heavy

Woollen District. My father worked at Dormy Blankets, which was the largest wool blanket mill in the world at that time. Even the Queen covered herself with Dormy blankets. In fact, all of the beds in Buckingham Palace were wrapped in the warmth of my father's blankets. I felt proud of that.

"Our terrace house was small and crowded. My mum worked very hard in the home, caring for me and later, for my two sisters. She always baked desserts for each noon meal. My favorite was treacle sponge pudding and custard."

"That's *my* favorite English dessert," Mom chimes in.

"I know. We're two peas in a pod." He chuckles and continues his story.

I cannot write fast enough.

"My memories begin in the middle of World War II. I was 'invented' a year and a half after the war started, along with the ballpoint pen and color television. My family had no car. No phone. This was not unusual for those days.

"There was not much food in England, as imports were limited, and all the money was used to pay for the war. There were no supermarkets or packaged foods. Everything was purchased in a small shop. Every family received a book of ration tickets, like coupons for necessities. Each person was allowed to purchase one egg, three pieces of bacon, one-fourth pound of sugar and a small piece of butter per week. Butter was cut from a large block and wrapped in brown paper. Sometimes there *was* no butter. I remember having bread with just treacle on it. The thick syrup made my bread hard and crispy. I hated it. Without butter, it were awful!" (The memory makes him speak Yorkshire.) "Something as extravagant as chicken might only be seen at Christmastime."

Mom reaches over and taps his forehead. "You have a good memory, Mr. P."

"I always *was* interested in food," he laughs. "Like most children, I also liked candy. Once a week I stood in the long queue, sometimes for up to an hour, waiting with the other children for my two-ounce ration of licorice allsorts. Sometimes we waited all that time only to be given four humbugs or a packet of Wrigley's gum."

"What's a humbug?"

"It's a hard candy, like the horehound candy Grandma used to love," Mom answers.

"But what flavor is it?"

"They are black and white and taste like mint," Mr. P replies. "I liked them, but not as much as allsorts."

"How close were you to the bombing?" I open my phone to voice memos and press record. I don't want to miss any details.

"My Mum got a fright five days before I was born when Leeds was bombed. Forty bombs from German aircraft came down just eight miles from our home. Of course, London was nearly two hundred miles away, but they once got bombed for fifty-six days in a row! I do remember hearing the warplanes fly overhead many evenings, searching for the ammunition factories in nearby Leeds and Manchester.

"Everything was so dark at night because of the blackouts. The old gas lighter was forbidden to walk around our village lighting the streetlamps as usual. People were not even allowed on the streets after sunset. Large, thick, black sheets were pinned on the windows so no light could be seen outside. Lights would show the Germans where our houses were. Darkness was so important, if someone forgot to pin up their sheet, they could be imprisoned!

"I remember the bomb shelter where we fled when there was an air raid warning. Dug into the ground near the bottom of the garden, its corrugated iron roof was an eyesore among the lupines and delphiniums. When the sirens began, Mum grabbed me, quickly put my Mickey Mouse gas mask over my face and called out for my sisters. We all ran to the shelter, just like in the movie we just watched. I remember shrapnel dropped on our street once and killed our next-door-neighbor, Mr. Weatherford. We lived in constant fear.

"Dad didn't go to war. His job at Dormy was important. He was a spinner, making blankets for the soldiers in the trenches. I used to visit my dad at work. I liked the way the mill smelled because they washed the blankets in a special soap from France. What felt like one hundred years later, I learned it was Marseille soap, which my wife and I purchased on our honeymoon in Menton." He reaches over and runs the back of his hand down his wife's arm.

"We've had a block or two in our bathroom ever since." Mom says. "That scent makes me happy."

"That's why your bathroom always smells like . . ."

". . . the south of France," the P's say in unison.

"Do you have any happy memories of that time?" I ask.

"I always enjoyed music and Saturdays. Sometimes Auntie Cora took us to the fish and chip restaurant. Every Saturday afternoon there was wireless music at the cinema before the film. After the film we queued in line for a quarter of a mile for our candy ration.

"And I had a few toys. I remember making a bow and arrow from the tree branches and pretending to be Robin Hood. I also had three marbles. I made a hole in the dirt and rolled them in. Most parents made toys for their children. My favorite was a woolly stuffed sheep, sewn by my mum. I had a special stool, which I turned into a theater by laying it on its side. Mum made small curtains and cardboard actors. I made up stories or acted out scenes from the cinema films. Later, when I was older and my sisters were young, we made paper mâché puppets that moved with strings. We couldn't go to toy shops to buy things. We made them ourselves.

"I feel strange doing all this talking about myself," Mr. P says abruptly.

"I like it. It's very interesting. Keep talking."

"Tell about the scarlet fever," Mom prompts.

"Okay, if you will turn out the overhead light," Mr. P concedes. "It's 'urting my eyes."

I stand and start to pull the string.

"That's the fan," they chorus.

I pull the other string and slide under the covers next to Mom.

Mr. P almost whispers as he begins to talk again. "At age three, I started feeling sickly and got a high fever. Mum was fearful because she heard of a fever ravaging the school children in our village. She sent for the doctor immediately. In those days he came directly to our home. After examining me, he looked up at Mum's worried face and nodded. 'I'll call for the ambulance,' the doctor said soberly.

"Mum wrapped me up in a blanket, holding me tightly. It was Christmastime. Pitifully I cried out, "Mum!" as the ambulance crew placed me in the back for the six-mile ride to the hospital. I was locked in a sealed room, alone. I had to be quarantined because scarlet fever is extremely contagious. My home was ordered disinfected and all my books and toys were burned in the garden, even my little stuffed lamb. I didn't see it happen, but they told me afterward. That would make a child cry, wouldn't it?

"I waited longingly for Mum and Dad's weekly hospital visit. When they finally arrived, I could only see them outside the window to my room. They waved and blew kisses. Sometimes they sang, "In Bleak Midwinter," my family's favorite song. I could see their mouths moving behind the glass and I sang along with all my strength."

Mr. P's tenor voice trembles in the dark as he fills the room with his sacred song.

What can I give him,
Poor as I am?
If I were a shepherd
I would bring a lamb,
If I were a wise man
I would do my part,
Yet what I can I give Him —
Give my heart.

Christina Rossetti

We lay silent. I'm glad the light is off because I cannot hold back my tears as I envision that sweet little boy singing through the glass. The ceiling fan's click, click, click brings me back to the present. My throat feels tight as I think of the two people beside me in the bed and all their untold stories. Eventually, Mom asks, "How long were you in the hospital?"

"For one month. That's a long time for a three-year-old boy to be in bed, alone in a room. Finally, the day arrived when I could go home! Dad and Mum brought me a sturdy pair of clogs. I was thrilled because they were new, with a shiny metal horseshoe on the soles. When I walked, they made that clip clop sound horses make on cobble streets. In those days, shoes were made to last. I skipped home holding Mum's hand.

"Two months after I turned four, the war ended. We celebrated VE Day on May 8, 1945. I was ecstatic because I got to have a balloon! I remember holding tightly to the string as my red balloon flew high in the sky. There was a huge celebration. One road outside Dewsbury was blocked off and the townspeople put tables together extending a quarter of a mile. We all sat together and ate potted meat sandwiches with jelly (English Jell-O) for dessert. Musicians played and people danced in the streets. The unanimous joy and laughter were unusual and incredible!

"The joy continued right on into spring. I got a brand-new suit for Whitsuntide!"

"What's Whitsuntide?"

"Maybe it's just a British holiday. It was near Easter time, to celebrate the Holy Spirit's arrival after Jesus was resurrected. All the children from church marched through the streets with a brass band leading the procession. Everyone received hymn sheets for the singing. I couldn't read the hymn sheet, but I knew the songs from going with Mum to the Methodist services. I recall being overcome with emotion, even at four years old because all the people singing in harmony sounded so beautiful.

"To me, the important things, the foundation of who I am, was laid early in my life and modeled by my mother: having a family, caring for the destitute, going to church, singing songs of praise to our God. These are the principles that took root in my soul, the pillars I could return to after I lost my way in the future. Now I am old, but these simple things are still important, especially singing to my God and praising Him."

"Years later, you wrote a poem for your mum and mailed it from Switzerland," Mom reminds him. "I found it in the suitcase with all of her old letters. It alludes to the times you went to church together and played theater with the stool. I think it's on the table downstairs, JuJu. If you want to find it."

"I'll look in the morning. I'm tired now. Goodnight P's," I whisper as I leave their cozy rouge room and creak across the hall to my guest bed. It doesn't have red satin sheets, but I don't care. I'm happy about the way this chapter ends. I will sleep well.

Mum

I was happy by your side
behind the old stool to act and hide.
Roast beef and Yorkshire pudding I still smell,
The world's best cook—I can tell.
We walked down the street for a visit or two.
No TV then to watch and be glued.
Sunday evening to church we would go.
You gave a glimpse of the God I know.
Let this be a consolation
From your son in another nation.

You shall not be afraid of the terror by night, nor of the arrow that flies by day, nor of the pestilence that walks in darkness, nor of the destruction that lays waste at noonday.

Psalm 91:5-6 NKJV

West Tanfield, Yorkshire

Chapter 3

MY EASTER SWEATER

God uses sorrowful tragedy to set the stage for surprising triumph—whether in this life or the life to come.
David Platt

My eyes are half closed. Morning sunshine warms my face as I pray on the P's back deck. *Scrape, scrape.* Mr. P's trowel moves quickly. He sets red pavers in dark earth, creating a walking path between impatiens, echinacea, sweet basil and kale.

Heavenly Father, I whisper, *today's topic is difficult. Please send the Holy Spirit to guide our conversation, to help him remember, and to help me write only what is useful for helping others understand they are not alone, there is a name for their abuse, and there is hope. In the name of Jesus, amen.*

The P's always have a pretty patchwork of flowers and vegetables in their garden. Unlike Mr. P, I grew up calling the outside areas around homes the 'yard.' As kids, Annie and I played either in the front yard or the back yard. The garden was a separate area where we grew cucumbers, tomatoes and summer squash. Simple. To Mr. P, it's all a garden. He doesn't really pronounce the r, and the a is drawn out like ahhh, so it sounds fancy. "I'm going to water the gahhhdden" can mean he's watering the lawn or he's watering the plants. When life gets hard, he usually escapes to the garden.

Perhaps that's why he's here this morning. I watch him work. His hands move quickly, confident of what they will do next. Slowly he unfolds his six-foot frame, standing to survey the path he's created.

It's like a miniature roundabout with square pavers leading from the deck steps toward the fence, but not in a direct route. The lane splits, going either way around a central area filled with tiny cypress trees, Italian terra cotta pots and deep red geraniums. The pavers meet again and continue in one line toward the gate where gladioli lean against the wood, their purples and pinks forming a backdrop for the layers of flowers and plants.

"You P's always have lovely gardens." I wave from my plastic chair.

"Buongiorno!" He greets me in Italian. Although Mr. P grew up English, I'm sure he's got Italian DNA. When speaking Italian he becomes someone altogether different—animated, excited and bold. He always says, "When I'm in Italy, I'm my most authentic self."

"I hope you are ready to be your authentic self this morning," I say as he walks toward me, wiping dirty hands on the sides of his short-sleeved button-up shirt.

"I'm not feeling very excited about this part of the story," he confesses, untucking a chair from the round outdoor table where I wait for him to tell me about the day that skewed his world.

"Where did you learn to do this?" I ask.

"Do what?"

"All of this!" I gesture toward the miniature Italian garden that is the P's backyard. "The stonework, flowers, the symmetry, all of it."

"Well . . ." he pauses. "Your mother actually designed this garden after watching gardening shows on Netflix when she was sick in bed last winter. But we always work together to make things beautiful. In school I took rockery and really enjoyed it. I've used those skills a lot over the years. I suppose my first interest in plants and things came from my father. All his life Dad had a beautiful garden. That's one thing we did together, because I wasn't into sports like my dad wanted.

"Dad was athletic. I was not. He won medals for rugby football, but nobody went with him to a match—apart from my uncle. I *would* go and watch him play bowls, though. He played in tournaments and the whole family went to cheer him on."

"Do you mean bowling?"

"No. English bowls. It's different. Sometimes it is called lawn bowls because it's played outside on a bowling green. I never really cared about it, but it was all the rage when I was young. Sometimes we played at home on the back garden lawn."

"What are you two doing out here?" Mom interrupts our conversation with a smile and two cups of fresh mint tea. "The mint is from our garden," she says, pronouncing the r like a true Southern American as she carefully sets her tea tray on the table.

"Oh, we are discussing gardening and sports," I respond, reaching for a wedge of lemon.

"I hated sports!" Mr. P adamantly proclaims. "I refused to play ball in school—wouldn't even *take* my football boots for gym class on Fridays. There were about four or five other boys who did not want to play either. Coaches called us sissies and made us run cross-country instead."

"Not in all the centuries was football the mark of manhood," my mother emphatically states as she hands him a McVitie's digestive biscuit. "Not everyone plays football. There are different kinds of people." She wraps her freckled arms around his neck.

"My father wanted me to play rugby. Instead I was behind the footstool playing with papier-mâché dolls!"

They crack up laughing together as Mom sits down.

"We have to laugh. We must just laugh because what else can we do?" Mr. P says.

"You had other interests, didn't you, P?"

He nods and brushes cookie crumbs from his mustache.

"Like what?" I ask.

"Well, when I started primary school, I enjoyed fishing with my friends. We used to go to a duck pond in the park. We made fishing nets with sticks and a piece of wire." To Mom he asks, "You know those thick lisle stockings women wore in those days?"

"I'm nearly nine years younger than you and lived on a different continent, so I don't remember lisle," she reminds him, "but I do know about thick tights from living in Switzerland."

"Lisle was a very strong cotton thread, used for gloves or winter stockings. We would cut the foot out and fasten it to the wire, making a fishing net. Kids nowadays are spoiled to death. They have no imagination.

"I always liked creative things—photography, art, and music. Still do. Even now, when I go to the Christian men's group in town, I feel lost because all they talk about is ball. I don't know a thing about it. When men discuss ball here in America, is it baseball or what? I don't know the difference between the Bruins, the Browns or the Buzzards."

"Usually around here," Mom waves her hand in the air, "they are talking about football. Or basketball. They used to talk about baseball more when I was a teenager."

"It depends on the season," I explain. "There is football season, basketball season and baseball season."

"How ridiculous," Mr. P mocks. "What ever happened to spring, summer, autumn and winter?"

"I don't know, but we are getting off topic."

"Maybe not," Mom suggests. "Who he was as a boy affected his relationship with his father, which affected him as a man."

"I was never close with my father like I was with my mum. It's like he was there, but not there. Emotionally absent. Mum, I was very close to. I was often out and about with her alone. We went shopping, to the moors, to church. Mum was spiritual. Dad never went to church. Mum and I would walk a mile to go to church. We didn't have cars. People thought nothing about walking."

"Were your parents close?" I test the tea. It's still too hot, so I pick up my pen and continue scribbling notes.

"Not really. After I grew up, Mum told me my dad used to put money on dog racing. She nearly had to beg him to spend money on clothes for us kids because Dad spent his money on the dogs."

"That would definitely cause some tension in their relationship. Especially if money was tight," I comment.

"Mum was overprotective of me. I was a sensitive child. I always felt a nervous anxiety as far back as I remember. I never felt relaxed. Never."

"It would have been very difficult for your mother to be nine months pregnant and running for the bomb shelter! I can't imagine!" Mrs. P empathizes with her deceased mother-in-law. "I'm sure she *would* be protective."

"Yes, but only later in life did I understand the concept of codependency and be able to connect some of my issues to having a distant father and a mollycoddling mother. By the way, that bomb shelter stayed in our garden after the war. My sisters and I played in it."

"I'm sure all that affected you— the fear you felt in the womb, the war, the poverty," I say. "No wonder you had childhood anxiety."

"People in England *were* traumatized. When we went to visit your family twenty-some years ago, they still talked as if the war just happened. Childhood trauma has a lot to do with setting us up for future addictions and struggles," Mom adds. "Plus, it's a big trauma for a little one to be in the hospital with scarlet fever, and to have all your clothes and toys burned. To have your little lamb burned. Poverino." (She uses an Italian word meaning 'pitiful little one' as a term of endearment.)

"I suppose so. I never really thought about it like that. I just always remember feeling nervous. As I got a bit older, I felt ashamed, because of my legs."

"What was wrong with your legs?" I ask.

"They were fat. I was called 'fat slab' by the mean kids. I had a satchel to carry my books to school. I remember I would walk holding my satchel in front of my legs. To hide them."

"Didn't you wear pants to school? Who knew what your legs looked like?" I ask.

"Little boys didn't wear long trousers in those days. Up to age thirteen, we wore shorts."

"And knee socks," adds Mom.

"Even in winter?"

"All year round," he explains. "That meant you were still a little boy."

"I'm learning so much British trivia as I write your story, Mr. P. Your life is interesting."

"Oh, dear!" he exclaims. "I wish it weren't so interesting. After I grew up, I felt angry with people who hadn't had any trauma in their life. I thought, 'Why have *you* sailed through life and just been able to find a girl and get married?'"

"You felt different from others?" Mom asks.

"Yes. As if I were dog droppings on the pavement. But, that would be at a later date. There was a small window of time when I felt somewhat happy."

"Tell me about that," I prompt.

"Well, I guess I grew out of the fat phase and started doing things on my own. I delivered newspapers after school in the evenings to earn a bit of money. I put them in people's letter boxes and came home after dark."

"How old were you, coming home in the dark?"

"Maybe around twelve or so. My mum often walked to the ladies' meetings at church alone and came home in the dark. Back then, who was afraid? Nobody."

"Nowadays you'd have to worry about being stabbed to death. Every day on the BBC news we read about some poor Brit getting knifed. It's awful!" Mom exclaims, scrunching up her nose.

"Well, we didn't think of things like that back then. After I bought my bicycle and joined the cycling club, I would spend entire days riding alone all over the countryside. Sometimes I rode so far from home I ended up staying in youth hostels for the night. That was normal."

"And those days were long before cell phones! I would have freaked out if I were your mother. I want my teenagers to text me *all* the details—where they are going, who they are with and when they arrive," I say.

"It wasn't like that then," he repeats. "I became obsessed with old villages after discovering H. V. Morton's timeless travel book, *In Search of England* at our local library. That's when my travel addiction began. I'd read about a place then take off on my bicycle to find it. Exploring took my mind off things. It was exhilarating!" Mr. P's blue eyes light up like they usually do when he's planning an adventure.

"I felt my life was going quite well until an incident happened, which embedded self-hatred in my soul."

Mr. P. shifts in his chair. Looking straight at me he says, "This is very difficult and embarrassing to talk about."

"Thank you for telling your story. I know it's difficult, but I believe God is really going to use it to give people hope and understanding of their own stories."

My tea is the perfect temperature now. I hold my cup with both hands and wait for the story I've been waiting for.

"I feel stupid telling things. But it's *not* my fault. When something like this happens to you, you must tell yourself, 'It's not your fault. You didn't choose.'" He reaches for his wife's hand. Mrs. P already has tears in her eyes. She's heard this story before.

"My mum had stayed up until the early morning hours, lovingly knitting a red and blue striped Easter sweater for me. I came downstairs for breakfast and proudly put it on. Mum carefully straightened the shoulder seam. Quickly, I finished my porridge and treacle, and kissed her goodbye. I had a long ride planned, with an overnight stay at the end. How could I have known my bright new sweater would be like Joseph's coat of many colors—an extravagant gift from a loving parent that would go with me into the pits of hell?

"My bike had satchels on either side. I put my new box camera in one and my Pears soap, toothbrush, pork pie and a bottle of orange juice in the other. The sun felt lovely as I rode toward the youth hostel at Ellingstring, a village on the edge of the Yorkshire Dales. I enjoyed biking through the countryside, breathing the spring air. Daffodils bloomed by the side of the road. I remember them. Yellow flowers are my favorite, you know." He gestures toward a pot of yellow chrysanthemums near the table.

"After pedaling for about fifty miles, I made a short detour to picturesque West Tanfield, another quaint village in Morton's book. I stopped on the Ure River bridge to catch my breath and photograph an idyllic view of the gray stone houses by the river and the church with its 15th century Marmion tower. I can see it now in black and white—the picture I took that day. I developed it myself.

"I walked my bike across the bridge and entered the St. Nicholas church. Inside was cool and dark except for the light filtering through several stained-glass windows. Thinking I was the only visitor, I quickly peeked behind a curtain at the sandstone monuments of Sir John Marmion and his wife, then sat down to rest on a pew near the entrance. As I stared at a stained-glass story of Jesus surrounded by children, an older man sat down beside me.

"Where are you going?" he asked, simultaneously putting his hand on my bare knee. Immediately terrified and repulsed. I answered him honestly, "I'm going to Ellingstring." Then I quickly ran for my bike and set off in the opposite direction. I was stupid, telling him anything."

"It wouldn't have mattered. He had his vile plans," Mom contradicts. "You weren't stupid. You were a kid."

"I felt imminent danger and peddled as fast as my legs could carry me. The road became extremely narrow with an unusually high hedge bank covered with hawthorn on either side. It was so steep I could not see the fields above. This man must have searched the lanes. He must have gone up and down and around to find me because suddenly his large black car was beside my bicycle.

"The car pressed in, too near, forcing me to stop or be hit. I tried to yank my bike up the steep bank to get away. I was terrified for my life. Terrified of what this stranger might do to me.

"I heard his voice getting closer, but I don't remember what he said. Trapped between the car and the high bank, I was forced to stop running, forced to go along with his evil intentions. Forced into his car.

"After I-don't-know-how-long, he released me. As I clambered up the hillside for my bike, my abuser tossed a half crown at me and sped away. It clinked on the pavement and rolled to a stop. Shame flooded my soul as I bent to pick up the coin. I dropped it into the pocket of my khaki shorts.

"My carefree spirit was destroyed. I felt defiled and immediately hated myself, feelings which lasted for decades. I was only a boy and my life came to an end that day. My head whirled with disgust as I jerked my bike away from the hedge. My body was not dead, but my soul was in hell. My legs shook as I mounted my bike.

"Tears streamed down my face as I pedaled toward Ellingstring. They blew like raindrops onto my new sweater as I sobbed into the wind. I escaped the reality of what had just happened with the thought of my mum's hands, working through the night to knit a gift just for me. I forced my mind to concentrate on her hard work and felt the comfort of her love."

Mr. P stops talking. It doesn't matter that my tea is now cold or that I haven't even taken a sip. My heart is broken for this precious man in front of me. I have so many questions.

"Why did you pedal toward Ellingstring? Why didn't you go home? Did you tell your mother what happened? Did anyone file a police report?"

"I don't know. I don't know! I just kept going toward the youth hostel. There was a young guy and his girlfriend staying there that night. They were kind to me. I got a photo with them. We made friends. We kept in touch and even met up another time in Dewsbury.

"Did you tell them what happened to you?" I ask.

"No."

"Did you tell your mother when you got home?"

"No. I never told anyone."

"Not even the psychologist in Switzerland?" Mom lets go of his hand and leans forward to look into his face. "Didn't it *ever* come out in therapy?"

"No."

"Who was the first person you told?" she asks again.

"Maybe you. Before we married."

"Me? That was nearly forty years later!"

"You held this horror inside for forty years?" I say.

"Yes."

"Why didn't your therapists get to the root of the problem?" Mom questions. "We must always get to the root, not get lost in the topsoil."

"My soul was worth more than twenty cents, wasn't it?" Mr. P's tone is flat.

"Of course! Your soul is worth the life of the Son of God!" My mother raises her decibel level. "*Why* did he throw money at you? Throwing money down is another abuse. It's part of the vileness. Was that supposed to ease his conscience?"

I start to say something, "It's kind of like Judas. When he realized what he had done, he threw the dirty silver back at the priests . . ."

Mom interjects with a minor temper flare, "Didn't you just want to slap him up one side and down the other?"

"I was scared, wasn't I?" Mr. P says quietly.

Mom's anger is subdued by the tears in her voice, "You probably went into shock, didn't you, P? I hate it. I hate that this happened to you."

"Yeah," he says staring at his favorite yellow garden flowers.

"Maybe we should pray before we talk any more," I suggest, wondering if he is shutting down on us—if it's wise to continue.

"Good idea," both P's agree in unison.

I begin. "Father in heaven . . ." We grasp hands around the table. "Thank You for Mr. P's life, for his story. Thank You for preserving his physical life that day, and for helping him to heal from the trauma. Please protect his heart now, as we have opened some painful and confusing memories. I ask for the Holy Spirit to comfort him and each of us as we walk through the rest of this difficult chapter."

Mom continues, "Bind up any fresh wounds with Your love, Lord. Even though this is an old story, it can still hurt. I plead the blood of Jesus over each of us and declare in the heavenly realm that no weapon forged against any of us will prosper. There will be no demonic retaliation because we are sharing this testimony, in the name of Jesus Christ."

"I bind and rebuke the spirits of shame and guilt off of me, in the name of Jesus," Mr. P declares. "I am redeemed and restored and covered by the blood of Jesus Christ. I will not believe any lies from the devil, my enemy. The truth of who God is and what He says about me in His Word has set me free from the bondage of fear and shame and guilt. Thank You, God. I praise You! In Jesus' name, amen."

"Mr. P, may I ask you something?" I have a burning question.

"Okay."

"Was that your first sexual encounter?"

"Yes, but I remember a couple of previous incidents of inappropriate behavior by males," he responds.

"Do you want to talk about it? Or have you had enough?" Mom asks, protective of her Mr. P.

"I'm okay. I don't really remember what happened with the podiatrist, but I think he must have done something to me. Otherwise, why would I remember after all these years that he made me take my underpants off to examine my feet? It was embarrassing. I had flat feet and I had to do exercises by standing on a pole on the floor of his office."

"Without your underwear?" Mom and I chorus.

"I also had to wear something in my shoes," he says.

"I don't care about the orthotics." I feel anger rising. "I want to know why a podiatrist made you take off your underwear. How old were you?"

"I suppose I was around five years old."

"Where was your mother?"

"I can't remember."

"Do you sense she was there?"

"I don't know. She trusted him. Doctors and such knew best."

"When we were young, that was our culture. We didn't question anything," Mom agrees. "But something wasn't right or you wouldn't remember it like this."

"I remember it because it was so shocking. I can see his face now if I think about it. He was cross-eyed and strange. He was touching my legs. I'm there without any underwear on. Maybe something inappropriate happened, but I cannot recall anything but his face. I felt uncomfortable in his presence each time I had an appointment afterwards. I didn't want to go anymore."

"What's inappropriate is that he made you remove your underwear. Regardless of whether anything else happened, he was already crossing boundaries!" Mom nearly shouts the last sentence. Then more softly, "You poor child! What on earth? Your mother was always overprotecting you, but you weren't overprotected."

"How awful! Do we even dare ask what else happened?" I wonder. "Is it important for the reader to know these stories?"

"I'm not sure," Mr. P replies. "Do you think the teenager who brought the bread and played with himself in front of me makes any difference to the reader?"

"I would definitely say, yes because this series of incidents is a setup from Satan. My opinion . . . but I believe you were conditioned to have a proclivity toward same-sex attraction because your first sexual experiences took place with males, even though you were a victim in each circumstance."

"Some would say boys do that sort of thing all the time," Mom replies. "They compare their size and stuff like that. Does that make it a sexual experience . . .or abuse?"

"I believe so, but usually they are older and more like peers when they do that, right? Mr. P, how old were you when this incident happened?" I ask.

"I don't know exactly. I'm a little kid. Maybe six or seven."

"That's definitely a power imbalance if Bread Boy was a teenager."

"Maybe a year or two after that something similar happened in the Methodist church bathroom," he remembers.

"Now what, P?" Mom questions.

"A boy around my age demonstrated masturbation on himself. I must've been about nine. It's not *just* seeing someone's penis!" He raises both hands, palms up. "It ruins your whole life and causes tremendous agony and torment."

Even now, after all the years, I see pain behind the lenses of Mr. P's glasses.

"I agree," Mom says. "My therapist told me once that certain personalities can be physically molested and not be as psychologically affected as a highly sensitive person who may be damaged by a lustful look from someone they trust. I mean, look at *my* life. Look at what happened to me . . .the abuse by my father, my uncle, and what my cousin did in front of me with his sister's lipstick! For a long time you don't talk about it. You are defiled—whether it's intercourse or not. There are levels of defilement."

"True," I say. No one ever touched *me* like that, but I felt overexposed and violated when my little friend and I discovered her dad's porn-stash. We were too young to see that stuff. And like you, Mr. P, my first exposure to someone else's genitalia was same-sex exposure. We can't unsee things. It affects us."

"You never told me about that," Mom says.

"I know. I was ashamed. And I thought I would get in trouble. I was afraid you might not let me spend the night over there anymore."

"I wonder why we don't tell our mothers?" she asks. "I didn't tell *my* mom about some of Dad's weirdness, either. But I did tell my Aunt Zina about my cousin and the lipstick! He got a stick of kindling on his rear end and I can hear him yelling in my head right now. I don't know why I'm remembering this story. We can hear things that trigger a bunch of garbage."

"Mr. P, where was your mom when the bread boy delivered more than bread?" I ask.

"Next door, lighting Auntie Margaret's coal fire. Every day, Mum popped over in the afternoon to light the fire so Auntie Margaret's house would be warm when she came home from work. I was alone when the bread boy knocked on our door.

"He usually came 'round a couple of times a week. I asked him in, saying, 'My mum will be back in a few minutes to pay you.' He put our bread on the table and sat on the sofa to wait. Suddenly, I was shocked to see him exposing himself right in front of me!

"My first thought was, *Oh, no! He will touch someone else's bread*! Bread wasn't in plastic wrappers then," Mr. P explains. "My next thoughts were, *What is that? Why did he do that?* I felt scared and embarrassed. He just stared at me. I never forgot his lewd behavior."

"Ewwwww! Did you tell your mom?" I wonder aloud.

"No."

"Why didn't you tell your mother?"

"I don't know. Because we wouldn't have had any more bread, would we? That's the way a child thinks."

"You were a sweet, sensitive little boy. I'm sorry those horrid things happened to you," Mrs. P empathizes with her husband. "We seem like such a refined couple and there is all this muck in our childhoods. Have you forgiven all of your abusers?"

"Yes, of course. A long time ago."

"It's amazing when we can forgive unforgivable behavior," she says. "I'm thankful Jesus gives us that ability, because otherwise it's impossible. Even though I have forgiven, when people cross a boundary and are in my personal space, I react. I feel violated with seemingly small things. I think I'm overly sensitive that way because of the boundary violations I experienced as a child."

"I understand," Mr. P agrees. "Although my struggle was different. When a person is molested, it seems to take over our brains. In our lack of self-worth and the destruction of our souls, we end up being damaged people who damage other people. This is the homosexual thing as I see it. I was trying in a sexual way, to get something I should have gotten from a father's love. We will see it later in my story.

"To all who have suffered in this way, I say, 'Persevere with God. Tell Him, 'I will not let You go unless you bless me with freedom and healing.' I hung on to that promise, even when it seemed like I wasn't hanging on. That's why we can't judge anyone. We do NOT know where they've been or where they are in their experience."

"It's true! And here's another point," Mom adds, "I believe people access demonic spirits through molestation or rape."

"Now that's heavy," I say. "It doesn't seem fair for a child to access that kind of darkness."

"But it's true," Mr. P confirms. "You end up with spirits of insecurity and anxiety and depression and fear—spirits of suicide and confusing sexual propensities . . .until someone can spiritually help you."

"Wow! Do we want to introduce spiritual warfare right here in the beginning of this book?" I ask.

Mom says, "I don't know. Many Christians don't even acknowledge it. Lots of people play church, but they don't always spiritually help people. Warfare is simply using God's Word to fight the lies of the greatest liar of all. One of my favorite scriptures is 2 Corinthians 10:4-5."

For the weapons of our warfare are not carnal but mighty in God for pulling down strongholds, casting down arguments and every high thing that exalts itself against the knowledge of God, bringing every thought into captivity to the obedience of Christ.

2 Corinthians 10:4-5 NKJV

"The way I first memorized it was from the King James version. It says, 'Casting down imaginations . . .' I love this scripture because garbage gets into people's heads when abuse happens. They don't know they have spiritual authority to cast down those imaginations, those arguments against God's truth. They don't know of God's power to break the strong hold the enemy has on their thinking."

"The scripture that really helps me is Romans 8:1," Mr. P begins, "There is therefore . . ." Mom and I join him for the rest, "now no condemnation to those who are in Christ Jesus." THIS is the truth! If we believe this, we can move forward by faith in Him who can and will set us free. My favorite verse of all though, is John 17:23. It reminds me that God loves me as much as He loves Jesus.

"If you are reading this, and you have feelings of guilt, I want to tell you that God does not condemn you. He loves you as much as he loves his own Son. I felt too ashamed for too long. Before I received God's healing grace and understood the truth of how much He loved *me*, nothing helped."

Mr. P begins to pray aloud. "Dear lord Jesus, it's my desperate plea that anyone reading this now will search for You and search for help, so they don't have to go through all the years of hell. I bind Satan, in the name of Jesus from making them feel too ashamed to talk to someone."

Mrs. P says, "I have such compassion for those who are hurting and those whose boundaries have been violated by a touch or a word or a look. I want to also pray for you, dear Reader: 'Dear heavenly Father, I come to You with tears because these are really sad stories that happened to my husband. I lift up any innocent child, teenager or person who has experienced sexual abuse, whether they remember or not. I lift up anyone to You who is triggered by reading this book. Please send Your Holy Spirit to minister to them as they seek You for healing. I pray for the love of God to bring healing and restoration to their broken sexuality.

"God, you say in Matthew 18:18, 'Whatever we bind on earth is bound in heaven. Whatever we loose on earth is loosed in heaven.' I bind and rebuke the evil spirits of guilt, anxiety, and lack of self-worth now in the name of Jesus, the great Healer. In His precious name, amen."

Dear Reader,

You are God's child. It's not your fault. You are loved. You were always loved, no matter what. God will bring healing. God will restore. If He did it for Mr. P, He can do it for you. Just you watch and see.

You intended to harm me, but God intended it for good to accomplish what is now being done, the saving of many lives.

Genesis 50:20 NIV

YOUNG MR. P

Stokesay Castle, Shropshire

Chapter 4

BUTLINS HOLIDAY CAMP

I envy her happiness. I envy his happiness.
Laurie, Little Women

"I think I'm going to have a piece of chocolate. It's the right time of day to have one." Mr. P winks at my mother as he peels thin foil wrapper from the extra dark chocolate bar he keeps in the door of their refrigerator.

"When is it *not* the right time of day for a piece of chocolate?" I ask.

"Numbing with food seems like a good idea after Chapter Three," Mrs. P replies from the dining room table where she and I sit surrounded by stacks of yellowing letters from yesteryear. She briefly touches my shoulder asking, "What would you like? I'll make some popcorn balls."

I laugh. "We all turn to something, don't we? Some numbs are just more socially acceptable than others."

"Well, same sex attraction was definitely *not* socially acceptable in the UK in the 1950's. I felt like an alien from outer space!" Mr. P mumbles through a mouthful of chocolate.

"Let's talk while Mom makes the popcorn. Why did you feel like an alien?"

"Are you aware that it was not until 1967 that homosexuality was decriminalized in my country? For years, I lived under the shadow of the fact that if I followed my feelings, I would be considered a criminal and could be incarcerated. For years before that, I never even knew there was a name for what I felt after that horrible Easter-sweater-bike-ride-day." Mr. P plops down and props his feet up.

"Tell about your life after that day. Where did you go from there? How did you cope?" I ask.

"I felt too gross and embarrassed to think about it. I pushed that nightmare to the back of my mind for years, thinking it had no effect on me. I immersed myself in activities and dissociated from the details of that trauma.

"Sometimes I attended the youth group at the Methodist Church. One night, when I was about fourteen, they played a game called 'truth or dare,' for what godly reason I don't know. Anyway, the boys ended up kissing the girls. Naturally, I thought I should join in, curious to see what kissing would be like.

"I thought it was alright but did not feel as enthusiastic as the other boys appeared to be. I felt a bit confused, different. Inside my being, there was always a nagging anxiousness, which never left for several decades. Something was missing. There was an inferior feeling inside, like I was the only person suffering from the emotions I experienced. I did not understand what was wrong with me. There was no one to talk with about it. I could not let my real self be known. Boys would talk about girls, but when I talked about them, I was pretending. I did not have sexual feelings toward the girls. The only thing that made my heart sing was music.

"A year or so later, I remember the boys blabbing about one girl who was 'easy.' Wanting to see what all the excitement was about, I let her know I was interested. She invited me home when her parents were out. I will not go into detail, but it was a disaster. I could not go through with it. I pulled my trousers on and fled. This experience left me more ashamed than ever."

Mrs. P stands in the kitchen doorway wielding a wooden spoon. "I've never heard *this* story before!" She swipes her finger across the spoon, tasting her maple syrupy concoction. "I'm glad you didn't. Glad you couldn't. Glad I was the first woman you were ever intimate with." With that, she does a little curtsy and disappears into the kitchen.

Mr. P and I glance at each other and laugh. "Your mother is hilarious!" he says.

"She certainly is. And she has really good ears, too," I whisper.

"I can hear you. What are you whispering about?" Mom singsongs from the kitchen. We laugh again.

"What else do you want to share from your teen years, Mr. P? I want our readers to feel like they know you."

"I became obsessed with photography, cycling all over Yorkshire photographing villages and castles. At fifteen, I began working for Mr. Field at the camera shop in Batley, where I had my film developed. I worked in his shop for four years—learning the art of photography and film developing, which required much more patience than modern digital photography.

"The film came in a long roll. Mr. Field taught me to lift the film with both hands, dipping it into a plastic dish that held the chemicals. Part of the film went into the solution then I lifted it out and submersed the next part. My fingers were always brown because of the chemicals we used to develop the photos, like I had smoked for a hundred years.

"I had to work carefully, because if I left the film too long in the solution, the pictures would be totally black. Sometimes they did not turn out, but Mr. Field never blamed our work. He told customers there must be something wrong with their camera.

"We also took professional photos. Sometimes interesting people came in to have their portraits made. Once I was behind camera making a portrait of the director of our local Operatic Society. "Can you sing?" he asked abruptly.

"Yes . . . ?" I answered with a question in my voice.

"Would you like to audition next Tuesday? We need a 'Toreador' for our upcoming musical."

"I leapt at the opportunity because I secretly dreamed of becoming a famous singer. My low self-image craved the accolades whenever I sang solos at our Methodist Church. Perhaps the need for affirmation was partly why I wanted to become a professional entertainer. *Just maybe*, I thought, *The Toreador will be my ticket for the train to fame.*

"Because of my church singing experience, I had a bit of confidence to proceed with the audition. With a mixture of trepidation and determination, I tried out for the part on Tuesday.

"'Mum! Dad!' I remember shouting when I got home, 'Guess who is *The Toreador* in the Batley Operatic Society's winter show?' I danced around our tiny kitchen singing, 'Will you come and watch the show?'

"I fought no real bulls on the Operatic Society's small stage, but for me it was an exciting adventure. We did several shows a year, 'The Gypsy Princess,' 'The Country Girl,' 'Bonaventure . . ." I even played Laurie in 'Little Women.' My whole family came to all my shows for four years. These were the humble beginnings of my singing and acting career.

"I continued working for Mr. Fields. He even left me in charge as manager when he went on holiday. My chest puffed up with the sense of responsibility. When I wasn't working or singing, I was planning my next travel adventure. I voraciously read travel books. In my mind, I was always away on some excursion. By age sixteen, if anyone asked me the names of the most beautiful villages in England, I could name them all.

"My first big adventure outside a book was when I hitchhiked to the coast and took a boat to France. I got a ride to Milan, Italy then hitchhiked to Rome. The film director who gave me a lift was making a movie starring Liz Taylor. We drove south through the night, chatting about Italy and our favorite films and actors. He dropped me at 5 a.m. at the Piazza Navona. That expedition was the start of my love affair with Italy. I was seventeen."

"Italy has been tough competition through the years," Mrs. P enters the room with a silver bowl full of the best homemade caramel popcorn ever. "She is the only one you've cheated with.

And just for that, JuJu and I get all the popcorn," she jokes, setting the bowl in front of me.

"Thank you, Mother. I hope you've been listening. Mr. P's life is like a movie. Sit down and enjoy the show."

"Oh, dear," he says reaching out his hand for popcorn. Mom gives him just enough to make him want more. "If my life is like a movie, the next part is the sad part."

"I thought we already had that part," I lament.

"My agony lasted until I truly understood the Gospel. It eased up when I met your mother, but the only reprieve from suffering I've ever had was that glorious first year of our marriage. Shall I continue?"

"Go on, P. We will have a pain-free life in heaven. God never promised us life without sorrow. Look at what happened to His Son," Mrs. P puts things into perspective. Mr. P continues with his story.

"As I became more confident in my skin, I began developing more than film, I developed friendships. Fred was my close buddy from the cycling club, and Ralph from church. After all these years, I still receive a card from Ralph and his wife each Christmas.

"Sometimes we went dancing at the Mecca Dance Hall in Wakefield with the Methodist youth group. I did enjoy dancing with the girls. I became friends with a few, but nothing more. I was a good dancer—especially after Ralph and I took lessons at Mr. Newsome's Dance Studio. We learned to dance the Foxtrot, the Quickstep, and the Waltz. Old Mr. Newsome always took the lead. The ridiculous part was he made us stand on his feet while we danced with him. It was a bit awkward, and way too close for my comfort. I think he secretly liked it.

"One of my guy friends stayed overnight at our house once. We slept in the same bed. I felt extremely uncomfortable. Later, I made another friend, Martin from the Operatic Society. He slept with *loads* of girls. One night, after a few drinks, Martin grabbed me, kissing me passionately, like a nutter. Our other male friends stood around laughing, drunk, acting like fools. Even though Martin's breath smelled of alcohol, I enjoyed it all. That was the first time I was kissed by a man.

"After that night, I went to church and prayed fervently because I knew my desires were different. It was torture, knowing I was strange and could not talk to anyone about it. I grew into manhood with terrifying feelings inside. I was never happy—always had that nagging pain in my soul. I can't remember a day passing for decades that I did not have a headache. I was a bundle of tension and nerves, believing I must be the only person in the world with affection for individuals of the same sex. Friends teased me incessantly because I was not interested in girls. It was torture not being able to tell them why. This agony went on for decades, even after I broke down and spoke to someone about my feelings of attraction for males.

"Despite my confusion, I *did* think girls were pretty. I was fascinated by certain movie stars and collected picture postcards of Elizabeth Taylor, Susan Hayward, and Jean Simmons. Film, theater, and singing became my escape. I could reinvent myself each time I walked onstage. Eventually I worked as a singer for three years at nightclubs, holiday camps, and pantomimes. Just after my nineteenth birthday, I moved to London for the first time. I lived like the pauper I was, but thoroughly enjoyed the thrill of getting a glimpse of the royals or other famous people."

"Oh, that reminds me," chirps Mrs. P as she hands him more popcorn. "I remember reading a letter you wrote your Mum after seeing the royal wedding party of Princess Margaret and Lord Snowden. It definitely reveals your interest in the Royals. Should I get it? Maybe it will lighten the mood for a moment."

"I'd like to read it," I say as Mom moves toward the stairs. "I'm interested in who he was as a young man and rubbing shoulders with celebrities is always fun."

"I wouldn't say I rubbed shoulders with celebrities," Mr. P protests, "but I certainly wanted to be one and craned my neck to see what they looked like! I've forgotten all about that wedding."

The Poplars
Poplar Avenue
Willesden
London, NW2
Friday, May 6, 1960 4 PM

Dear All,

I've just got back from the wedding and labor exchange. I arrived at Trafalgar Square this morning at 10:45. It was impossible to get anywhere near the Abbey as the sides of the roads were packed with people. Eventually I found a place in the mall where I could see very well. I was near the front of the causeway and felt awful being so tall, as no one would see behind me. I had a smashing view.

The cars started leaving the palace about 11:15. Most of the people we didn't know at all. The crowd did recognize the Duke and Duchess of Bedford, who waved to us. Then came Princess Anne with the other bridesmaids. Princess Marina of Denmark was recognized. Then princess Margaret and Lord Snowdon passed, followed by the Queen and the Duke with Phillip. Then last of all, Princess Alexandra. Didn't she look lovely? I also saw the Queen Mother and Mr. Ogilvy.

It was all very exciting; I can tell you. You would have loved to have been with me, Mum! When they had passed, I went and got a good view in Whitehall by the Horse Guard Parade. There were two TV cameras there. It would be nice if you saw me. I was among the tallest of the crowd. I don't think I would be too hard to see. I stayed and saw them all again coming from the Abbey. It was a lovely site. Especially seeing all the royalty in one day. I heard the service on someone's transistor while we were watching. It was surprising there were as many men watching as women.

Some of the guests caught the same train as me with their top hats and tails. Fancy, them not traveling by car.

All told it has been a lovely exciting day. I hope you enjoyed it all on telly, Mum.

Cheerio for now and God bless.

All my love, Geoff

x x x Thanks for the insurance card.

"Your letter is so detailed! Young people don't write like that anymore," I remark. "My sons are nineteen like you were and I can barely get a five-word text message out of them. Your Mum was fortunate. It's obvious you had a close connection."

"Yes. We were too close. She was my best friend."

"And she saved *all* your weekly letters!" Mrs. P returns with a stack of envelopes. "They paint such interesting word pictures of life back then. I'm grateful your mother kept them," she says to Mr. P. Mom winks at me, "Despite the fact that we have lugged that suitcase from house to house for years."

"P!" she blurts after opening another envelope and scanning for a moment. "Here's your original hiring letter from Butlins Holiday Camp."

"Butlins was ages ago! Let me see." Mr. P reaches for the yellowed envelope. His right-hand trembles slightly as he unfolds the thin paper and begins to read:

Dear Mr. Pennock,

Are you still available for Redcoat duties at our camp this summer season? I am now in position to offer you employment from July 11 and would be grateful if you would advise me as soon as possible.

Yours Sincerely, Bill Martin
Entertainment Manager for Butlins' Limited

"I've never heard of Butlins," I say.

"If you were British, you certainly would have!" His eyes smile as he hands the letter back to Mom. "Butlins Holiday Camps in the 1950's and '60's were THE place to gain experience as an entertainer. Many well-known singers and actors had stints on stage at Butlins—Cliff Richard, Clinton Ford, even Julie Andrews and Catherine Zeta Jones, when they were young. Comedians Des O'Connor and Michael Barrymore got their start as Butlins Redcoats like me. I longed to leave home and take on the big stage at Butlins."

"I love old letters!" I exclaim. It's like reading someone's diary after they are dead."

"I'm still here," Mr. P's tone is droll. "Even though I feel like the person who wrote those letters is dead."

"I've gleaned the most interesting ones and organized them according to date," Mom explains. "Here are the letters from your first summer at Butlins."

"How long did you work there?" I ask.

"Just three seasons," he responds. "What am I supposed to do with these?" He waves the letters toward my mother.

"Don't you want to read them to us?"

"Not really. I feel silly. You read them." Then he adds, "Aren't they boring?"

"No!" Mom and I exclaim in unison.

"They are priceless and charming," Mrs. P explains. "They are full of such details of your life."

"But honestly, who really cares about the details of my life as a wanna-be singer at a holiday camp in England?"

"I do, for starters. In our modern Snapchat, and Instagram world, letter writing is a lost art. May I read another?"

"Go ahead. If you think it matters."

"Thank you, Mr. P. I believe it does matter. Your story matters. It's important for our readers to understand who you *were* in order for them to appreciate who you *are* and what God has done in your life. Your story will give hope to so many who struggle in the aftermath of sexual abuse, or who experience sexual identity crises, same-sex attraction, or any other proclivity to sexual sin. I open an envelope, unfold the nearly translucent writing paper and begin to read aloud:

> *Butlins, 1961*
>
> *Dear All,*
>
> *I arrived here at Butlins Holiday Camp at 3 p.m. yesterday. I spent last night looking around at the hotels. And I went to a dance.*
>
> *I share a room with a bloke called Ted. He is married and is a comedian on the show. He seems a decent chap. This morning was free, this afternoon I have to help with the running of Tombola (a raffle).*
>
> *Tonight, for two hours, I have to sit and keep kids from falling into the swimming pool.*
>
> *I have just got my rig out. The white trouser bottoms are wide. Anyway, it doesn't look too bad. I have got some white shoes to wear.*
>
> *As a Redcoat, when we have our meals we sit at the same tables with our guests.*

"One of my duties was to dance with the guests," Mr. P interjects. "I used to pick out all the lonely souls and dance with them."

> *I have settled down all right, and everyone seems to be okay. The meals are good. And so is my room and bed.*
>
> *Altogether there are nine hotels here, with different entertainment in each one. We flit about from one to another. I have a nice next-door neighbor, Jeanne.*

She says if anything wants ironing or sewing or anything, she will see to it for me.

Please don't worry about me, as I am okay and enjoying myself.

All my love, Geoff

"So, a Redcoat was like a steward?" I ask.

"Somewhat. We had many duties. We were supposed to socialize with the guests—be their dance partners, organize games, go on walks with them, even attend the church services. It boiled down to making all guests feel comfortable and engaged. I applied for the job because I wanted to sing in the nightly shows."

"I think your next letter tells of your disappointment at not being able to do that initially," Mrs. P says handing him another envelope.

He hands it to me.

Butlins, 1961

Dear All,

At midnight on Friday, some of us went swimming in the sea. We had a great time and the sea wasn't much colder than during the day. Although it seemed eerie in the dark.

"When I was a boy," he interrupts, "I had a traumatic experience in the sea. The waves rolled me and dashed me against the rocks. I love the sea, but I like knowing I can always touch the bottom and keep my head above the water. You know, some things affect you for the rest of your days."

On Saturday I was greeting guests at the station all day. I had only a half hour off today, with barely enough time to have a shave and wash my hair.

I haven't had time to have a bath. And I have a shirt, vest, work pants, and a towel and pajamas to wash— if and when I have time. I think we should have more time off, especially with the poor wage we get.

I still haven't sung since a week last Friday. I don't think this is fair as most of the Redcoats are in the bars and in the shows every night. And they are no better than me.

I washed some underpants the other day and left them in the drying room and they were stolen!

I miss your meals, Mum. We'd some Yorkshire pudding today and it was like poo. I'm not kidding.

Sorry about all this grumbling, but I came here hoping to sing and I'm doing everything under the sun but . . . I mean I was just as well working at Newsomes as this and earning more money for less hours. It wasn't as though I was unhappy at home or at work. It seems to me I've just come here as an ordinary Redcoat. Anyway, I'm hoping things brighten up, or you'll be seeing me home sooner than you think.

All my love and thoughts are with you.

Your Geoff

"Awwww, P. Were you a little homesick?" Mom asks.

"I think so. And obviously upset I was doing everything except singing."

"If someone stole my underwear, I'd be upset, too," I joke. "I notice you say, 'Dear All' in the greeting. You were writing to your whole family?"

"Yes, to my Mum, Dad, and my sisters. Jean would have been about fourteen and Jennifer around twelve or so. I adored my sisters."

"Did anyone write back?"

"My mum always wrote back. Dad wrote twice, to ridicule me. But that part comes later. My mother never had a phone, so I couldn't phone her. Letters were our only way of communicating."

"How long did it take for your letters to get home after you mailed them?" I'm interested. I think I would have gone nuts waiting for a reply. If someone doesn't answer my email or text within the day, I gnaw my nails."

"No more than two days. Sometimes our letters crossed in the mail."

"This next one has you singing in church each week." This time Mom reads:

From Butlins, 1961

Dear All,

To my dismay I shall not be home on Saturday after all. Anyway, let's hope it's the Saturday after. Not that I've got unhappy here or anything. But I was thinking I should be home on Saturday and was getting so excited at seeing you all again.

This morning, as is usual every Sunday, I went to the church service. It was really lovely this week as they sang hymns nearly all the time, including "Jesus Lover of My Soul" and "Abide With Me."

All my love, Geoff

x x x

P.S. I've just gone mad and bought a bar of chocolate and I am making a glutton of myself. And Mum, don't say the photo looks miserable—for I have enough photos with me grinning. Anyway, for a studio photo you have to look serious.

"Church and chocolate. Definitely two of my favorite things as well," I laugh.

"Some things don't change much," Mom says. "Please, P— don't go mad and eat the whole bar today. You know what your doctor says."

"I know. It takes me nearly a week to go through a bar. I think I'm alright."

"Should we read another?" I ask, reaching for just one more handful of buttery, maple syrupy popcorn.

"Maybe just one more. We don't want to weary people with details of my Butlins life."

"Okay, but this one is short. It speaks of the upcoming pantomimes. That was definitely a steppingstone on your way to fame, right?"

Mom hands him the popcorn bowl. He finishes the last bits, licking his fingers.

I read:

Butlins 1961

Dear All,

On Monday, I'm going to London for an audition to be in a pantomime at either Bradford or Sheffield. Anyway, I shouldn't accept anything until I've written and told you the details and see what you've said. (That's of course, if they accept me.)

I may be home next weekend. Let's hope so. I'm longing to see you.

All my dearest love.

Yours, Geoff

P.S. I've just been up the road to buy a dinner. Butlins' fish and chips and jam, I can't bear. They are like cold poo.

"That's funny!" Mr. P exclaims.

"See, you always *were* a picky-pants about food," Mom takes the bowl as he tries to run his finger around the rim for one more lick of caramel.

"I remember going to a pantomime with you P's. Years ago, when you lived in England. It was so silly! Men dressed in drag, audience shouting back and forth with actors."

"Yes!" Mr. P remembers. "We saw *Cinderella*."

"Weren't you in *Cinderella* with Danny La Rue in Bournemouth?" Mom peeks around the door frame from the kitchen.

"Who's Danny La Rue?" I ask.

"Danny La Rue. He was quite famous. And quite glamorous," Mr. P says. And by now he must be quite dead, because he was older than I in 1963 when we worked together at Bournemouth Pavilion. But we are getting ahead of ourselves. First, I do the Panto *Aladdin* in Sheffield.

"You got the job?" I'm excited.

"Yes."

"Perfect!"

"*I* thought so. It gave me something to look forward to. And it was close to home, so I could enjoy my mum's cooking and my family could come to the shows."

For what will it profit a man if he gains the whole world, and loses his own soul?

Mark 8:36 NKJV

MR. P SINGING AT BUTLINS

WINSFORD, SOMERSET

Chapter 5

THE ENTERTAINMENT BUSINESS

It is strange to be known so universally
and yet to be so lonely.
Albert Einstein

"Today is the day I'm going to get castrated!" Mr. P shouts to his wife from their red bedroom.

"Oh, I thought we were going to Big Lots today," Mrs. P responds from the bathroom where she pins her ponytail into an "up-do."

I smile. *They crack me up!*

A few minutes later, the P's and I sit in September sunshine around their deck table. Mom's mismatched blue and white Spode bowls hold the last of the season's fresh berries. Mrs. P is the only woman I know who serves breakfast on china. She has always been fancy like that.

We have much to discuss. I hope The P's are up for it. Mr. P's forehead is creased with the pain of a headache that hangs around like a hungry dog. It's been two weeks already and I can see it's wearing him down. Apart from the headache, he has a stent in his ureter in preparation for a looming kidney operation. He often winces when the kidney issue out-pains the headache. Despite it all, he retains his sense of humor.

"I'm finally ready for castration," he jokes again. "When I was twenty, I certainly wasn't."

"Why do you keep talking about castration?" Mom wonders aloud as she pours our tea.

"Because this is the part of my story when I finally break down and tell someone about my sexual feelings. Castration was the only hope they offered!"

"Wait. *What?*" I stop chewing and stare at him. I am stunned.

"It's true." His blue eyes sparkle with mischief.

"I always wondered what was wrong with our love life," Mom teases.

"Seriously, P's. Tell me everything. That is ridiculous!"

Mr. P leans back in his plastic deck chair. The tremble in his hand is worse today. Rooibos tea jostles inside his cup as he struggles to hold it steady. I open my black and white composition book, clicking my pen into gear as he begins to talk.

"I was in Sheffield, in a pantomime, when I mustered up enough courage to speak with a doctor. But first I had to go to London to audition. I lived in a cheap flat and borrowed money from my mum and dad to pay the first rent until I got a paycheck from my two jobs."

"What did you do for work?" I ask.

"I was a stock boy at Woolworths and I also worked at a pub, much to Mum's dismay."

"Oh, I read a couple of letters about that. You stayed in a tiny room and hated cooking for yourself," Mom says, disappearing into the house to fetch the letters. I sip my tea and doodle tulips in my composition book.

"Who wants to read aloud?" Mom returns, waving several faded envelopes.

"Go on," Mr. P replies. "I'm just finishing my tea."

"Let me see," Mrs. P says softly as she opens envelopes and scans pages. "Hmmm. I think you're still finishing your summer at Butlins in this one. It says you're 'skint.' What does that mean?"

"It means I had no money, as usual," he laughs. "That's Yorkshire for broke."

"You go to the beach and the 'pictures' in this one."

"I'm sure I did. I've always loved swimming in the sea. And back then I watched nearly every film that came out."

"You must not have been *that* skint if you could afford the movies." I try my hand at the colloquialism.

"Listen to this," Mom chuckles. "You even write home about having a cold and cleaning your room."

> *. . . Today my cold is much better. I have been taking Aspro's and a Vicks inhaler. It's awful having to buy all these little things yourself. Not like being at home when YOU buy them. It seems awful quiet having the room to myself this week, as Ted was always talking and acting (the silly fool).*
>
> *The cleaner has been off for two weeks. My room has been piling up with dust. So this morning I had two hours off, which was marvelous. I shifted the beds and furniture, dressing table, wardrobe and Hoovered all around. Then I got the tin of polish out and gave everything a right good do. Next, I made my bed, the first time it had been made in a week. I must admit, when I had finished everything, it looked smashing.*
>
> *I think when I come home, you'll have to put all the washing and cleaning jobs from folk you get on to me, Mum. I don't dislike ironing, so I can help you.*

"That's so sweet—you offering to help your Mum with chores."

"He was a good boy." Mom kisses him on the forehead. "And he still is! Especially when he irons for me. I just can't anymore with my crooked little arm."

She continues skimming.

"This next one is short. It says you are 'lovely and brown from the beach' and ate 'a pound of plums, a pound of grapes and a pint of milk for dinner,' with a P.S. confessing you 'pinched' envelopes from the office for all your letters."

"I think that means stealing. Mr. P. Maybe you weren't such a good boy after all," I banter.

"This next one mentions your sister, Jen and your voice teacher. Shall I read it?"

"Why not?" he says, leaning forward.

Maybe these letters are sparking memories.

Dear All,

I hope Jen is still going on okay. Did I ought to have sent a card for your anniversary? I forgot. Anyway, I hope you had a nice one. It wasn't your silver wedding or anything like that though, was it?

I went up to London and saw my singing teacher, Mable, who just had a talk with me. I start lessons next Tuesday. She seemed okay, and by the way she talked I think I have a lot to learn. If I take a tape, she will give me some skills so I can practice back here. So I'll have to get my recorder when I come up home.

In the afternoon I saw the film Barabbas. I was expecting it to be really good, but it was nothing marvelous.

Cheerio for now.

All my love, Geoff

"Yes!" Mom cheers. "This is the beginning of your ascent to stardom. Wasn't Mable famous?"

"Well, if I wanted to sing professionally, I needed professional singing lessons. Madame Mable Corran, at that time, was the voice teacher of anyone who became anyone in London. And I wanted to be *someone,* didn't I?"

"Here it is—the one about your first lesson with Miss Mable. It's hilarious! Who wants to read?"

Mr. P reaches for the letter.

> *Dear All,*
>
> *On Thursday at the singing teacher's, it was a real scream. I was there an hour. Mr. Sullivan took me in the car. The things the woman had me doing. I could hardly keep my face straight. She is getting on in years and said the first few lessons people usually think she's mad. She had me putting my hands on her chest, on her head and on her Adam's apple to feel the vibrations while she was making the most stupid, hideous sounds. Then we went on to do exercises. Touching my toes, rolling my head around and pretending to be flying, among other daft things.*
>
> *Also singing, "Ne, Ne, Noooo, Nah, Nay." I felt stupid. I was almost bursting my sides holding the laughs back. Among a few who have been to her are Mark Wynter, Valerie Masters, Marion Ryan, and Dickie Valentine.*

"Marian Ryan was a famous British pop singer at one point," Mr. P explains. "Also from Yorkshire." He continues.

> *She seems to know what she's talking about and is really very nice.*
>
> *On Friday night, I sang at this pub—a really high-class place at Hackney. I was singing with their group (a pianist, guitar, drums, and sax). John took me to the drummer's, where I had my tea. Then we all set off from there. I was rather nervous at not having practice. I had no need to be as the group backed me marvelously and everything was a great success, I'm glad to say.*
>
> *All my love, Geoff*

"Wow! That's all very exciting. So, your summer at Butlins gave you some experience and confidence to push to the next level?" I ask.

"Maybe. I just wanted to perform all the time. I dreamed of becoming a star."

The sun sits warm on my neck as we wait for Mom to find the next letter. I look at Mr. P, a seventy-eight-year-old man with trembling hands, a heart stent and a giant kidney stone, sitting in his back garden awaiting an operation.

We dismiss them, I think to myself. *We shake their hands at church or give them a brief hug at family gatherings, but we miss the richness of the elderly experience, ignore the lives they've lived and the stories they hold within their weathered skin.*

God, please don't let anything happen to him before we can share his story with the world. Even if he never topped the charts as a British pop star, his life matters. His story has potential to impact this generation. Please preserve Mr. P. Let his surgery be without complications, in Jesus' name.

My silent prayer is interrupted as Mom fans paper in front of my eyes. "Here is the letter where he auditions for *Aladdin*. Things are starting to move now!"

"Let me read this one." I grab the letter. "I'm loving this, you know. It's kind of like watching a movie."

> *Dear All,*
> *Sorry I forgot Dad's birthday.*

"Oh, dear! I'm forgetting everything. I don't sound like a nice person," Mr. P interjects.

> *I'll buy him something when I get some money in hand. Do you think you can send me 2 Pounds Mum, please? Then I'll owe you for 5 Pounds, as I don't think I'll survive until I get my wage.*

I've just had my dinner—potatoes, sausage and a lamb chop. I've put some peas to steep for meat pie and peas tomorrow. Thank goodness I shan't have this to do when I have my dinner at work next week.

Thursday night I went after an evening job in a pub as a trainee relief barman. I have to go down tonight from 7:30 until 10:30. I'll earn 12 Pounds/6 pence. It's just for a few odd nights per week. Hope you don't mind, but it will only be for three weeks and I'm at rock bottom with my money.

The pub is in Dagenham, about as far as Batley is from home. I get the bus at the end of my street and it stops outside the door. The pub is a new building, which has just opened and looks as though it's real select and posh. Anyway, the money will come in nice and handy for Christmas.

Yesterday morning it started snowing and was freezing cold. I went to the agent I had written to earlier in the summer. He was holding an audition for me. I told you I rang him on Tuesday and was told to ring again Thursday. He said he only wanted four singers and told me the time I had to go for my audition, which was 10:30 till 12:30. He said to come as early as possible.

I arrived at 10 o'clock and an older man was already there. The audition had been advertised in the 'Stage.' So that meant there would be a good few people there and I wouldn't have an earthly chance. The audition was held where I used to go for my singing lessons.

There were just three of us there when the agent came. He was only a young bloke and really nice, not like the big-headed things half of them are. The bloke before me was supposed to go in the other room where the piano was, to sing first. But the agent called me and said, "Are you Geoff Pennock?" So I went in first.

The pianist was good, and I sang "Portrait of My Love" and was saying my prayers at the same time.

He then asked me if I could get any higher. So I sang part of the song again in a higher key. I never thought I should get the notes, but I did.

He then said, "I will naturally set you on."

From then on, I was in a dream. I was really in tears and could hardly talk. I don't think I've ever felt such a sensation in all my life. It felt wonderful that after all these years of trying, I'd got a start. No one will ever put me off now. With the help of God, I'll get to the top! If I didn't put my faith in Him, I might as well have given up.

The agent, Bob Perkins said with me living down here, he would put me in at Bristol. But I noticed on his sheet he wanted someone at Sheffield. So I said, "I live up north." And he put me there. I signed a contract of which I have a copy—and left Week's Studio the happiest person alive yesterday.

I was all out of a shake and couldn't believe what had happened. I still can't. I keep looking at the contract.

Straight away I went and sent to the telegram. I had to see how much it was first, as I really couldn't afford it. It cost 5 Pounds/3 pence.

I then had some dinner and went and told Mrs. Barnes the good news. I felt like going around with a loudspeaker and telling everyone! Last night I went over to Barry's after ringing Claire and calling and telling Graham. I should have been celebrating but could not afford to. I wish I could've been home to tell you the news myself.

I might as well stay down here until I come up for rehearsals. Which I was told would be round about 10 December. He said he would let me know all the arrangements within the next week or so and I shall get my fare paid up to Sheffield.

I'll have to write those people I know in Sheffield and see if they know anyone who will put me up. I should be able to come home Sunday mornings and stay till Monday morning every week. That is 14 weeks of enjoyment I have to look forward to.

The panto starts Christmas Eve. Did I tell you it was Aladdin?

See you in three weeks time then. I don't think I've written as much in one letter in all my life. I think I'll have a nod. I hardly slept a wink last night. I was that excited. God bless.

All my sincere love. I hope you are as happy as me. Please write soon.

Your dear son, Geoff
x x x x x x x x x x x x x x x x x

"I love this letter! You sound so delighted!"

"I *was* happy singing in the chorus. There were four of us singing together. When you're in front of an audience, it's a happy time. Can you imagine being in a pantomime? It's a joyful, creative thing! Nothing like Walt Disney's *Aladdin* movie. A panto in England is completely different.

"Somewhere I read pantomimes developed from sixteenth century Italian street theatre. The Brits have been mad about pantos for years. I don't know how you would explain the thrill of them. You'd have to grow up British to really understand. The audience interacts with the stage. They become a part of it."

"They *are* a bit lewd." Mom interjects. "With the vulgarity, villains and jokes."

"You know the British sense of humor includes tons of innuendos. I'm not defending it. It *is* our culture. The cross-dressing is from Shakespeare days. I mean, *that's* something really British, isn't it?

"In our version of *Aladdin*, the prince would be a woman. Aladdin's mother would be a man dressed as a woman—a silly character. I didn't play any main character. I was just one of four male singers, backing up the mains, but to me it was a dream! I was on stage every night for three months! It kept my mind off the other, unexplainable parts of my life."

"Thanks for the description," Mr. P. "Thanks for sharing your story. I really am glad your mother saved all these conversation-starter letters."

"Yes," he says, "but all through the years the letters I wrote to my mum were not the real me. Not who I was."

"Why?" I'm curious.

"Because she didn't know the pain I was going through. There is a lot of pressure to go out with girls, you know. And your friends always asking, 'Why don't you have a girlfriend?' I knew something was wrong, but I never let on to my mum."

"That's heartbreaking. I'm so sorry you suffered like that."

"Let's read the next one." He steers our conversation toward the safety of describing the details of his department-store day job. I know these are difficult topics for him. He lives a different life now. I'm sensitive to this and choose not to press.

> *Dear All,*
>
> *Thanks for the 2 Pounds I received this morning. It just saved my life as I pay the landlady 2 Pounds/10 per week on a Wednesday and I only had 1/10. Sure it seems dear, doesn't it? But if I had got any rooms near London it would have been three or 4 Pounds per week at the cheapest. I'll get through now until I get my wage on Saturday.*
>
> *I've just got back from Barry's. I nearly live around there. I went for a bath as we haven't one here.*
>
> *I think people who come down to London on their own, not knowing anyone must be mad. If I hadn't known a few people, it would have been awful.*
>
> *When I went to the pub to work on Saturday, we had to clear everything away after it had shut, and I missed the last bus and had to walk three miles back*

here and didn't arrive until 1:30. I'm glad I am not going again. I don't fancy doing that on a Saturday after working all day. I should also have to dash straight in and out after work to get there on time.

Woolworth's isn't too bad. The worst thing is getting up on a morning and getting my breakfast which has consisted of a cup of tea, All-Bran, brown bread and an apple most of this week.

In the same stockroom as me, work three more kids about my age. They are okay to get on with, although I hardly see them, as we are that busy. The women from the shop come up and down most of the day for different things. They are all nice and friendly and usually stop to speak. Most of the day we are carting and unpacking crates and boxes. It is fairly heavy work and I have ached all over this week. It is to be expected, as the last time I did owt [something] like this was May.

The boss does not let us stop for a minute. It's not like being in most places, with everyone having a break time every so often.

It's marvelous how much stuff they have in the stockroom. There are two rooms. How they know where everything is, I don't know.

The dinners are really lovely. They have a canteen on its own for the girls and the men have a little room at the side. I can understand you, Mum, when you say if you were at home on your own at dinnertime, you wouldn't eat owt [something]. I felt the same. I'd rather do without than get it ready. If I've been hungry and got something ready, by the time I've cooked it, I'm not bothered. I think you enjoy it all the more when it's got ready for you.

Anyway, I'll soon be back to the good old Sunday dinners at home. Only two weeks. Hope you're all keeping well.

God bless. All my dearest love,
Geoff
x x x x x x x x x x x x x x x x x x x x x x x x x x x x x x

"I can definitely see some of the old Mr. P in the young Mr. P," I comment. "You *still* notice and appreciate salesclerks who are friendly and speak with you."

"Why aren't there any letters from Sheffield? When you are in the pantomime?" Mom looks up from the pages she's spread across the table.

"Because I went home once a week. I could tell all my stories in person at the dinner table. Well, not *all* my stories. Some I never told."

"Like what?" *I can't help it. I need to ask.*

"Like I finally went to speak to a doctor about my problem."

"What kind of doctor?"

"Just an ordinary doctor."

"What was the catalyst?"

"I just plucked up courage. I felt embarrassed. I wanted to know, but I daren't go to our family doctor. At that time, anyone who was gay was considered a pervert. I realized I was different . . ."

Mr. P stalls. A neighbor's weed eater fills the silence until he speaks again.

"I'd heard of Oscar Wilde, who ended up behind bars, sentenced to hard labor. And Lord Byron . . . Only in 1967 was homosexuality decriminalized in the United Kingdom." His voice escalates. "So, in 1961, what was I thinking? I could be put in bloody jail!"

"Shhhhhh! Don't tell the neighbors!" Mom gestures toward the house next door. "They think we're a lovely old couple."

Mr. P laughs and lowers his voice. "In Tunisia you go to jail for three years, even now.

"At that time, I was going through all of these things in my head: *it's against the law . . . I'm bloody nuts . . .* whatever!"

"That's why you were sneaky and went to a doctor in a city away from your home?" I inquire.

"Yes."

"What did you want him to do for you?"

"I don't know. I didn't know *what* he could do, did I?'

"Do you feel the doctor was an advocate, or compassionate toward you at all?"

"No! I thought he was a bloody nutter, didn't I?"

"Why?"

"Because his advice to me was, castration! *'It is the only solution!'* he said. "Of course, I declined."

"Thankfully!" Mrs. P interjects. "Our marriage would have been much less interesting otherwise."

I glance at my mother. She's wearing an expression Mr. P affectionately calls 'the bird face.' It's the perfect combination of saucy and sweet.

"So . . ." I venture, "What went through your mind as you left Dr. Castration's office that day? I really want to understand."

"I don't know. That was sixty years ago, wasn't it?"

We wait for a full minute before he continues. "From a doctor's perspective, if that was the only cure, my situation felt hopeless."

"Did you know anyone else who had these feelings?" I have so many questions, but I don't want to overwhelm.

"Of course I didn't. I thought I was the only person in the world."

"So, what did you do?"

"A person would cover it all up with the joy of being on stage, wouldn't they? Just get on with the show. That's what *I* did. I lived for those moments when the audience clapped and cheered, and I tried to forget everything going on inside of me.

"After Aladdin finished, I moved back to London to work in B.B. Evans department store until I could get a break in entertainment. I wanted to be near Miss Mable and try to get signed with an agent. Somehow, I managed to support myself through the spring until my second season at Butlins, Margate."

"Were you at a Clifton Hotel?" Mom asks. "There are a few letters from Clifton Hotel, Margate. I put them in a separate stack."

"Yes. That's it! I got another summer contract."

"I'll be right back!" Mom scoots away from the table. "That second summer is when you get a little famous with the Butlins crowd."

"Did you know," she stage whispers dramatically, "until just a couple years ago, he still received Christmas cards from some of his fans?"

"That was so long ago. They're all gone now. Nobody writes any more," Mr. P laments.

"Well, they sure must've loved you, Steve Parrish, because they wrote for more than fifty years! One woman even included him in her will!" she says, carefully stacking her Spode bowls. "We were already married when the money order arrived from the lady's executor."

"The madam was a middle-aged spinster when she came to Butlins. I remember she had a little mustache." He shakes his head at the thought. "'Steve Parrish' inherited 800 Swiss Francs when she passed away."

"Steve Parrish?" I repeat. "I'm confused."

"It was his stage name. That's what he called himself. Didn't I tell you there are many Mr. P's?"

"Tell me more! Where did you get *that* name?" I quiz.

"Years ago, there was a movie called Parrish, it was set in New England. There was a blonde-haired actor. What was his name?" He thinks for a moment. "Troy Donahue."

"Oh, I remember him!" Mom recalls. "He was cute. But so were you, Peedy P."

"I want to Google him so I can see," I comment.

"Why don't we all go inside? It's a bit warm out here now anyway." Mr. P picks up his tea with shaky hands. I follow the *tink*

tink tink of a teaspoon clinking against the side of his cup all the way to the kitchen.

After resettling ourselves in their sunny sitting room I search "Troy Donahue" on my laptop. Images of a dreamy, California-looking guy pop up. I share a bit from a Wikipedia link.

> *Donahue later admitted that he began abusing drugs and alcohol at the peak of his career and increased use after his career began to wane:*
>
> *"I was loaded all the time... I'd wake up about 6:30 in the morning, take three aspirins mixed with codeine, slug down half a pint of vodka and then do four lines of cocaine. That was just so I could get the front door open to peek out and see if I could face the day."*
>
> *Stark, John (August 13, 1984). "After 20 Years Awash in Booze and Drugs, Troy Donahue Prizes His Sobering Discoveries." People.com. Retrieved May 23,2014.

"It's sad, isn't it?" Mr. P says softly. "I can understand it. If a person doesn't have Jesus, where do they go with all their pain?"

His words hang in the air like a dark fog. Mom kisses his forehead saying, "I'm sorry, Peedy." Then she hands me a Margate letter dated 1962:

I skim two paragraphs about the weather before reading audibly.

> *The guests have been a great lot. Two middle-aged widows who were here on my first week last year arrived today for two weeks. They're really lovely folks and think the world of me. Last year when they left, they said, "We wrote to Billy Butlins saying how wonderful Steve Parrish made our Holiday."*
>
> *I'm on the show tomorrow and I'm thrilled to bits as I'm on the top of the bill at the end. So I just pray I shall be okay. I'm having a rehearsal with the orchestra tomorrow afternoon. So everything should go off alright . . .*

"Sounds like you were a big deal, Mr. P. I guess "P" could stand for Parrish *or* Pennock," I joke.

"Maybe I was more popular the second season because return guests already knew me. Redcoats spent a lot of time making the guests happy."

"Read this one," Mom says. "It's about an audition he has in London."

> *Butlins, Cliftonville Hotels, Margate*
> *Wednesday*
>
> *Dear All,*
>
> *We had a glorious day on Sunday. I think it must've been the nicest day this summer. 12 hours of sunshine we had. I managed to get a couple of hours on the beach and had a swim, which I really enjoyed.*
>
> *Both our bosses this year are as miserable as sin. Not a bit like Bobby, our boss last year, who called at our house. One of the Redcoats had a row with them last Tuesday and gave his notice, and another yesterday. The only time they smile at you is when we take money for the darned raffle tickets we sell.*
>
> *Yesterday was a lovely day and I was wishing I could stay and lay on the beach instead of going up to London. I had arranged to see an agent at 2:30 and had a real rush as the train was late and I didn't arrive until 2:30.*

"You never did like late trains, did you, P?" Mom interjects.

"He's very Swiss that way," she tosses an explanation my direction. "When it comes to travel, the transportation must not be late."

I continue reading.

> *I looked good, as I got a bit brown from being in the sun on Sunday and an hour Tuesday morning.*

What a ramshackle old place I had to go for my audition—some shabby little rehearsal rooms. The agent was a real friendly family woman. No airs and graces. Just like anyone back home. She made me feel at ease as soon as I walked in. We talked about everything under the sun besides singing. The pianist was really good, and I sang well.

She was thrilled to bits with me and kept on saying so (I don't know how many times) as we went across the road to her office. She took all my particulars and said with my looks and voice I should get somewhere. I think she gave me more confidence in myself than anyone ever has.

She took my home address and my address here and said she would do her utmost to get me some work. She meant it as well, as I could tell she was sincere—not like those who say they will let you know and never do. If I hadn't been any good, she'd have told me at the rehearsal rooms without wasting her time taking me to her office, which was a couple streets away. So I am now hoping and praying for the best.

Afterward, I went for my singing lesson from 5 o'clock until six. I thought I would have an hour this week and give it a miss next week.

In the evening we went to the pictures to see Audrey Hepburn in "The Loudest Whisper." It was a real wonderful and touching film. A woman sat next to us having a good weep. Tell Jean she must go see it if it comes to Dewsbury, as it's one of the best films I've seen for a while.

Cheerio for now. All my love and God bless.

Yours, Geoff
x x x x x x x x x x x x x x

"Wasn't Aubrey Hepburn the one who lived up the road from us in Switzerland?" Mom asks. "When you worked at La Ligniere?"

"Yes, she lived about twenty minutes away. I always thought she was lovely somehow. I mean, she wasn't beautiful, but there was something nice about her, wasn't there? She was in all those funny, innocent kinds of films. She also helped children and the poor throughout her life."

"Audrey Hepburn may have been a very sweet person," I say, glancing up from another letter, "but you *do* realize her character in *Breakfast at Tiffany's* was a sex worker, right? While Holly Golightly appeared innocent enough, she was actually a prostitute. I think Hollywood just glossed over it, like they still do about sexual things that are quite spiritually serious."

"I never thought of *Breakfast at Tiffany's* that way," Mom admits. Then she turns toward to Mr. P, "I'm quite sure God rescued you from the underbelly of the entertainment world before you were in too deep. All the glitz and glamour in those old Hollywood movies must've been fascinating to a poor boy from Dewsbury."

I change the subject. "Speaking of poor, you must've been out of cash at Butlins if your parents had to send you hair cream. Listen to this.

> *Butlins, Clifton Hotel,*
> *Margate. Kent. 1962*
>
> *Dear All,*
>
> *Thanks for your letter and the hair cream. Please don't keep putting in your letters that you miss me. I miss you all terribly and it only upsets me when you keep writing that.*
>
> *They put me on the show on Friday. I sang "I'd Do Anything" and "Portrait of My Love."*

As if on cue, the P's burst into song.

"It's from Oliver! Mr. P explains. "I think it was in the top ten."

"How do you two know all the same songs with him being nine years older?" I ask my mother.

"I had older cousins, so I was into all that teenage stuff from a young age."

"Carry on reading," Mr. P's voice is merry. Things are getting interesting. I feel as if I'm watching a movie of my own life listening to these."

"Okay. Where was I?"

> *It went down really wonderful and the audience went mad, shouting and clapping! I felt really great. The orchestra played wonderfully! At the dance afterward, I was overwhelmed with compliments.*
>
> *You know the song, "Honeybun" from South Pacific? Where she is dressed as a sailor, and there is a man dressed in a grass skirt with coconuts and a wig, dancing? Well, four of us were dressed like that while one of the girls sang the song. The audience really died with laughter. They are putting that in the Friday show every week now.*
>
> *I am just in the chorus tonight. This week we are having two sittings for the meals, as we are getting busier. There will also be two shows a night, so I should get more experience than ever. I better leave now, as I'm going to the morning church service.*
>
> *All my love and thoughts are with you.*
>
> *Yours, Geoff*
>
> *x x x x x x x x x x x x x*

"Well, now we have proof in your own handwriting that you were a cross-dressing singer in your twenties!" I needle.

"I guess so, if you consider a coconut bra and a hula skirt as cross-dressing," he laughs.

"Seriously though, did you ever desire to dress in feminine clothing? Don't some gay men like to cross dress?"

"Noooo! I Never did." His voice is forceful. "I would say very few. I think that's a different thing altogether. I've never personally known anyone who would want to."

"Maybe that's a trans thing." Mom says. "It's a bit of a different slant. But don't you think some guys in the pantomime *liked* to dress like women?" she asks him. "Like Danny Larue?"

"Oh, dear! He *was* different. Danny was an exception. I would say that's an exception," Mr. P repeats. "In those days, which was a long, long time ago, although homosexuality was not accepted, strangely enough, *he* was accepted.

"For decades Danny Larue did the Christmas pantomimes. There were only a few flamboyant people like that around back then. More often than not, shows would have a comedian who was not at all gay."

"So," I venture, "when you started working with cross-dressing show people, you didn't feel like, 'Here's my tribe?'"

"Not in any shape or form. I kept my sexual thoughts and feelings to myself. I didn't fit in anywhere. I wasn't comfortable inside myself. I hated myself."

"You mention church in this letter. You went to church, even when you were away from home—away from your Mum?"

"Yeah." He doesn't elaborate.

"Through all the stories," Mrs. P looks at her husband intently, "it seems you're always seeking God."

"I was seeking God because I didn't *want* that thing that made me feel strange and unusual. I was always trying to meet some need by going to church. I needed significance, security, and self-worth. I got those words from a book, but it's true. All my pain and confusion was overwhelming at times. I wanted God to do something, but I didn't even know what to ask.

"I don't know Danny Larue's story, but I know mine. And I know the stories of many friends through the years who struggled in some way with their sexuality—lesbians, homosexuals, some who couldn't decide what they were. We were all damaged people, acting out our pain and numbing in unusual ways. No matter the pain or the anesthetic, there was only one answer to it all. I kept going to church to find Him, but He wasn't there."

I am convinced and confident of this very thing, that He who has begun a good work in you will [continue to] perfect and complete it until the day of Christ Jesus [the time of His return].

Philippians 1:6 AMP

CASTLE COMBE, WILTSHIRE

Chapter 6

LETTERS FROM LONDON

It is only because he became like us
that we can become like him.
Dietrich Bonhoeffer

Seven full months dawned and disappeared—Mrs. P's seventieth birthday, Mr. P's kidney operation, a wet winter filled with doctors and dentists, and bank dollars disappearing by the thousands. On the August afternoon we last wrote together, Mr. P sat with a teabag on one bloodshot eye, a throbbing headache and a painful stent in his groin as he awaited a third kidney procedure. Today the whole world is different.

Perhaps the only similarity between then and now is we three are together, still writing this powerful testimony of God's redemptive power to rescue a life and transform it for His glory! As I write these words, the P's are with me in a pandemic-inspired lock-down in Spain. Mr. P sits in the only armed chair in our AirBnB apartment, comparing Spain and Italy's death tolls from Covid-19.

Mrs. P leans back on the sofa, legs crossed, Bible and pen in hand. She's reading Revelation 6 about end-time pestilence. I'm at the table, typing words on my laptop keyboard—praying there is time for Mr. P's story to be told far and wide before we see our Jesus face-to-face.

"Listen to this," he says, tears in his voice. "More than 10,000 Coronavirus deaths now reported in Italy."

"It's absolutely heartbreaking." Mrs. P peers over pink-rimmed readers to catch his eye. "I read earlier many nurses' faces are bruised—marked from hours of wearing tight protective masks."

"The Spanish government just added another fourteen days to our lock-down," I add to our disjointed discussion.

After more than two weeks in a tiny foreign apartment with my husband and the P's, I am accustomed to these confusing conversations. Sometimes the four of us (my husband is here too) sit quietly on our devices until something we watch or hear causes us to blurt out a statistic or new mandate pertinent to our situation.

It's surreal. None of us can recall anything even remotely similar in the histories of our lives. Because of something that never should have happened in Wuhan, China, thousands of people around the world are dead, dying or fighting for life as a ventilator breathes for them. Most tourists fled home before governments closed borders and airports. Cafes and restaurants shut down. Streets are empty and police are patrolling. Fear, uncertainty, and a twinge of sheer panic pervades every communication with friends and family in other countries.

"I'm going to work in the other room," André, my pastor-husband announces quietly. "Thoughts are starting to flow for my next chapter." He's using this time to author a book of his own.

"That's our cue, P's. Let's finish reading our previous chapters so we know where to go from here in your story. Mom reaches for Mr. P's hand as I begin. She looks glamorous today in her royal blue kaftan. We are supposed to be in Morocco. Mom is dressed as if we were.

They both listen intently, sometimes nodding in agreement. I hear Mr. P sniffle as I read the last sentence of Chapter 5, "I kept going to church to find Him, but He wasn't there."

"I'm crying. It's my life. I'm hearing about myself, but I feel as if it's someone else. It's so long ago. It makes me cry." He wipes his nose with the back of his hand.

Mom and I chorus, "Don't touch your face!" Face-touching is a Covid-19 no-no.

He laces his fingers together and continues. "From when I was a child, going to the Methodist Church with my mum, God was always there, somewhere in my life. Until I was forty years old, though, I believed he hated me. I felt I was worth as much to Him as the excrement Spanish dogs leave on the sidewalk. That lie affected everything in my life, as I was always searching for my worth."

"Your letters in your twenties certainly give us a glimpse of the you who was searching for God and you who was seeking your value from the applause of others." Mrs. P's eyes are moist with empathy.

"I'm so thankful you took time to type a bunch of his letters into emails, Mom. At least I have those, and my notes from last summer.

"What happened next in your story?" I ask.

"Well," says Mr. P, "I had fourteen weeks at Butlins that season. They didn't pay so well. I was always borrowing 2 Pounds from my mum."

"There's a letter about that in the emails," Mom reminds me. "His mum kept an envelope with a running tab. He didn't just sponge off her.

"You always paid it back, didn't you Mr. P?" she affirms.

"Yes, but then I'd borrow again," he chuckles.

"Here we go!" I exclaim after finding the email. In this letter you don't pay it back right away because you buy yourself some 'smashing' new pants. Listen to this.

> *Dear All,*
>
> *Sorry I did not send any money to you last week, but now I enclose 2 Pounds. I have just bought a new pair of trousers at 2 Pounds 10. So I couldn't send you owt. They are really fabulous; an olive shade and they look smashing with my new coat and shoes.*

Everyone was admiring me last night and saying how fabulous I looked.

Yesterday was a really wonderful day. Absolutely boiling. It was my day off. I did some shopping in Margate and had my hair cut. Then I caught the bus to Canterbury. From there I went to a village called Chilham, which is one of the most beautiful villages in England. It was really one of the most enchanting places I have ever been. I was thrilled to bits. Wish you were with us, Mum. You would have really enjoyed it. It was one of the most wonderful days since I've been here.

Cheerio for now!

Love, Geoff

"Oh, that's Mr. P." He refers to himself in the third person. "You've been there with me to Chilham," he says to his wife. "I love these places."

"There are so many Mr. P's," she teases. "The American Mr. P, the Italian Mr. P, the Swiss Mr. P. Life with you is never boring. Chilham wasn't where they filmed Pride and Prejudice was it?"

"No, that was Lacock."

Mr. P is wearing plaid pajama bottoms, the brown and tan striped house socks we bought from a kind Chinese man's shop the day before Spain shut down, and a button up shirt with a sailboat pattern. I think I see the bottom half of his outfit flapping in the breeze on the balcony clothesline. He doesn't look at all like his usual dapper self, but obviously feels right at home discussing English villages.

"I'll show you a picture of Chilham on the iPad." He smiles. "That's what I miss when I live in America—all these quaint places." One finger pecks on his iPad until he finds what he is searching for. Mom leans over to look.

"Isn't it beautiful? A lot of these places are spoiled now with a load of cars, which wouldn't be there at that time," he laments.

They stroll through English villages on their iPad. Mr. P's eyes sparkle with memories.

"This is Mr. P!" He turns the iPad around to show me a thatched-cottage-lined street at Welford-on-Avon. "This is the real Mr. P."

"You're a street? A cottage? An English Village?" Mom teases.

"I'm a man who appreciates unspoilt, quaint places. My mum liked all these places I liked—castles, abbeys, and cathedrals. Dad didn't always go. Did I tell you I once hitchhiked with my mother?"

"Now *that's* something not many kids can say they did with their mom!" I blurt. "Tell us the story." *I'm ready to type every word.*

"I can't remember much. It was . . . in the Cotswolds."

"Can you spell that?"

"C-o-t-s-w-o-l-d-s—an area with the most enchanting villages in England. Buildings are made of honey-gold limestone. When the sun hits just right, they glow. That one famous row of Cotswold houses is even pictured in our British passport.

"I can't recall details about hitchhiking. I just remember doing it. We probably got part way on the bus and couldn't get to the next place, so we hitchhiked to Castle Combe.

"I've been there three times, once with once with *my* mum, once with *your* mum and once by myself. It's quite remarkable. Castle Combe once won a prize for being the most beautiful village in England. Maybe you saw the movie *War Horse.* It was filmed there."

"Oh, I did! The scenery was amazing," I recall.

"This is why his mum was jealous of me when we got married." Mom winks and stage whispers. "She lost her traveling buddy."

"She *was* jealous," he acknowledges. "She liked me all to herself."

"This next letter is short." My eyes return to my emails. "You forget your Mum's birth date, but you are busy advancing your singing career. I hope she understood." I read again:

Butlins 1962

Dear All,

I haven't time to write a letter till Friday. I am so busy rehearsing and learning two new songs. All is going okay. Please let me know as soon as possible whose birthday is when. Is it Jean's on the 16th and yours on the 27th, Mum? Let me know right away.

Love, and God bless, Geoff
x x x x x x x x x x x x x x x x x x

"To this day, I get them confused! Even though my mum's not here anymore, I still switch their birthdays in my mind," Mr. P admits. "Jean just laughs about it."

"What I laugh about is the way you describe *everything*—from the weather to the details of what you eat or drink. Listen to this one . . ."

Butlins 1962

Dear All,

This weekend has been absolutely boiling! All I seem to do is buy glasses of cold orange juice to keep cool. Can't really think of much to write.

John has got in for his holidays in September. Whether I should be here or not, I don't know. Some people last week said the best thing for me to do is to come home. Anyway, I shall see what happens.

I was on the show on Friday and went down smashing. How I wish I could sing more, though. Lots of people say I am wasting my time here. I must admit, I sound good with the mic and orchestra.

I'm sorry I haven't sent any money yet, but I haven't had time to go to the post office, which is a bit away.

Hope you enjoyed your trip on Saturday. If the weather was anything like down here, you will be burnt to a cinder. Looking forward to seeing you.

All my love, Geoff

"I really just wanted to be on stage all the time, didn't I?" He glances sideways at my mother.

"Here's where you begin to have female fans," I say, skimming the next one. "Toward the end of the season."

Butlins 1962

Dear All,

I enclose 1 pound 15. I am sorry it isn't more, but I have to buy things to eat in-between mealtimes, as I leave some of the meals. They are that horrid! Don't worry. I make up for what I leave.

Is it okay for me to send you all these photos of myself with the guests? They are always asking to have their photo taken with me, so I ask them to send me one back.

Did you get an awful thunderstorm on Sunday night? It was terrible here. It must've been because it woke Ted (my roommate) up, and that's nearly an impossibility! He neither hears the alarm, nor the call of the loudspeaker. I have to shake him and shout—even then he goes back to sleep! Anyway, on Saturday, the last morning he's here, me and Jenny-next-door are going to throw some water on him.

Hope to see you soon.

All my love, Geoff
x x x x x x

"It's starting to roll!" Mom claps her hands like a happy seal at Sea World. "You're heading for fame, Mr. Pennock," she cheers.

"Yes, seems strange now. The girls wanted my autograph and photograph—maybe something more. Some girls would go to Butlins to sleep with guys from the shows, you know.

"I once shared a room with a young drummer. He would bring women back to the room saying, 'Come in. It's alright. Geoff's asleep.' I could hear everything they were doing."

"Looks like all *you* were doing was writing letters to the girls," I tease. "Listen to this," I begin to read.

Butlins 1962

Dear All,

This morning I received a wonderful letter from Mr. and Mrs. Watson. I've never received a nicer letter in all my life. In the letter was 1 pound! Mr. Watson said it had been given him to give to me, but he would not say who it was from. Do you know? I would like to write and thank them. I don't know why on earth they sent it though, as I don't need any extra money. Anyway, I am writing to them when I finish this.

Last night we had a rehearsal for the show, and I am singing two songs on Friday!

I shall have to buy a typewriter if I go on like this, as this morning, I received a letter from a girl who was here last week and there are some more who said they would write to me. Anyway, I can't write back. As all the spare time I have now is taken up in writing. It's nice though to think that someone is thinking about you and has not forgotten you.

Since Tuesday, the weather has been dull.

I bought a watch this morning, as I am hopeless without one. I'm nattered all the time about getting back late from the beach.

All my love and keep smiling. Geoff

P.S. Don't think I keep paying for all these photos. They bought the last one I sent to you.

"You still get 'nattered' about being late," Mom remarks. "You're very Swiss that way."

"I do. But now I don't need to worry about it, as I haven't anywhere to go. I'm going *crazy* stuck indoors every day! When my pants are dry, I think I will go for a walk to take out the trash or something!"

"Mr. P!" I interrupt. "You're becoming a Butlins party animal! Listen to this . . ."

Butlins
September 10, 1962

Dear All,

It was the end of the season party on Friday. Four of the Redcoats left. Saturday morning, two of them, twins, left. I was really sorry, as they have been my best friends here this season. I am missing them this week.

The party was great, and I kept sober. I think I ate too much to be anything else. There were about 16 crates of beer and about 14 bottles of whiskey, gin, etc. They also served pork pies and chicken legs and tons of different sandwiches and cream cakes. All I seemed to do was stuff myself with the buns. I really made a glutton of myself.

I didn't get to bed until a quarter to five Saturday morning.

"Oh dear!" he interjects, sounding very British.

I had to be up for work at 7:15.

And again, "Oh dear!"

I felt okay all day—didn't feel tired at all. I was on the show Saturday night. The audience was the best I've ever known. As Saturday night it's usually poor, with everyone being newly arrived.

I got more applause than anyone else. The audience was shouting for more. They went mad! I had more compliments Saturday night than ever and was thrilled to bits. It gives you more confidence to carry on. I think my lessons seem to be doing some good.

I think I shall be here until the beginning of October, as we are booked up until the end of this month.

Mum, do you think you and Mary could come down for a weekend before I leave? I could get you some digs and a pass to the shows.

All my love, Geoff
x x x x x x x x x

"Wow! Mr. P, your audience *loved* you!

"Was Mary a relative?"

"Mary was Mum's friend, a bus conductor. They called them that back then. When people got on the bus, conductors walked around, took money and gave a ticket."

"Did your mum ever come see you in a Butlins show?"

"She came down once, on a Saturday. But not my father."

"You were always wanting something from him that you never got, huh P?" Mom rubs his stubbly cheek with the back of her hand.

"Yes. And I would venture to say most male gays probably have bad relationships with their fathers and are too close to their mothers."

"There may be some truth to that statement," Mom ventures. "I've heard too many of these stories. They all have similar ingredients, but modern psychology will say otherwise."

"On another note," I grin at Mr. P over my laptop screen, "I think you might be hung-over in this next letter."

"Geoffrey! What's the matter with you?" Mom wags her finger at him.

"Pass the Limoncello," he jokes.

The P's *get* each other. Despite painful, confusing pasts, they truly understand one another. It's nice to see that. Many couples just don't.

Butlins (1962)

Dear All,

I don't know why I am writing cos I've now't much to tell you.

I am really glad you're having a nice time. Thanks for the little book. It's really nice. And the verses are lovely. Thanks for all the lovely cards, which are stuck around my dressing table mirror.

The cottage at Flatford seems to be everywhere. I'm sure there can't be many places that have been photographed more.

Mr. P interrupts. "There's a famous painting of a white house by the river. That's the Bridge Cottage at Flatford. John Constable did it. He was a quite renowned British artist."

I nod and keep reading.

All the Redcoats had a party last night. We had a smashing time. Lots of grub and drink. It finished at 3:30 AM. And I had to get up at 7:30 to awaken everyone on the loudspeaker system. I put all four alarms on, and never heard one of them! It was a good thing Barry (the drummer) woke me up. I had a head like a log and have felt awful up to this evening.

Everyone at the party had to do a turn. So I put on my best Yorkshire accent and sang "On Ilkla Moor Baht 'at" and it went down well. I don't think they expected owt like that.

"Oh, Mr. P, this is hilarious! But are you seriously sowing some wild oats here?

He laughs aloud. "It's hilarious? Maybe to you! Nobody who reads this will know 'On Ilkla Moor Baht 'at."

"Probably not, I chuckle. "But *I* remember the three of us standing together on Ilkley Moor not long after you two married. You sang your Yorkshire anthem at the top of your lungs and scared up a red grouse. As a birder, I was grateful. As an American, I had no idea what on earth you were saying!"

"I've been married to this Brit for nearly thirty years. Heard that song numerous times. Still, I couldn't tell you what it says in plain English." Mom stretches out on the sofa as she says facetiously, "Mr. P. I didn't know you had a drinking problem."

"I didn't have a drinking problem *at all*. If there was a party or something, I might have a drink, but I did not go to the pubs."

"I'm reading on, P's. I need to know what happens next! I think I need a Yorkshire dictionary though. Some of these words!"

> *This morning I was on duty for a ramble. I was hoping none of the guests would turn up, and then I could go back to bed. Anyway, two middle-aged women turned up.*

"I can see them now," he interrupts again. "Two middle-aged spinsters. I have a photograph with those two in my book at home."

> *It was a lovely morning, and it blew the cobwebs away. We walked all along the clifftops right out into the country to Kingsgate Castle. I really enjoyed it, as I'd never been before. We had tea and biscuits and then caught the bus back.*
>
> *I didn't tell you before, the folks from last summer who were here the other week with the lad who has leukemia gave me 10 Pounds before they left! And again this Friday, a woman and her daughter gave*

me 10 Pounds for being 'nice and friendly towards them,' she said. I was thrilled to bits! It's nice to think you are appreciated sometimes. I was really surprised, as I hadn't bothered with them more than anyone else.

"Aren't my letters boring?" Mr. P inquires again.

"I find them detailed and interesting. They describe a culture and era I know practically nothing about. More importantly, they describe you. Perhaps not the deep down real you who is struggling with your sexual identity, but the outside you who is painting a word picture of your life as a rising young British star in the 1960's.

I scan Mom's emails for another from this time-frame.

"Here's one more. You aren't partying in this one. You're exploring!"

Dear All,

Yesterday it was a lovely day up to about 3 PM. I caught the 9:15 train to Tonbridge, an old country town with a castle. Around there about 11 AM I had my dinner, which consisted of a pork pie, three cream buns and half a pound of biscuits.

"Three cream buns and half a pound of biscuits!" Mr. P blurts.

"You were a hungry boy! Mom laughs. "I'd sure love a cream bun right now."

"I've never eaten a cream bun, but I'll take anything cream: ice cream, Krispy Kreme, clotted cream," I reply. "Three weeks cooped up in this apartment has given me the munchies. Every time I read one of Mr. P's letters, I get hungry! I think you were a 'foodie' before there was such a thing, Mr. P."

Then I caught the bus through some beautiful countryside and villages and walked a mile and a half over to Chiddingstone Castle.

"Wherever I was, I found where the villages are. It's quite funny." Mr. P's face is relaxed. I can tell he enjoys Memory Lane today.

"It's quite YOU, Mr. Pennock," Mom wiggles her forefinger at him. "Villages, food, singing, art! It's all you. Back to Chiddingstone Castle."

> *I looked 'round the castle, then walked around the lake and looked in the caves—said to be the haunt of smugglers at one time. I was the only person there. It surprises me there are all these lovely places in England and no one visits them.*
>
> *From there I walked through the orchards to the lovely old village, renowned for its beauty and owned by the National Trust.*

"Was that Sissinghurst?" He wonders aloud. "The National Trust probably owns all the houses in that village now. They buy up all the old manor houses and villages, keeping them pristine and tourist-friendly."

> *In the churchyard was a truly beautiful magnolia tree. In the village itself, there were only about ten houses and a post office. In the post office, I bought a pint of milk. It was freezing cold, so I went back and bought another. I thought it would do me as much good as spending money on a deal meal.*
>
> *From there, I walked to the next village to catch the bus. I sat on the side of the road as an artist, sketching the oast houses, which are prominent landmarks around here.*

I pause. "Explanation please, P."

"Oast houses? They were buildings for drying hops—that flower beer is made from. They had cone-shaped roofs over the drying rooms, quite picturesque. There were fields of hops in Kent back then.

"Oh, I think I've seen those houses in photographs. I didn't know what they were," I reply. "They remind me somehow of the Italian Trulli village we visited in 2007."

"I can see that. They both have cone-shaped roofs," Mom agrees. "People live in oast houses now. Some have been transformed into nice bed and breakfast hotels."

She motions for me to keep reading.

> *I saw a sign pointing out a pathway across the fields, to the village I wanted to reach. So I set off down the path, thinking it would be a shorter route than the road. (By the road, it would have only been two miles.) It then began to rain, and I lost the pathway. I climbed over walls and fences and got lost among the hop fields. Before long though, I saw a farmer and followed him back to the road. It only rained for about an hour. It stopped when I got to the village.*
>
> *I got the bus to Tunbridge Wells, a spa town similar to Harrogate. I arrived back at Margate at 8:30, had a meal and went to bed at 9 PM. I got up at 12 and went to a party until 2 AM! I am on second sitting (shifts for breakfast) this week and didn't have to get up until 9!*
>
> *Hope you're all keeping well. If they go by my contract of 14 weeks, I shall finish two weeks on Saturday.*
>
> *All my love, Yours, Geoff*
>
> *P.S. I am going to get the music 'Once in a Lifetime' I think it's fabulous!*

"I don't know *that* song," Mrs. P admits. "Maybe it was before my time."

"Let's Google it," I suggest. "Hmmm. Here's one by the Talking Heads. I'm pretty sure that's not it. Wait, there's an older one by the same title. Sammy Davis Jr.?"

I click play on the YouTube link. Sammy's smooth voice croons about the role of 'fate' in a person's life.

"That's it," Mr. P confirms. "When I moved back to London after Butlins, I felt like fate was working. In the end, it wasn't fate, but God."

"I start out hopeful." He begins speaking in the present tense—as if he's right there in his mind. "I'm working with agents and have a couple of auditions. Mable arranges a recording test. If I pass, she feels sure I will be making a record."

"That's exciting!" I type every word he says.

"I do end up recording a demo with 'A Teenager in Love' on the A side. I'm thrilled to bits to have a real record, but I quickly find out how ugly the industry is and what I might have to do in order to get promoted."

"Uh-oh."

"I knew what that man was up to." Mr. P switches to past tense. "He was an agent who promised to get me into the Top 10 if I came to live with him!"

"Oh, no!"

"Oh, yes. He even wrote a letter to my mum. It said, 'Geoff should come live with me so I can work on him better.' Those were the exact words. She didn't understand the underlying message, but I did.

"I threw his letter away just the other day before we came on this trip. I felt violated all over again when we found it among the other letters. A lot of those movie stars in the olden days, that's how they got on—by sleeping with agents and producers. I don't think it works that way now. They go to drama school and stuff."

"You might be surprised Mr. P," I counter. "What did you do with his proposal?"

"I didn't go!" He nearly shouts. "I didn't even want to think about it. Hadn't I *already* been abused by an older man?"

Mr. P rarely raises his voice. Memory Land isn't so pleasant anymore.

"Afterwards, I was out of work for some time," he continues. "I ended up living on government assistance in some scruffy room with a board covering the broken window, and no bath. I wanted to take my life but didn't have the guts. I pleaded with God for hours in that little room, 'Let me die or have an accident.'"

"That man's indecent proposal may have triggered something," I venture.

"The 'something' was always there. I just didn't have enough entertainment or villages to drown it anymore. My emotional being was in such a state that I could no longer bear to live. Constantly, I felt a terrifying sense of guilt from a God who hated me for having feelings I wasn't acting out but could do nothing about. I prayed. I went to church. My Mum would send me those daily reading things, but I didn't have a grasp of the gospel—not at all.

"One day I was walking down Regency Street, one of the main streets in London, when I noticed an advertisement for some Christian meetings. I signed up and began attending Bible classes in the evenings.

"Often I would chat with a woman there. She was a Greek from Cyprus, a really lovely lady. She gave me a book about Jesus. When I get to heaven, I will look for her and say, 'One of the stars on your crown has my name on it because in 1963 when I wanted to take my own life, you introduced me to Jesus.'

"The more I heard about Him and read about Him, the more I wanted to know. I began to hunger for something I believed He could give me, something that could not be found in villages or art or music—something the entertainment business could never offer, even if I became as famous as the Beatles."

And we know that all things work together for good to those who love God, to those who are the called according to His purpose.

Romans 8:28 NKJV

STEVE PARRISH, GEOFF'S STAGE NAME

MILTON ABBAS, DORSET

Chapter 7

FINDING RELIGION

Faith is the realization that God's pleasure in you will never be based upon your performance for him.
David Platt

"The Coronavirus has killed 11,000 people here in Spain. We are second only to Italy now."

"I can't bear to even think about it. Can't we talk about your story rather? Even though you were depressed and suicidal in Chapter 6, at least I know you make it out of the darkness because here you are, having tea with me fifty-seven years later."

Mr. P and I sip ginger tea and chat as another grey April day disappears into darkness outside our rented apartment window. Mom is Face Timing my sister Annie in their bedroom. André is in a Zoom meeting in ours. Today begins our fourth week on lock-down in Spain.

We've stopped watching every news brief. Daily reports of rising global death tolls have taken their toll on each of us. We are weary of being indoors. Weary of hearing how people and places we love will never be the same after this pandemic has shut down the world. I'm not indifferent to the collective suffering on our planet. I'm just tired of talking about it.

Maybe you feel that way, dear reader. Maybe the suffering in the lives around you, or the suffering in your own soul has you worn out, too. Maybe you feel stuck, with no apparent way forward. Has reading these memories of one young British wanna-be star made you wonder where his story intersects with yours? Are you connecting with or feeling his pain, his emotional isolation—his fear of being different?

I hope so. Because all of humanity is intertwined—across cultures, generations and faiths. Where our stories intersect is where we connect. Connection is the antivenin to addiction. And addiction appears to be humanity's default response to pain. Stick with the P's and me, dear friend, because there is much wisdom to unpack between 1963, when Mr. P first meets Jesus and 2020 when he is vulnerable enough to tell us how this Jesus completely transformed his life.

Change often comes slowly, but it comes. This lock-down will end, the Coronavirus will be contained, and people will go back to their lives. Whatever is keeping you stuck and crushing the life out of you can also one day disappear, just as it did for Mr. P. But I'm getting ahead of myself. We've got to go back to 1963 in order to move forward. Are you ready?

"I notice your letters change after you begin your Bible lessons," I comment.

Mr. P reaches for another digestive biscuit before responding.

"That's because *I* was changing."

"You share bits of what you are learning and always add 'God bless' at the end instead of just your usual 'All my love.' You also never let on that you are depressed and suicidal."

"No, I wouldn't. I didn't want to worry my mum. Things got a bit better though. The excitement of learning new truths from the Bible seemed to overshadow everything else I was suffering. At least for a time."

I open my laptop and search for a file called 'Letters 1963.'

"This one doesn't have a date, but it must be around that time frame. Looks like you are still enamored with the lifestyles of the rich and famous while cutting lawns for cash. Should I read it?"

"Sure. Right after I get a piece of that new cheese, I discovered at the Mercadona. I'm still a bit peckish. It's goat, cow, and sheep cheese. Would you like some?" Mr. P stands and moves toward the kitchen. I shake my head.

"Go ahead," his voice booms from the other side of the wall. "I can hear you from here."

> *Dear All,*
>
> *Do you know who I saw in person last night? Bette Davis! She was making a personal appearance at the cinema where her new film is showing. So I waited outside with a big crowd until she came out and got into her car. I was next to the car window and got a good view. She looked really nice.*
>
> *One thing about being down in London, there's always something going on. Things are moving slightly now, but I better not say anything until I start working. I got 6 Pounds yesterday for an hour of lawn cutting and have to go every two weeks to do the garden up.*

"Are you two starting without me?" Mom enters the room with her phone in hand. "Your sister says hello. Where's Mr. P?"

"This is just the first letter. I'll call Annie later. He's getting some cheese."

Mom scoots a chair up to the table and puts out her hand as Mr. P passes with his slice of cheese. He gives it to her and returns to the kitchen for another.

I keep reading.

> *Tell Jen she can have her birthday present at Whitsuntide when, if all is well, I shall come home.*

"He was close to his sister, Jennifer. They were good friends," Mom says as she tears the cheese into four pieces. "I wish I had something to put this on."

This morning I sat in the park. The weather is really fantastic. Some of the Coronation Street lot are coming down for the gala at Battersea on Saturday. Look out for me if it's on telly.

"*Coronation Street*! Ju, have you ever seen it?"

"No."

"It's a British soap. I've watched with P's sister Jean a few times." She shouts toward the empty doorway. "Some characters are my age and have played their roles for 50 years, maybe more, huh P?"

He doesn't answer. *Probably didn't hear*. I keep reading.

We have the gasman in today as the pipes are blocked. I have just washed the floor and I am off to the Launderette. Then to the singing lesson and Bible class.

Cheerio for now! God bless.

Love, Geoff

xxxxxxxxxxxxxxxxx

"P! You are trying to put on a good front," Mom says as he suddenly appears with a packet of gluten-free crackers, "but it's obvious you are lonely and bored if you are writing about the gas man and doing laundry. Thanks for the cheese and crackers."

"You're welcome. The cheese is very good, isn't it?"

"Yes. Tastes quite goaty."

"This next letter is also without a date. But you mention Easter music, so it must be that same spring." I redirect the conversation away from goaty cheese.

Dear All,

I forgot to thank Jen for the joke. I have stuck it on the wall. I think it's very good.

I stayed in tonight, wrote some letters and listened to the wireless. There is a good series on about a vicar.

Will Jen please record "How Do You Do It?" on the tape? And "The End of the World" or "So It Will Always Be" by the Everly's.

Also, next Sunday morning there should be some Easter music on.

"I'm a teenager in Arkansas when these songs are popular!" Mom interrupts again. "If this is the letter, I think it is, next he'll mention some high-level Italian thing. I know *I* never listened to opera on the radio! You were quite interesting, Pennock."

"That was the 'Italian Mr. P' before there *was* an Italian Mr. P," he jokes.

Please, if you can, try and record the Easter hymn from La Traviata Rusticana, which goes, "Rejoice for The Lord has Arisen." I think you know what I mean, as you heard me say I liked it before. They are forced to play it Easter Sunday. They always do.

I shall be able to go to the service Good Friday morning. It should be a nice service.

Jen can erase Cliff Richard and the Beatles and the stuff we recorded before I left, if she wants. I hear them about half a dozen times every night on my wireless. It's been a godsend, the wireless. It's a lot of company.

We haven't a bath, and I hadn't had one since I left home. I think I was beginning to smell. I didn't know where any baths were, and I kept forgetting. Anyway, today I popped into the YMCA and had a bath there. Nobody knows if you're a member or not, popping in and out. When I can afford, I think I'll join, as it's always somewhere to bathe.

P.S. For my dinner I had three eggs and made an omelet. I had it with a fourth of mushrooms.

All my love, Geoff

"Mom, would you and Jennifer have been around the same age?"

"Yes. And we enjoyed the same music! I would have liked her, I can tell."

"She *were* a sweet person—friendly, very pretty, but the cortisone bloated her up," Mr. P's Yorkshire dialect kicks in with the memory. "We were close. I think she were more like me in a lot of ways, was Jennifer. We understood one another's humor."

"Why cortisone? I ask. "Was she ill? This next letter sounds like she missed some school."

"I don't remember what illness she had. It was something . . ."

I skim the rest of the letter. "You're a real-church hopper in this one, Mr. P. Listen to this."

> *Dear All,*
>
> *I hope you all are keeping okay. How's your blood, Mum? And Father's belly? I'm glad Jen is much better now and going to school.*
>
> *I have just had my breakfast and dinner. Three raw carrots, a tomato sandwich, a sponge cake with custard and a pint of milk.*
>
> *I went to the Bible class again last night. He's a wonderful chap who speaks—the type of person like Billy Graham. I shan't know which religion I am, soon. Easter Sunday it was Church of England. Last Sunday morning, it was Baptist's church, in the afternoon—revival center and at night, Methodists. And every Thursday the Sabbath keepers.*

"Sounds a bit schizophrenic!" Mom teases.

"I was hungry for something, searching for something more than formal religion, something that could make sense of the confusion inside of me."

"What did you find?" I inquire.

"I found legalism and formalism—in *every* church. At first, I thought it was God. It took many, many years to unlearn my wrong ideas of who God really is.

"Go on." He motions me to continue.

> *I think I enjoy the Thursday service best, as it is on Regent Street. It's a bit far to go on Sunday as well. When I go on a Thursday, afterwards I go and have my bath at the YMCA.*
>
> *Tonight I may go and see Joe Brown, Mark Wynter and Susan Morghan, who are on stage at a local cinema.*

"That Mark Wynter was famous in England, like Cliff Richard at that time. He went to the same singing teacher as I.

"I wonder what he's like now?" Mr. P grabs his iPad and Googles Mr. Wynter.

"Oh, he's old!"

Why am I surprised he sounds surprised?

". . . But so am I."

He turns his iPad around to show Mom and me *"then and now"* photographs.

"You wore your hair the same," she says.

"It was the '60's. What can you expect? It says here he is *still* touring with an Agatha Christie theatre company."

"You could've been famous like that."

"I'm glad I wasn't. It would have destroyed me. And I might never have met you." He reaches for his wife–his expression a merger of tenderness and jest.

I keep reading.

> *I'm wishing I could afford to set off every day, as the weather is great. The Daffodils in Regent Park look lovely. I'm hoping to get home for Jen's 15th birthday.*

Cheerio for now and God bless. Always thinking of you.

Love, Geoff

P.S. Give Jean and Jen a big kiss from me. Tell the sweet little booger to write soon. She hasn't put in any rude remarks lately.

"That was April. I musn't have gone to Butlins that year."

"What did you do?"

"Don't know. I must've been hoping I would get signed for a record or something. I didn't just want to be on stage at Butlins Holiday Resorts, I wanted to be famous like Cliff Richard. I think I spent the summer doing odd gigs and going from church to church."

"That makes sense because in this next letter you are all fired up about the coming of Jesus."

Torbay Road
September, 1963

Dear All,

Please excuse the paper, as I ran out and this is an envelope. Thursday night was the last of the Bible prophecy meetings for five weeks. I received my certificate for attendance. I've only missed going twice, since April. I shall miss it very much. Although I can go Tuesday, Wednesday, or Friday, I enjoy the Thursday meetings best. Anyway, I'm glad I finished the course. It has been awfully enlightening.

Pastor Henderson is really wonderful. We have dealt with six prophecies in Daniel, and how they came through the ages in history. The only and next thing to be fulfilled is the return of Christ. We believe it will happen in the event of nuclear war, when, before we all destroy each other, God will intervene, and the righteous will be raised to everlasting life.

Friday night I went to the pictures to see the VIPs, starring Elizabeth Taylor. It was okay, but not as good as I expected.

"Maybe we *will* all destroy each other with the Coronavirus and be done with it," Mom blurts. "Or some other bio-terrorism."

"This pandemic does feel a bit like the end of the world, doesn't it?" he agrees, moving to 'his' chair in the corner of our small, shared space.

Today's news was something from a sci-fi movie. Since when is it a crime to hold a church service in America?"

"Or a wedding or a funeral?" I add, interrupting their banter. "Let's go back to the safety of the 1960's." I continue reading.

The group was playing for a wedding Saturday night, and they asked me to go along and sing just a few numbers to fill in. They hardly knew any of the songs, so I could sing six! The reception was in a hall with a stage and we had sandwiches and drinks on the house (pity I don't drink). I had to blow myself up with lemonade, as they had no tonic water.

The group played from 8 to 11. It seemed smashing to be on stage again. I felt real good inside, and very happy. Although I only sang a few songs, I enjoyed it tremendously. And when I didn't sing, the girls kept shouting up for me to sing. I went down well, thank goodness and got paid 2 Pounds 10 and got brought home by a car, so I think I did well.

Next week we are getting ready for a dance. We have 45-minute slots. In between, they want us to do Beatles numbers. I've got them to learn.

Tonight was the start of the autumn evangelistic campaign with Pastor Henderson. A while back, I helped send out 15,000 leaflets and invitations. We received only 150 reply cards, and there were only 160 extra people in the congregation. It seems a pity that 15,000 people had an opportunity to find out the true meaning of life and turned it down. You can't say they go to other churches, as only 2% of the population of London goes to church.

It was in the paper the other day that one child in six born in London is illegitimate. They say we are living in a wonderful modern age, but the world has never known such sin and goings on than now.

"The world has never known what?" he leans forward.

"Such sin and goings on than now," I repeat, a little louder.

"1963 was *nothing* compared to now—like a lullaby," he retorts.

The countries keep saying they are trying for peace. How can they do this when most of the people of the world have a lust for power and money? People must be mad! What a happier place the world would be if all were Christians. Everyone would be happy at work. No nattering old bosses. (I am quoting part of tonight's sermon.)

"So I'm preaching to my family now," he laughs.

"What did *they* think?"

"My mum would be interested. My dad thought I was a nutter. But, that was a bit later."

Mom moves to the sofa. Fluffing a flattened pillow she says, "P, between all the church meetings and the Beatles singing, it's like you are living two different lives."

"I suppose so. I didn't know *who* I was. It was years before I found my true identity and value in Christ, but the meetings made me want something I knew I didn't have."

Enclosed are the cards that were sent out to people. Good luck with the Bible course.

God bless you; you are always in my thoughts.

All my love, Geoff

Extra note: Got your letter this morning. Thank Jen for hers.

"Who took the Bible course?" I wonder aloud.

"I don't know. Somebody must've, because they ended up going to a series of tent meetings in Dewsbury."

"The whole family? Even your sisters?"

"Don't think so. Just my parents."

After a moment, Mom says, "Papa (she sometimes calls Mr. P Papa), I see you changing in these letters. You used to only worry about who liked you, who clapped for you, who gave you tips. Now it's like you're being touched in a way to solve the world's problems. Inspired—like you begin to get out of yourself and think about things more important than what you ate for breakfast!"

The P's chat for a few minutes. I skim through letters on my laptop, trying to decide which to include in this manuscript. I don't want to tire you with too much trivia from a twenty-something sexually repressed guy's letters to his mom sixty years ago, but I want you to see and know and understand where this man came from and how God called him out of his personal darkness into the light of the truth he walks in today.

Mr. P has been my stepfather for nearly thirty years. He's not the first man who has loved my mother, but he's been the *best* man for my mother. Watching them dance their unique dance of marriage for three decades has taught me much about how a man loves a woman, much about romance, and mercy, and the miracles of God.

A lump of emotion squeezes my throat even now as I type these words while watching them love each other in small ways on the other side of this room. Like any of us, they are less than perfect, but The P's place their faith in a perfect Savior. They choose to trust His perfect love—love that casts out the fear of the past and gives hope to those who feel stuck there. Of all the redemption stories I've read or heard, theirs rests on top. Being a witness to their lives has unveiled the power of God to transform a character and bring healing to the deepest of soul wounds.

Let's get back to the 1960's, where we see the seesaw beginning to shift as spiritual things carry more and more weight in young Geoff's life.

"P's!" They jump like teenagers when a parent opens the bedroom door without knocking. I laugh.

"This next letter is like watching a film. I see every detail in my mind. You know what, Mr. P? Reading your letters aloud reminds me of that 80's movie with Anne Bancroft and Anthony Hopkins.

"84 Charing Cross Road," he remembers." It's a true story. Judi Dench played Hopkins' wife. I've always liked Judi Dench."

"Yeah, well, reading your letters gives me that same kind of longing feeling I had watching that movie. I'm in the present getting lost in your past and I'm laughing and crying with these characters. You write words about biscuits and Bible lessons, but there is so much more going on here. Remember when Bancroft's character Helene talks right at the camera? That's me, talking to the reader. Yours is also a story of two worlds, connected by hand-written letters. You've gotta hear this one."

Torbay Road
September, 1963

Dear All,

I've just finished off the last of the cake and biscuits, which were delicious. There always seems to be something missing on a Sunday and I am wishing I could pop home like when I was at Sheffield. I have just had a leg of chicken and fried egg for my dinner. It made a change. I must eat three times as much at home than down here! Mum, your cooking is the best in the world. And you know it.

It seems ages since I was home. On Thursday, I didn't have much tea [dinner] and I was so nervous.

> *Not of singing, but of forgetting the words of the new songs I learnt. When I came off stage, I was starving, and without thinking started to eat a boiled ham sandwich, which one of the lad's mothers gave me.*

"Oh, that's funny!" Mr. P laughs. "I had read in the Bible about pork being 'unclean.' I had this idea—if I religiously obeyed everything God said, He would give me relief from my agony and turn me into someone I thought I wasn't, a heterosexual."

"So, eating a ham sandwich broke your contract with God?"

"It wasn't a contract. Just a mindset I had. I don't know where I got it. I was always bargaining with God, 'If I do this, You do that.'"

> *I don't have any more bookings for about a fortnight, so that gives this singing group time to become accustomed to each other, as it's different in a group than with just a piano.*
>
> *Friday was our birthday celebration at work, and we had a bit of a sale. There was a long queue outside. The boss got so nervous he went to the lav three times before we opened. Like a little kid, he was. It was so funny! He expected us to be rushed off our feet.*
>
> *When the doors opened, all the folks rushed past our department, and we didn't have one customer until 9:30. You ought to have seen the boss' face. He was furious! Me and the others could hardly hold ourselves back from laughing. All we have to sell in our sale is trash anyway.*
>
> *The lad in the group who lives near me, his dad was saying our boss is always causing bother in the pub near where he lives. He knows him very well. You can tell what he's like.*
>
> *A new girl started as a window dresser last week. She's only 16, and a nice kid. She had got some fluff on herself off a carpet and came into our department*

to borrow a brush. Our boss said to her, "Clear off! It's like a bloody brothel in here!" If I had been her, I should have reported him to the manager. No one likes him.

"I must've been back at B.B. Evans department store. Despite the nattering boss, I quite liked working there. Busyness kept away the loneliness." Mr. P is obviously interested in his own story.

How's Dad?

On Friday I went to see Tom Jones at the pictures. It was very good and very funny. I got a real surprise! There was a manor house on. When I saw it, I thought, "I know that place." And then, when they turned the camera around to show a stagecoach coming up the village street, I could have recognized it anywhere. It looked as lovely as ever—Cerne Abbas in Dorset. It was lovely to think I'd been there.

In the movie, they lock the girl up in the abbey tower where I had my photo taken outside, sitting on some steps. It seemed funny to see it on the film with the hounds getting ready for the hunt by the wishing well, where you throw a laurel leaf in for a wish. It brought back some happy memories.

It was there I saw lampshades covered with photos. You must have heard me talk about the place with the giant in chalk on the hillside. Tell Jean, if she sees the film, to look at the little book in my drawer. It says on it "Cerne Abbas," also, the picture of me outside the tower is among the mounted photos.

"Mrs. P, haven't you been there with me?"

"Just after we married," she remembers. "And isn't that chalk giant slightly obscene?"

"Yes, one more obscene bit of British history. Obscenity is part of our heritage. I've had a lot to overcome," he jokes.

Last night there was a concert on at church, and a talent contest. I didn't enter, as they were all singing religious songs. I am not in practice with the few I have.

"That's funny!" he exclaims. "Now I sing about twenty Christian songs per day, don't I?"

"Yes, André and I can hear you through the walls most mornings."

"Praise songs are powerful spiritual weapons. I learned that from the book, *There is Dynamite in Praise.*

The church is having a color slide competition this month on landscape. But I forgot about it. It's too late now to send my entries. I'm sure mine are better than some showing on the screen last night.

They are also starting socials for the young on Saturday nights, so that should be interesting.

Tonight the subject is, "The Return of Christ." I'm wondering if I ought to look for another job until I get fixed up theatrically again. I could then keep the Sabbath and be baptized, and I'm sure if I were baptized, I should see my future more clearly and know what to do for the best. It says in the Bible, "Repent and be baptized and you shall receive the Holy Spirit." So I think it's worth it. I've spoken with people at church and they've said what a difference it has made to them. My life, been as complicated as it is, I think it's the best thing I can do.

Cheerio for now! God bless.

Love, Geoff

x x x x x x x x x x x x x x x x x x x x

P.S. Please keep the Bible certificates in a special place. They aren't much, but they mean a lot to me.

"I thought if I got baptized, God would change my feelings, you know? If I did that for Him, He would do something for me. If only people knew the Gospel! God is big enough for anything." Mr. P punctuates his words with his Italian gestures. "We don't have to bargain with Him. Jesus already did everything. I didn't know that then. I was putting my faith in *my* works—what *I* did. The true Gospel is not about me at all. It's all about Him."

"How long did it take before you figured that out?"

"Years! Twenty-four years of emotional hell."

. . . always learning but never able to come to the knowledge of the truth.

2 Timothy 3:7 NIV

Lincoln Cathedral

Chapter 8

FAITH & PRESUMPTION

Going to church doesn't make you a Christian any more than standing in a garage makes you a car.
Billy Sunday

"I don't like carrying umbrellas. Lord, please stop the rain, in Jesus' name. Thank you."

Mr. P slides the glass balcony door closed behind him. Another grey day dawns as we enter our fifth week of lock-down in Spain. Only one person from our apartment is allowed out. Today is Mr. P's turn to shop at Mercadona.

"It will stop."

It's pouring.

He sits down, peels a tangerine, then returns to the window. "In Jesus' name. It will stop now." His command is soft, but firm.

The tangerine's fruity fragrance lingers, so does the rain.

He goes into his bedroom and comes out dressed in black jeans and a long-sleeved shirt. He looks outside again. "I think it's stopped raining," he says with no surprise.

I wonder at his faith as I watch him pull on his black leather sneakers.

This is how Geoff Pennock operates. Seven months ago, food would not stay on his fork. Three kidney procedures and way too much anesthesia left his hands trembling violently. He would not tolerate it. Mr. P did exactly the same as he just did with the rain.

"In the name of Jesus, I will stop shaking. This is not God's will for me. I will not accept it." He declared those words through a mouthful of scrambled egg that he scooped up with his fingers because using a fork was hopeless. His physician referred him to see a specialist who wanted to prescribe more medication for the "tremors." Mr. P refused it all and clung to his faith, proclaiming Hebrews 12:12, ". . . so then, strengthen hands that are weak and knees that tremble."

Each morning during our lock-down, I'm reminded of God's response to Mr. P's faith as I pass his chair on my way to the kitchen. By the light from the balcony window, he holds a tiny New Testament with steady hands, feeding on his daily dose of God's mighty Word. As I type these lines, the sky has lightened and holds its moisture. Once more, almighty God honors the faith of one human bold enough to believe the kingdom of God is within us through the power of the Holy Spirit.

"Blind people shouldn't wash dishes." Mom's voice from the kitchen interrupts my thoughts.

"What?"

"These cups in the dish drain are filthy. I wonder who washed them?"

My mother despises dirt of any kind. Since the moment the door closed behind her husband half an hour ago, she's been sweeping and mopping and picking up clutter.

"Do you need my help?"

"No, keep writing. What you are doing is more important. I just wish Mr. P would leave the washing-up to someone who can see."

I smile to myself. They rarely argue. His inability to get tea stains out of mugs is one of their few points of contention.

"Maybe he needs to pray about his eyesight," I holler through the wall.

"I wish he would," Mom replies.

I organize some notes and create an outline for this chapter while waiting for his return. I have questions about faith.

Bzzzzzzzz!

The door buzzer is alarmingly loud, even when I expect it.

Mr. P enters with one shopping bag in each hand. I take the bags. He removes his rubber gloves, mask, and shoes. We have strict routines for anyone entering the apartment. All outer garments are hung outside, hands washed, keys disinfected. Mom and I wipe down bags of arugula and packages of pasta with alcohol wipes. I am vigilant about protecting all of us from COVID-19. The virus has already killed more than 20,000 people in Spain.

As I sanitize our front door handles, I wonder at the difference between Mr. P's faith and mine.

When Psalm 91 says, "No plague shall come nigh thy dwelling," does that include the Coronavirus? Where is the dividing line between faith and presumption?

"Mr. P, I have a question for you."

We sit—me on the hide-a-bed sofa, he on his chair in the corner.

"What's the difference between faith and presumption?"

"I think," he responds, "if a person's got a relationship with God, He's going to tell you about things. He lets you know with strong impressions. He wants us to test Him. If something will give Him glory, we ask in Jesus' name."

"Isn't it presumption to leave the house without an umbrella when the forecast says 100% rain?"

"It's difficult to carry an umbrella and two bags of groceries. We don't have a car here. Do I need to get drowned going shopping? Is *that* God taking care of me? It's all for His glory. I try to go out when it doesn't rain, but if it's going to rain all day, I don't think it matters that He stops the rain for thirty minutes. I don't do that every time I leave the house, do I? Otherwise it would *never* rain!"

"I think he's rebuked the rain about three times since we've been here." Mom plops down beside me. "Ooh. This sofa doesn't have much give, does it?"

"Hard as a rock," I agree.

"P," she says, "You *are* kind of a modern-day Elijah. Remember the Capri miracle? It's your story, but can I tell it?

He nods.

"Geoff's sister Jean and her family were visiting him in Italy. This happened before we met but is one of the faith stories that helped me fall in love with him. Jean had never been to the island of Capri and this was going to be the highlight of their trip. They were in Naples, ready to go, but it was pouring down rain. Mr. P insisted they get on the ferry anyway."

"I remember!" he interrupts. "I said, 'When we get to the top of the island and get off the funicular, the sun will come out. If that doesn't happen, there is no God."

"Now, some would definitely say *tha*t was presumptuous," I interject.

"I wasn't presumptuous. I *knew*. Sometimes God tells you things, doesn't He?"

"So, what happened?"

"Let *me* tell the story!" Mom throws open her arms proclaiming, "When they arrived at the top, the sun burst through the clouds and they had the most wonderful, memorable day out!"

"That time was for my sister," he explains. "She didn't have much faith that God cares about the things important to us. I believe He wanted to show her a glimpse of Himself that day."

"She's never forgotten it," Mom reminds him. "She's the one who told me! I don't know anyone with as much faith as you, Mr. P. Your life is like a movie."

"Maybe one day someone *will* make a movie of your life. First, though, we need to finish writing your book. Are you ready to go back to 1963?"

"Are we still there?" he moans. "I'm ready to get on with it. Get me into another decade. Please!"

I transition to the table and open my MacBook.

"We are at the place where you fire another agent."

"It was probably John. Let's hear it."

87 Torbay Road
Kilburn NW2
Tuesday, 10:30
Oct. 1963

Dear All,

I have talked everything over with the pastor and Mable. Time to be finished with John, my agent. It is a load off my mind, I can tell you. I'm over everything and that's God's truth. If I go on like this much longer, I shall be able to write a book of my life story. It's certainly had its ups and downs so far. It's marvelous though, how I've always scraped through.

"What was wrong with your agent?"

"He wasn't getting me any work. I felt I was on a string for a long time."

I do hope Jen's jaundice is soon okay again. It's taking a long time.

"That's what it was Jennifer suffered from—jaundice. I couldn't remember before. She was quite ill. There must've been something wrong with her liver. I started reading about healing, even then."

"Because of her?" Mom asks.

"Yes, but because of myself really. It was all in a superficial way. Everything was about me, how much faith *I* had. How good *I* was. Dear!

"I'm trying to think of the first healing book I ever read," he says. "I believe it was called *Healing the Sick.* Let me look it up."

I move back to the sofa and sit next to Mom. Monk parakeets screech loudly from treetops in the park across the street. I envy their freedom. Four weeks is a long time to be stuck indoors. I'm so ready for this lock-down to be done.

"Here it is!" Mr. P shows us the book cover on Amazon: *Healing the Sick: A Divine Healing Classic for Everyone* by T.L. Osborne. "Published in 1955. He started something, Osborne did. His work was definitely my first introduction to healing. Then I got on to Katherine Kuhlman, and Henry Nouwen—who wrote some very deep things. In the end, it turns out *he* was gay. I didn't know it then, but I identified with his suffering.

"Healing became my life study. I read everything I could get my hands on."

"But, what do jaundice and homosexuality have in common that you sought the same books for answers?" I ask.

"One was destroying my sister's life and one was destroying *my* life. Anything against how God made us—perfect and whole, is of the devil. God loves us so much; He doesn't want us to have jaundice or be mentally tormented in our spirit.

"I could not bear to live with the torment. It drove me insane. Physical illness and mental illness—one is as bad as the other. To me, it was a torment I could not accept. I had a headache all the time. And a pain inside my heart—like a heavy pain. I have gay friends who have been 'married' forever, long before it was legal. They could accept the torment somehow. I could not."

"The suffering this man experienced. It's terrible," Mom empathizes. "Religious people don't know what to do about evil spirits or gay people. They have no idea how they suffer."

"People think you're a piece of poo! A fruitcake with marzipan. Speaking of fruitcake, my gay married friends make the best Christmas cake. They are getting quite old now. One has cancer of the prostate. I really need to write to them," he rambles.

"How is this Coronavirus pandemic affecting *them*?" Mom wonders. "They really are nice people, even though they don't know Jesus. We have stayed in their home, you know."

"You two always have interesting friends."

"Have we gotten off track?" Mr. P asks.

"Not really. Well, maybe a little, with the fruitcake." I move back to my computer and find where we left off.

> *Also, my father's behind.*

"My father's behind!" Mr. P repeats.

"That's what it says. Was there something wrong with your father's behind?"

"He might have had hemorrhoids, but do we need to include that?"

"Maybe not. I'll read on."

> *I hope Mum and Jean are okay. I think we all deserve a win on the pools and a good holiday. (I should not have said that; it's gambling.)*
>
> *The landlord and landlady are really nice people. I hang my washing out in the garden and she airs it in the airing cupboard and lends me her ironing board.*
>
> *I'm quite content, no lie and I swear it on the Bible. I had to say that as I wondered if you believe me, especially when I used to say I was okay in some letters when really, I was down in the dumps.*
>
> *Must close as I've an interview for commercials. Please pray for me.*
>
> *God Bless You.*
>
> *All my love, Geoff*

"Wow! You admit your past letters weren't always a true reflection of your heart. That's a new level of honesty," I observe.

"My family would only get a little crack of the truth, though. They wouldn't get any more than that."

"Why not?"

"Would you tell *your* mother you're gay? No! Put yourself in that position. Let's say you're a lesbian. Would you tell your mother?

Back then it was a crime! It's like kids who take drugs. They don't want to tell their parents, do they? That's how I felt, but I wasn't doing anything wrong. I wasn't *doing* anything!"

He continues blasting me with rhetorical questions, waving his hands like he's conducting an orchestra.

"Do you tell your mom everything? Does *anybody* tell their mum everything? Did I think she could do anything? What would *she* do? Make it worse! Maybe it's even her fault!"

"Calm down, P." Mom strokes his arm.

"Why do you feel having a homosexual son might be the parent's fault?" I query.

"The father is distant. The mother is too present. The devil stacks circumstances against a person. You get molested. It all goes together. There are books that explain things now. Back then there was nothing—a person had to suffer through on their own."

After all the years, Mr. P's memories hurt. We sit quiet as his palpable pain fills the room.

"Here's a question," he says softly. "Do you think a real fight, a real battle is necessary to find Jesus? Must we suffer deep pain in order to know Jesus deeply?"

"What's *your* answer, Mr. P?"

"It used to make me angry—that some people's lives seem so simple. They just get married and have kids and live happily-ever-after. I wondered, 'Why should I have to go through all this pain and other people don't?'

"I think Jesus may be more precious to those who have suffered and fought to know Him, just like my wife is precious to me, because I suffered and fought for her. A person like me will have a very firm foundation and faith. We can face anything and know, 'Jesus got me through *that* and *that* and *that* and He'll get me through this. Suffering builds faith somehow."

Mr. P is silent. The cheap wall clock above the TV ticks ten seconds away. Then he adds, "Suffering also destroys faith—at least in some people. They blame God."

"What makes one person respond like biblical Job, who said, 'Though He slay me, yet will I trust Him,' and someone else, who suffers far less than Job goes off the deep end or becomes an atheist because something awful happens to them or someone they love?"

"I don't know. It must have something to do with *choosing* to trust God, even when we cannot see the outcome. If you struggle with homosexuality and you think, 'God doesn't want me to be like that, but He won't help me to do anything about it,'—that's very discouraging. People commit suicide because of that kind of thinking. The truth is, He *will* help you. You just have to realize it."

"How did you get to *that* place?"

"It took a long time. I waded through loads of legalism before I discovered the truth about who God is and who I am in Him. Legalism made me a God-hater. But that was later."

"If legalism includes a 'holier-than-thou' attitude," I observe, "I already see some of that cropping up in your next letter."

87 Torbay Road
Kilburn, NW6

Dear All,

I wrote to John, my agent, explaining everything again as I told him last Sunday. I gave him my home address. So maybe you got a reply up there. I had to let him go. I'd got so fed up I didn't know what I was doing really. I've no regrets anyway. I know he was good to me, but I could not live on promises indefinitely. I've had a week to think things out, and in my own mind I feel sure I did the right thing. If I had kept on, I should have been a wreck, whereas now I have peace of mind.

I don't know what you put in your letter to John and would like to. Anyway I'm not nattering about the past anymore. What's done is done. You say that I've done the dirty on him. I don't think I have. If I have, God forgave me whether you have or not.

"You sound quite bold here," Mom comments.

"Yeah, we haven't seen this side of you in any previous letters," I agree.

"I was fed up. After trying for years to get ahead, I needed an agent who would open the right doors."

> *After church I went and sang as usual at Hyde Park Corner. It is really nice, the hymn singing outside.*
>
> *I was listening for a while at Speakers' Corner to a bloke who thought he was condemning Christianity. But all he was condemning was the Catholic religion, which all true Christians are against anyway. He was classing us all as Catholics—which is a bad thing. I felt like having a row with the bloke.*
>
> *Where in the Bible does it say to shut yourself up in a monastery or to be a priest and can't marry. And how can a priest forgive sin? Only Christ can do that. Look at the gambling and sweepstakes Catholics do. Any true Christian knows this is wrong. I don't wonder their service is in Latin. If it was in English, they'd know they are mislead.*
>
> *Did you know in Rome outside the Vatican there is a statue of Mary, underneath which is a chest in which Catholics put money and jewelry—believing the more they put in, the better chance of getting into heaven? (As if paying your fare—the stupid nits.)*
>
> *I bet you think I'm daft carrying on about religion as I do. But it's got me really interested lately. Fancy Christine Keeler getting 25,000 Pounds for her life story in the news of the world. How much better they would have done to have the life story of Christ for free. People laugh and scoff at Christ now. How they will weep for forgiveness on the Day of Judgment, when it is too late.*
>
> *Always thinking of you.*
>
> *God Bless, Geoff*

"Oh dear! I sound extremely critical. But that's what the spirit of legalism does to a person. It causes them to focus on following the rules. Then it becomes easy to notice when someone else is not doing that as well as you are. As I learned about different religions and beliefs, I began to criticize those I didn't agree with. It took my focus off my Savior.

One of the best friends I've ever had is Catholic. I would *never* call him a 'stupid nit.' He has a beautiful spirit and a deep relationship with Jesus. A person can know Christ in any Christian religion, but religion itself is a broken system of man-made rituals."

"Well said, Mr. P. I agree with you one hundred percent. It was religious people who crucified Christ. People with that spirit can become very dangerous."

"With a little bit of religion, a person can easily begin trying to be their own savior by 'being good' and following all the rules. Then everything becomes about them and not about Christ, who 'became sin for us . . .'"

Mom chimes in and they finish the verse in unison. ". . . that we might become the righteousness of God in Him. 2 Corinthians 5:21."

Mr. P continues, "In church people tell children, 'If you aren't a good little boy, Jesus won't love you.' People used to say that to me. I've remembered it all my life. If you ask most people now, they think you are going to heaven for being good. Until you unlearn that way of thinking and go forward to experience Christ *in* you and have that deep relationship—that's who you are. You are a legalist. That's what happened to me. I drove my family crazy."

"I understand. Legalistic theology could drive anyone crazy," I concur.

"What happens with me next?" he asks, changing the subject. "I should be going to Bournemouth soon."

"Ummm, let me see." I scan the next letter. This one's not *so* interesting. You wish your mum would come visit. You need a new pair of shoes and you are earning some cash as a wedding singer. I'll just read from the end, where you have another audition."

> *I'm going for an audition tomorrow afternoon. I didn't tell you what happened at the one last Thursday. The woman was really nice and sincere. She said if she had any word from Mabel that I was okay, she would get me a weekend booking at Butlins for 10 Pounds per night and if I was good, she would work on me from there. I've nearly finished working a decent act out for Mabel to approve of first.*
>
> *I've now run out of paper, so you can read what Pastor Henderson has to say.*
>
> *The service on Sunday was really lovely. The subject was, "Will Christ Return in Our Day?" Enclosed are the two sermons, or part of them for the past two weeks.*
>
> *All my love. God bless you.*
>
> *Yours, Geoff*
> *x x x x x x x*

"Is that when you auditioned at The Palladium?" Mom asks. To me she says, "The London Palladium is only the most famous theater in all of Britain."

"It's where the Beatles first played," Mr. P remembers.

Mrs. P declared, "I know! I was fourteen when they came out with *I Wanna Hold Your Hand*."

While Mom sings her sixties memory, I skim another letter. "This one actually mentions the Beatles, but there's no date. Let me see when that song was released."

Google takes me to 'The Beatles Bible.'

"You had to have written this letter in October of 1963," I say. "Listen."

87 Torbay Rd.
Kilburn
Thursday

Dear Mum,

I hope you had a nice birthday and got your flowers okay. I hope they were nice. It seems funny sending something I never saw. I hadn't any idea what to buy, so I hope they suited. You are worth all the money in the world to me. But I'm afraid I haven't that to give you.

"That part makes sense, because your Mom's birthday was in October, right?"

"Yes," he says.

"Here's the interesting part."

I passed the Palladium on Sunday going to church. There are crowds outside hoping to see the Beatles.

"P's!" I interrupt myself. "Listen to what The Beatles Bible dot com says about that Sunday:

"The Beatles made their debut on the television show *Val Parnell's Sunday Night at The London Palladium* on 13 October 1963."

"And guess what, Mom? It also says, 'I Want to Hold Your Hand' was recorded at Abbey Road Studio just four days after that!

"Mr. P! You were running with some famous people," I half-tease.

"Oh, dear! I wasn't running with them. I did want to follow in their footsteps though. When I got the Palladium audition, I thought that would be my lucky break."

I continue reading:

Bob Perkins, the agent I was with last year, rang Mabel, my voice teacher up to see if she had any worthwhile singers for the Palladium parts. 20 weeks at 19 Pounds a week!

Friday noon:

This morning I went for the audition. This is a preliminary one and then a final one on the stage at the Palladium. I passed this one this morning and have to go to the Palladium for the final on Tuesday.

We are moving departments at work and I should be working Saturday evening. So that will make up for the time I have off work.

Got your letter this morning. Glad you liked the flowers. Have no time as I've had to come home and change on my lunch hour. I'll write a long letter on Sunday.

God bless.

Love, Geoff
x x x

"There were 18 men auditioning," Mr. P recalls. "They needed six and I was down to the last eight. I was so close to having a break, but I didn't get it."

"This next letter explains what happened."

Dear All,

At 1:30 I got a call from Bob Perkins asking me to ring him, which I did. It was his wife who answered. She said, "Go along to the Prince of Wales Theatre tomorrow." She said she thought Bob was going to fix me up with the pantomime at Bournemouth. She also said my voice was not strong or powerful enough for the Palladium and that I had done very well to get as far as I did.

I was dead beat but managed to make it to church a half hour late. The sermon was about the Jews not believing in Christ, when in the Old Testament his death and coming are told there.

Tuesday, I got up and could not eat breakfast. I had so much to lose if I failed. By the time I reached the Palladium I was dithering with nerves. I went to have a sandwich and a cup of tea and felt much better.

At the audition there were 18 boys and about 20 girls. We were lucky to be at the most popular theater in London, where the famous perform. Only three girls were picked. They were nearly all good and some really nice girls.

We had to stand in a line under the glare of lights. I didn't feel nervous at all, really. It just seemed like being on stage in Sheffield. I stood there saying my prayers all the time.

He picked eight of us to stand forward. We then had to sing individually. After I'd sung, they asked six of the others to wait behind and for me and another kid to leave.

I was upset. I had banked on it so much. I really felt I would get through after being so near. All those singing lessons with Madame Corran (Mable)! She really encouraged me. I must get somewhere in the end. I'll never stop trying.

God Bless and thanks for all the prayers. For other auditions, I never really worried. But it was natural for me to get upset over this one. Anyway, I'm okay again now.

Geoff
x x x x x x x x x x

"I'm sad for you," I empathize. "Rejection like that, after coming so close must have been extremely disappointing."

"I'm impressed you got into the top eight, Steve Parrish." Mom reaches for his hand.

"How could I *not* have been disappointed? Until then, I could only dream about a chance to audition at The Palladium. But that was sixty years ago," he shrugs. "I've had so many worse disappointments since. How can I say how I feel about it now? That would be then. Would anyone like a cup of tea?"

And Therefore I say to you, whatever things you ask when you pray, believe that you receive them, and you will have them.

Mark 11:24 NKJV

Isle of Capri

Chapter 9

BARGAINING WITH GOD

Either we trust in God, and in that case we neither trust in ourselves, nor in our fellow-men, nor in circumstances, nor in anything besides; or we DO trust in one or more of these, and in that case do NOT trust in God.

George Muller

"26,000 deaths in England. It's the last day of April tomorrow." Mr. P hunches over his iPad quoting Coronavirus statistics.

Mrs. P pauses her broom. "Geoffrey, would you check France? How are we getting home?"

"We can't go home via Paris. 23,000 deaths. That's the same as England. It's awful."

"I don't think we're out of here until the beginning of June. And who knows what life will be like at home after this?" Her broom resumes. "We are supposed to be in Italy right now." Furious sweeping punctuates my mother's frustration with our situation.

"Italy will certainly never be the same again." Mr. P abruptly flips closed the iPad cover and disappears into the kitchen.

Six minutes later, the three of us settle around the table with white mugs of hot tea and a packet of sugar-free biscuits. We will distract ourselves from the pain of this pandemic with cookies and stories of Mr. P's past. Life ahead is uncertain. History doesn't change.

"So, what happens next?" I ask after catching them up to where we left off in Chapter 8.

"I receive a call to be in the panto *Cinderella* in Bournemouth."

"*Now* comes the Danny LaRue story!" Mom perks up.

"In Cinderella, as you know, there is one ugly sister and one beautiful sister. Danny LaRue was *always* the beautiful one," Mr. P remembers.

"He spent his entire lifetime in the entertainment world. That could have been *you*, Mr. P." Mom raises her mug in a faux toast. "We have your hilarious pantomime letter to your mum at home. Remind me to show you, Ju, if we ever get back to America.

"Okay. Let me check the ones you *did* send me, because I think I do have a letter from just after Bournemouth." I scroll through my emails.

"These biscuits are very good," Mr. P mumbles through a mouthful of crumbs. "I wonder what they are sweetened with?"

Mom hands him a napkin.

"I don't know," I reply, "but here's the letter I was looking for. Do you want to hear it?"

"Sure. If you will hand me one more biscuit."

> *1964*
>
> *Dear All,*
>
> *All yesterday and today I've tramped round to agents in the cold and sleet. What awful weather after sunny days in Bournemouth.*

"Bournemouth was by the sea," Mr. P adds. "I stayed in a lady's home while I played in the pantomime there."

He pauses. Obviously thinking. Remembering. My fingers rest on my keyboard, waiting for his next words.

"Her name was Madge. She was Sabbath-keeper. I had learned about the Sabbath, but this was the first time I actually witnessed someone observe it from Friday evening to Saturday evening, like the Jews. Only she wasn't Jewish. She invited me to church. I would go with her in the morning, and on Saturday afternoons would be in the pantomime.

"Papa!" Mom chides with a smile. "You were in church in the morning and Cinderella in the afternoon?"

"Yes, and it was a rush from church because the panto started at two o'clock on a Saturday. But you *know* me. My *real* church has always been outdoors, where I feel closest to God. My most spiritual times there weren't at Madge's church, but walking along the sea from Boscombe to Bournemouth on my way to work each day. That walk began my lifelong practice of talking to God as I walk in nature.

"I had a problem in Bournemouth though. It wasn't a new problem. It was the same problem that followed me everywhere. The devil knows how to set a person up. Just as I was learning new things about God, the old things I suffered with followed me to Bournemouth. I had a real struggle there."

He stops talking. Takes a sip of tea. Looks at Mrs. P. Takes a deep breath. Continues.

"Back then, I was attracted to a certain *type* of person. Not a macho know-it-all kind of guy, but a person with a sensitive kind of nature. There would be a spiritual kind of attraction.

"There was a guy who came to do Madge's garden in the mornings. I felt this kind of attraction towards him. There was something going on there, a battle in my mind. I remember sitting at her window gazing out at the gardener. I couldn't *bear* having those feelings. I hate talking about this."

Mom reaches for him. Their hands clasp.

"I thought," he pauses then repeats, "I thought, '*If I give myself to God, one hundred percent, this will go away.*'

"The guy went to the same church as Madge, so I also saw him on Saturday mornings. I hated myself for having lustful thoughts, even in church. Somehow, I got the idea, '*If I do something really big for God, He will give me what I long for—freedom from my unwanted feelings toward men.'*

"How I wrestled with Him on those beach walks! There were no shops, only the cliffs and the sea. I began praying—pleading with God. '*If I give up my singing career, something I've wanted to do all of my life, in order to obey You and keep Your Sabbath, then You will surely take these desires away from me.*'

"It was there, on the beach, that I decided to become a Sabbath-keeper. A difficult decision. I saw all the biblical evidence for the seventh day Sabbath, but there was no way I wanted to give up my singing career in order to keep it holy.

"I read all the books I could get my hands on against it. I wrote to Billy Graham asking about Saturday being the Sabbath. I went to the Catholics, Jehovah's Witnesses, even the Mormons. I tried all I could to fight the truth. In the end, I was convicted. If anyone asked, I would say, 'If the Sabbath was good enough for Jesus, it's good enough for me.' That statement wasn't the whole truth. It was a half-truth. I couldn't tell them about the other motive I had for wanting to follow everything in God's Word, could I?"

"But this next paragraph finds you looking for work on a Saturday," I say after glancing at my computer screen. Listen to this.

> *Three agents said they would try to fix me up with something. I hope they fix me up on Monday. If not, I'll go into B.B. Evans department store on Saturday. If I go back there they will let me off for auditions. I'll be glad when I get working. The local paper for jobs isn't out until the weekend.*

"Sometimes, even when you are convicted of something, it takes time to put it into practice," he responds. "Especially when that conviction is foreign to you *and* to most of the rest of the world."

"I can see the truth in that," I say. "Lifestyle change comes slowly. Especially when something affects your income."

"That decision not only affected my income for the moment. It affected my whole career, the trajectory of my entire life."

I keep reading.

> *I'll go to church tomorrow night for the meeting. I finished the course and got my certificate. I've started another one now.*
>
> *It is taking a bit of getting used to this week after all the excitement and happiness of only a few days ago. It would be silly to say I'm not lonely.*
>
> *One of the agents I saw today said she will get me into a summer show at Swanage, doing my own spot in sketches. She knows Mable. It would be nice.*
>
> *As soon as I get a job, I'll have a weekend at home. Maybe for Whitsentide.*
>
> *Cheerio for now and God bless.*
>
> *All my love, Geoff*
> *xxxxxxxxxxxxxxxxxxxxxxxxxxxxxx*

"You sound kind of pitiful here P," Mom observes.

"I suppose I was. Out of work. Nothing working out with bookings."

"But you continued with the church meetings?" I ask.

"Yeah, they kept me from throwing myself off a balcony or something. I was often deeply depressed. The meetings provided some fellowship, you know? I also started baptismal classes. Preparing to keep *my* part of my bargain with God.

The P's chat back and forth while I skim my inbox.

"Here's another letter mentioning Whitsentide. No date. This one's actually *to* you . . . from a girl named Diana."

Tossing a wink at Mom, I dunk the last biscuit into my tea. "Do tell, Mr. Pennock."

"Diana? We were in the Amateur Operatic Society together. Her father owned a butcher shop." Mr. P is nonchalant. "What can I say? We were friendly, that was all."

"Hmmm," I tease. "Diana sounds enamored from the first paragraph."

"Can I read this one?" Mom asks. "I remember it. She *is* gaga for him."

"Sure." I turn my laptop around.

> *Dear Geoff,*
> *Thanks for your letter.*

My mother reads in her best British accent. Not too shabby for a girl from Arkansas.

> *It's wonderful to hear you are coming home for Whitsentide. I can hardly believe it! Five months since we last saw each other! Doesn't time fly? It will be great—just like old times.*

"I *love* this letter!" Mom interrupts her British persona to comment.

> *I come home on Saturday morning, but I'm going shopping in Wakefield. So I think it best if you ring about 5 PM on Saturday. Roll on, Saturday! That's what I say! I'm feeling ready for a holiday.*
>
> *Just fancy, I've been teaching for four weeks now. Me, a teacher! Don't times change?*
>
> *I fully understand the situation about money, Geoff. I honestly will be willing to pay for myself. Money doesn't matter. We can have a lovely time, even if it's only going walking. There are some gorgeous walks around Chapelthorpe— about ten minutes from home.*

"Around where?" Now Mr. P interrupts.

"Chapelthorpe." Mrs. P mimics his Yorkshire inflection.

"I can't even think where that is." He shrugs and repeats, "Chapelthorpe. Never mind. Carry on."

> *I'm really excited and can't wait to see you. It seems a lifetime since you were here. By the way, how long will you be home? I'll be home a week.*
>
> *You say you don't drink now. Well, when I'm home I never want anything. I just don't bother about drinking.*

"Drinking? I didn't think I was a drinker," he says. But then I was determined to give up everything sinful, wasn't I? Trying to please God so He would set me free."

> *I hope you get this letter tomorrow. I bet you're all excited about going home. It's wonderful isn't it? You don't realize until you've been away.*
>
> *I was wondering if you would like to come to our house Saturday?*
>
> *Well, please excuse my terrible writing. I'm rushing to catch the post.*
>
> *Bye for now. See you at the weekend. It will be fab!*
>
> *Please ring on Saturday.*
>
> *All my love, Diana*
>
> *x x x x x x x x x x x x x x x x x x x x x x x x x x x x*
> *x x x x x x x x x x x x x x x x x x x x x x x x x x x x x x*
> *x x x x x x x x x x x x x x x x x x x x x x x x x x x x x*

"Wow, P. those are a lot of x's," Mom says in her normal Mrs. P voice. "How was my accent?"

"What?" He sounds confused.

"There are an awful lot of x's at the end of this letter." She turns the screen toward him. "I think she really liked you. She *was* quite cute," Mom teases. Whispering to me behind her hand she says, "I found a picture of them together."

"She was *cute*?" He sounds surprised.

"*And* you sent her a lovely gift from B.B. Evans department store, remember?"

"No, I don't."

"That's in another letter. At home."

Mom dishes out the details. "It was a necklace. A man doesn't just *do* that," she says to me. "I don't think he realized how she might have taken that. You don't just buy a *friend* a decent, fairly expensive piece of jewelry."

"I didn't realize I did that," he admits.

"Yes," Mom remembers. "And the clerk helped you pick it out."

"Really?"

"That's what you wrote to your mum. Diane was crazy over you, but she couldn't snag you. The poor girl didn't know why."

"She will if she reads this book," he replies, "but she might be dead. Everybody will be dead who knows me in the book, so I don't need to be embarrassed. I don't know how you can sit there and write all this about me."

I can tell he feels uncomfortable. Mr. P really does not like talking about himself. That's why days go by without any writing at all taking place. He needs time to recover from the vulnerability of sharing his stories.

"Why couldn't she?" I ask.

"Why couldn't she what?"

"Why couldn't she snag you?"

"Because I wasn't interested in girls. Not like that." He shakes his head.

"Was she the only girl you dated?"

"I didn't really date her. I can't remember anything. We were just friends. That was all. I always felt she wanted to be more than a friend, but what could I do?"

"Did you date *anyone*?"

"Yeah, I might have taken somebody out to the cinema or something."

"But not like a relationship?"

"No, Julie, just make something up."

"There's nothing to make up, Geoffrey Pennock." Mom wags her finger at him. "You led that poor girl on, that's what."

"Did I ever ask forgiveness for it?" he asks. His face says he's joking.

"That's between you and God," Mom shoots back, laughing.

"I shall go ask Him now," he says, scooting away from the table, "on my way to take out the trash and buy some croissants."

We watch him tie his shoes. As the door clicks closed behind him, Mom says, "Poor Mr. P. He can't stand to be stuck indoors all the time. Especially when there's a sunny day and an ocean outside. He's such an adventurer. Seven weeks in here is too much!"

"He might be pushing the lock-down limits, though, with his daily trips to the bakery. I hope the police aren't out this morning."

"I thought of something as you were reading about Madge." Mom straightens the sofa cushions before sitting down again.

"Madge?"

"Mr. P's landlady in Bournemouth. Did you know he took me to meet her the year after the accident?"

"No."

"There are so many P-stories you don't know. Come sit by Mommy." She pats the sofa. I slip off my flip-flops and sit next to my mother. Our arms touch. Her skin smells of lavender.

"Madge was on her deathbed. Geoff took her hand and introduced me as his wife. We were still newlyweds. He was so proud to say those words, 'My wife.' He wanted her to know his story."

"Mom, I think I don't know many details of those first couple of years after the accident because I was still recovering myself. And you guys were so far away."

"It's true. To tell you the truth, when I met Madge, I still suffered tremendously with my head injury. After Mr. P tracked her down, we went to Bournemouth. The wind off the sea made my head hurt so badly. He had to buy me a hat.

"I endured a lot to do that trip with him—that and many others in our first years of marriage. There was something in his psyche that wanted me to meet all of these people. It was part of his healing. I've stayed in gay guys' houses and hung out with singers from the pantomimes. He even took me through the backstreets of London to meet the little lady from Greece who first introduced him to Jesus. Possibly the most cathartic thing we did was retrace his steps to the church where the perverted man first touched Mr. P's leg. We signed their guest book and wrote the verse from the story of Joseph, 'What you intended against me for evil, God intended for good.'

"Mr. P is fifty-one years old when we journey backward to do all of this."

Mom switches tenses. She does that sometimes.

"It's like he doesn't want to hide anything from me. He wants to be completely transparent with who he was and is."

"Transparency is a necessary ingredient for emotional healing," I say.

"And for maintaining victory," Mom adds.

"We re-do everything" she continues. "Even watch the Cinderella pantomime in Bournemouth with Danny LaRue *still* playing the pretty sister! Together we walk the same beach where he wrestled with God about trading his career for freedom. As we went through each phase, we jokingly said, 'This is good for the book!' Never expecting there actually *would* be a book, at least not a book this deep."

"There *has* to be a book, Mom. This is Mr. P's legacy."

"Well, his intense feelings for *me* drove him to show me off because he never before had such feelings. When he finally got a wife, he took me back to those people who had watched him suffer through all those years—people who were steppingstones in his story.

"So, when I met Madge, this little old woman who had cared about my Mr. P spiritually, I became quite emotional because of the role she played in his life. He started a real relationship with Jesus when he lived with her.

"In my mind I see her lying there, small and fragile. I touch her hand and tell her, 'I'll see you in heaven.'

"I cried, actually, because my own Mamaw, who cared for *my* spiritual soul, had the same name—Madge."

Mom's eyes moisten with the memory.

"Madge wasn't just a landlady for a struggling pantomime singer. She was a kind, spiritual example. Not a legalist at all. Meeting her was touching for me because the Methodism he grew up with didn't do a thing for Mr. P. It was just religion. But he *did* get something from Madge. Through her example, he saw that relationship is more important to God than religion. He learned God gave us a whole holy day, set apart so we can be still and experience true rest and relationship with Him. He always remembered her example."

"Thank you for sharing that piece of his puzzle. We never know the role our example can play in another person's life, do we?"

"It's true," Mom says. Then, "I wonder where he is?"

She stands and whisks our empty mugs to the kitchen.

While Mr. P is gone, we tidy the living room, hang a load of laundry on the balcony clothesline and try to decide what to cook for lunch.

"Let's roast some of those little potatoes," Mom suggests.

"Okay. And I can make a frittata. We still have eggs."

We scrape past each other in our apartment's tiny kitchen as we open and close the undersized refrigerator, pulling out fresh vegetables to chop for salad.

"I feel like I'm in a Barbie house. Everything is so tiny," Mom jokes.

"Except for us. If we keep eating biscuits and chocolates, we're gonna be sorry."

"Well, what else do we have to do on Coronavirus lock-down? We write. We eat. We watch the news. It's not like we can *all* go on walks every day like Mr. P. He's a naughty boy. He pushes the envelope. Getting yelled at by the police once was enough for me. I'll stay indoors and eat biscuits, thank you very much."

Bzzzzzz!

"He's back!"

Mom unlocks the door. Mr. P hands her a brown paper bag. The smell of fresh croissants makes me think I'm hungry even though I'm not.

"Papa, you were gone for quite a while," she remarks.

"I *have* go out every day and walk and sit in the sun and sing and pray. I can't just sit in this building or I will go mad!"

"Wash your hands, P."

"I know."

Mr. P's tanned face is flushed with the exercise. After washing up and changing his clothes he settles into his chair.

Mom hands him a glass of water. "Drink Love! You're as red as a beet."

"The lady in the croissant place is getting ready for a leaflet."

He chugs the water and hands her the glass before continuing.

"She doesn't know yet, but she is. You've got to go slow with people a bit, before you pounce. That's what I've learned from working with the Muslims."

Mr. P likes people. He likes talking with them, listening to them, and sharing Jesus with them. Telling his God stories ignites the sparkle in his blue-grey eyes. For the P's, every trip is a mission trip. They never simply 'go on vacation.' They pray over destinations for months in advance.

Mr. P usually sketches a landmark, like the Alhambra, then creates 'leaflets' with favorite Bible verses in the local language. To date, they have handed out thousands of these homemade artsy pamphlets in villages and off-the-path places.

"Speaking of Muslims, I'm disappointed our plans for Morocco got foiled," Mom says, plopping down on the sofa. "We felt a passion for going and doing. We left home with a purpose, didn't we, P? Now everything has been blocked."

"It's true," he agrees. "We've spent money to come here in obedience to the Holy Spirit, to share Jesus with the Muslims. All we've been able to do is sit in this apartment for nearly two months now. I don't understand it. At all."

"There were going to be interesting ways of sharing the Gospel, huh Mr. P?" Their eyes meet.

"Yes." He smiles. "We should have been on a camel and putting papers in the camel's carry bag. With these Coronavirus travel restrictions those poor people who depend on tourists to ride their camels are out of work. I feel really sorry for them."

"I wanted to take your picture on the back of a camel, Juliet." Mom says.

"I don't remember agreeing to anything like that!"

"Morocco is extremely interesting from a travelers' point of view," Mr. P continues. "God has used my travel addiction to take us places we would never have gone otherwise. The first time we traveled to Morocco the entire family was nervous about us going, remember?" His eyes sparkle at his Mrs. P. "My wife wasn't nervous, except for carrying the Gospel in her undergarments."

"Mother!"

"She did. Right past the customs agent at the airport."

"It's amazing what little old ladies can get away with," Mom lilts with a glint in her eye.

"From the first time I went to Morocco," he persists. "I thought 'If the Bible is true, and Jesus is the way, the truth and the life—there is no way we can ignore these people who will be lost without Him.'

"Did you know," he leans forward in his chair, "in America there are thirty-eight evangelicals for every hundred people? I got that from a recent statistic book. People go to church, week after week for one hundred years and don't give a hoot about people who don't know Jesus!" Mr. P nearly shouts his last sentence.

"Calm down, Peedy," Mom hushes with a smile.

He lowers his voice. "In Morocco there is one Christian for every 10,000 Muslims. Shouldn't we care how many Muslims will experience hellfire if Jesus is their only way to eternal life and they don't know Him? Jesus says, 'If you're not willing to lay down your life, you are not worthy of me.' He didn't ask us to have some lala religion, but to take up our cross and follow Him wherever He calls. Hand me my Bible please."

Mom picks up his tiny Amplified New Testament from the coffee table. He quickly finds the verse he is looking for.

"Matthew 16:24 is very clear. Listen. *Then Jesus said to His disciples, 'If anyone desires to be My disciple, let him deny himself [disregard, lose sight of, and forget himself and his own interests] and take up his cross and follow Me [cleave steadfastly to Me, conform wholly to My example in living and, if need be, in dying, also].'*

"It is forbidden to give the Gospel in Morocco. They can put you in prison or throw you out of the country. But Jesus says, 'Go.' So we go. My seventy-year-old wife is willing to go to prison for having the Gospel in her knickers while other people sit in their pews not giving a single thought about the rest of the lost world. What kind of Christians are we if all we do is go to church once a week?"

Mom rubs his arm.

"P, at least we've been able to communicate with *some* of our Muslim friends."

"It's not the same as going to Marrakesh."

"Definitely not. But what can we do?"

Mr. P shrugs. "All we can do is pray for the people we meet here and trust that God cares as much for them as the Moroccans. Even if it's just one or two papers we are able to give out."

"That's one or two souls who will learn God loves them as much as He loves Jesus," Mom agrees. "I just wish it was like before, when we flitted up and down this coast leaving leaflets between here and Malaga."

"You P's have certainly been missionaries for Jesus."

"We started on our honeymoon," Mom recalls. "Giving out papers on Capri, remember, P?"

"Yes. That's a beautiful place, Capri. I drew the village square with the clock tower for those. Capri's square is a bit like the old part of Sperlonga."

"How many papers do you think you've shared?" I ask.

"Thousands, huh Papa?"

"Everywhere we go," he replies. "England, Switzerland, Spain, Portugal."

"What's the island off of Portugal?" Mom snaps her fingers softly, as if snapping will spark her memory.

"Madeira."

"Yes! Our feet flew up those mountains, putting leaflets in mail slots and under doors. I even tied one on a sheep's collar!"

"We did the same in France, and of course, Italy . . ."

Mom hijacks his sentence, ". . . where the Pope's lawyer got a good dose of the Gospel. Now *that's* a story! After our conversation, he even asked us to pray for him."

"We never gave out any papers in Austria, did we?

"No, but I don't remember why not."

They are silent for a moment.

"I'm trying to think. What else did we do, Papa? What about Liechtenstein?"

"Yeah, but don't ask me to spell it," he jokes. "And what about lunch? I smell potatoes."

Over lunch we check in with my husband about how *his* writing is going. André mostly works in our bedroom, coming out at mealtimes and prayer time, or to run the stairs in our apartment building for exercise. The P's and I hold our write-a-thons in the living area. The four of us compare notes and catch up around the table at least once a day. We've developed a pandemic lock-down routine that works fairly well for everyone.

"Writing is difficult. It moves slowly. I'm just beginning chapter eight," André says. "What about you?"

"Well, we're up to the part where Mr. P gets a scathing letter from his father," I answer. Maybe we'll tackle that bit this afternoon. I have a feeling it could trigger all kinds of emotions."

"I have a feeling you're right," Mom says.

"My father said I'd end up in a lunatic asylum," Mr. P recalls. "They used to be called asylums in those days."

"We all might end up in one if we don't get out of this apartment soon," I joke. "Who wants a cup of tea?"

"Ginger please," says Mr. P. "With a drop of honey."

Mom wants ginger, too. "Just half a cup."

"No, thank you," André declines. "I'll wash dishes so you can continue with your writing."

Three dings of the microwave later we take our teas to the coffee table and make ourselves as comfortable as we can on uncomfortable furniture.

Mom starts the conversation with, "Papa, do you remember about twenty years ago when we lived in England and I got curious about your old suitcase full of letters?"

"No."

"Well, I opened it one day to discover a jumbled mess of cards, letters and envelopes. I worked hard to organize everything into stacks—letters from your fans, letters from your mother, letters from you to your family. Then I found this letter from your father.

I remember reading it out loud. I sympathized with you and said, 'That was really mean.'

"Do you know what *you* did?"

"No."

"You didn't say one word to me. You just scooped everything back up and put it into the suitcase."

"I can't remember." He shrugs.

"I can. You didn't want to talk about it."

Mom turns to me, "I'll tell you about another time. We were going to write a book of our lives. I got that dilapidated suitcase out *again* and put it on the bed. Mr. P actually cried. Just seeing it got him too upset, and in a bad mood. I put it away and didn't pull it out again for all these years. I just left him alone."

"And now here I am, digging up this past all over again," I admit.

"I'm fine," Mr. P says. "I am a new creation in Christ. Nothing from the past can hurt me."

"I don't want to hurt you by reading it aloud."

"Dad's letter doesn't hurt me anymore. Talking about all you-know-what that comes afterward—that's what bothers me."

"One thing at a time. First, what does your dad have to say?" I begin to read aloud.

> *Dear Geoff,*
>
> *Glad to hear from you but disappointed at you not having fixed up with Butlins. You say you cannot save any sum of money. You have both me and your Mum worried—as we don't know what you will do next.*
>
> *I am not crabbing religion. Far from it, as there is many worse things you could do. But when you start talking about Saturday being the Sabbath day and we have all been brought up to know that Sunday is the Sabbath day and without, you are a Jew . . . Well, we are of the same opinion that you want to telly in the ad "Fruit And Nutcase."*

"What's he talking about here?" I ask.

"It was a television advert for Cadbury's chocolate. People were doing ridiculous things while this guy sings 'Everyone's a fruit and nutcase' to the tune of a song from *The Nutcracker*. Quite a famous ad."

"Quite a mean thing to say to your son."

"That, too."

> *After you must have spent around 200 Pounds in roaming about singing, and lessons. Don't you think you want your head testing talking about being baptized? What are you going to do for a living and save? Your Mum would be happier if you had a job at home.*
>
> *You asked her to come down and meet Pastor Henderson. Your Mum has had it rough these last two months, and besides—you should know by now that money does not come easy. I know, as I have had to work hard and so has your Mum, to bring you all up—though I do not begrudge her anything she wants.*
>
> *You asked Butlins for Saturday off. You will be lucky to get it off, as it isn't a day nursery. For the Lord's sake, stick to the religion but don't go crackers.*
>
> *Love, Dad, Mum, Jean and Jennifer*

"My dad was a bit like the poorer people in that Netflix football story, *The English Game*. It was a different era, but that was the type of people I grew up around.

"Dad signed the letter from everyone, but it was really from him." Mr. P glances at Mom. "I always hated my dad, didn't I?"

She nods. "*My* dad wasn't the thrill of life either. Dads can make or break a person's self worth, can't they?"

"Mhmm. Let's hear what I wrote back."

> *Dear Mum, Dad, J and J,*
>
> *I'm so glad to hear you have some new clothes for a change and that you look nice. I bought some Chelsea boots on Thursday. They're real smart. I'm going to save them until I get my suit before I wear them.*

"Chelsea boots? What's that?" he asks.

I Google them and give him a visual of the short, retro 60's mod boots.

"Oh, I have a pair in my closet at home. Bought them in Italy. I never wear them."

> *In regard to your last letter on being a fruit and nutcase, I fully realise that the way my career is, I should not be able to keep the Sabbath. But at the moment, things are not so. I feel though I ought to keep it as much as possible. That is of course, if I found a job suitable. I should not be foolish and jump into any job. I've been out of work too often for that.*
>
> *In regard to singing on a Saturday night—only in the summer is Saturday night the Sabbath. The true Sabbath of the Lord is from sunset Friday to sunset Saturday. Anyone who doesn't worship God on and keep this day is breaking the 4th Commandment. If I could go to church Saturday morning and afternoon, I should be much happier. I think you must think me mad, but the pagans and Catholics changed the Sabbath to Sunday and not God. No human being has the right to change the laws of God. All I want is to go to church on the day God gave us. Even in the field of entertainment I could do this.*
>
> *I'm quite happy and contented working where I am and got over the boss's nattering. I went after two jobs on Thursday afternoon unsuccessfully. I also had an audition, but the agent was out. So I*

went round to have a natter with the receptionist at church, from whom I got information about the Sabbath Observance Employment Bureau, where I shall go next Thursday.

If I change my job to worship on the Sabbath, I'm sure God will be nearer to me. We have many things to be thankful for. Can't we try to do something for the One who gives us many blessings? Because the majority go to church on Sunday doesn't mean this is the right day. Many don't know this isn't the right day. So they can't do any better.

Last night, as I said before, we played at a wedding reception held in the upper room of a pub. I've never seen as much beer scoffed in all my life. I had a whale of a time with the sweet stuff and Pepsi Colas. I didn't have time for tea, so I made up for it. We went down very well and didn't finish until 12 AM. We had a great time. If I'd have still been a drinker, I could have had as much as I wanted.

We got 2 Pounds each for staying an extra hour. They made a collection of 5 Pounds. So that was 3.10 each altogether. One of the lad's Dad has quite a few contacts and says it will be easy to have two or three bookings a week as we get going.

You know I worked the other Sunday. The boss said I could get paid. Now he says I won't. He's a lying old sod. How I hate lying! He will give me a day off for it. Anyway the day will come in handy, as I'll have another day for a three-day weekend.

I'm singing at our work dance next month. Next Friday, the group and I are entering a competition for 2,000 Pounds and a recording contract. I don't think we've an earthly chance, but still. They intend trying. I must try singing 'When You Walk Through a Storm.' I'm sure I could make a better job of it than Jerry and the Pacemakers.

Must close. My friend John is coming to London for a job. He must think the streets are paved with gold. Far from the truth, as they are paved with sin.

I bumped into one of the waitresses from Margate on Saturday. She only lives on the next road from me. The world is a small place. I'm always seeing people from Butlins.

I must bath and get ready for church.

Cheerio for now and God Bless you. I'll send the cake tin later.

Love, Geoff

x x x x x x x x x x x x x x

"I think you were quite respectful to your father in your reply," Mom says.

Mr. P remains quiet.

"Did you ever meet your father-in-law?" I ask.

"I never did. Geoff and I were only writing to each other when his dad died."

"P, he obviously liked you being in your singing career or he wouldn't be fussing so much."

"I suppose so. But he thought I was a nutter."

"I think you're right, Mr. P." I agree. "Here's another letter from your father to prove it."

Dear Geoff,

What a letter! It took me all dinnertime to read it. Well it is about time you made your mind up what you are going to try and be. If you decide you are going to throw all that time and money away, besides having to rough it many times, I think you need your head testing. And the girls and your Mom agree with me. You can be a God-fearing person without getting the religious mania like Mrs. Leach at the pork shop at Thornhill Lees. They had to take her to Stores Hall (lunatic asylum). You can be a Christian without going mad.

> *It's alright these people saying, 'You do this and that,' but where is it going to get you, as you cannot live on fresh air? So please stick to your singing. I'm not saying give up going to church—far from it. But when you have spent five years singing, it seems mad to throw it away.*
>
> *You will wish when you are as old as me that you had gone into the police force. In twenty-five years you would have retired on a pension.*

"Oh dear me! Can you imagine *me*—in the police force? Wagging my truncheon around."

"Truncheon?"

"You know, like a baton. The police always carried them."

He Googles. "Look! You can get me one on Amazon for $11.65. With a hat and handcuffs." His face is droll.

"I remember those Bobbies in London. They seemed so gentle, like my grandmother with a stick. You could have done that, Mr. P." Mom giggles.

"I can't imagine any vocation further from Mr. P's qualities. Obviously, his father did not know him well. Listen to this next bit.

> *What about getting a job carrying the flag for the Salvation Army? You could do worse, as you seem to have tried all the religions there is.*

"My father was being sarcastic there. Nobody would get paid for carrying the Salvation Army flag."

> *I'm very pleased you're settling at work with a better bonus.*
>
> *Our first bowling match we won on Saturday. It was a cup tie. W R Cup. Last night we played Batley CB and we won.*

"You see my father always wanted me to be interested in *his* type of things, like the West Riding bowling match. I wanted him to be interested in *me*, in my life. We did not understand one another. At all. It was always me and my mum who did things together. I've told you that before . . ." His voice trails. I finish the letter.

> *The weather is showery and cool, but on Saturday it was like summer.*
>
> *Our Jean has gone to the doctor because her hands are itching. What with having her feet scratched and now her hands, I don't know what next.*

"What was wrong with Jean?" I ask.

"Eczema. Dad had compassion for my sisters. They got on fine with him. It was just me he was strange with, especially after I gave up my singing career to be baptized. He said I would end up in a psychiatric hospital."

> *It is nearly time for 'Double your Money' on telly. Hope you can!*
>
> *Your loving Dad, Mum, J and J*

"Well, I certainly didn't double my money. In fact, after I got baptized, I lost everything I had worked so hard to achieve." Mr. P disappears into the kitchen. We hear the refrigerator door open and close. Then the water runs for several seconds. He returns with wet hands.

"Papa, before we get home, you need to get out of the habit of baptizing the kitchen floor or you will get into trouble," Mom declares emphatically.

Mr. P has a habit of shaking his hands dry rather than using a dishtowel.

"I get into trouble here, so what does it matter?" His face is mischievous and guilty.

"It's difficult to train a man who was a bachelor for fifty years." Mom sighs. "Let's get *you* baptized and leave the kitchen floor out of it."

"Yes, please," I request. "How does this all go down?"

Mr. P sits again. "I *could* have gone back to Butlins that summer. I wrote to the manager at Margate explaining why I needed Sabbaths off. He actually approved it. But I never went back. My desperation of wanting God to do something for me was bigger than anything else at that point, wasn't it? I was utterly miserable. Have you written somewhere I always had a headache, and a pain inside my heart?"

"Yes. I think I wrote it in another chapter."

"I felt nervous and anxious all the time for a hundred years. Medication never helped. I thought it would all go away. I only got baptized because I thought God would change me. I decided to give up my career because I thought God would change me. The God I thought I knew back then was a much different kind of God than the one I know now. I honestly believed if I did something for Him, like giving up my career, He would do something for me, like give me heterosexual feelings. My thinking was all works-oriented, like the Muslims. 'If I do this, I'll get Paradise.'"

"Actually P, your thinking was like the beliefs of many people in the world, even Christians. We are all inclined to want to work our way to heaven somehow," I counter.

"It's true," he agrees. "The pastor who baptized me believed it was wrong to wear jewelry. He told me to take off my signet ring before he would baptize me. I didn't understand. I felt upset because my ring was a gift from Mum and Dad for my 21st birthday. My parents were hurt. They thought I was ridiculous. Years later I agreed with them. In the book of Haggai even God has a signet ring, so why would He want me to take off mine? At the time, though, I was willing to do anything if only God would do *something*. The Gospel doesn't work like that."

"I don't think the pastor gave you the Gospel," Mom says. "If you had the full Gospel, you would have been saved, healed, *and* delivered."

"He didn't give me the Gospel. He gave me the beasts of Revelation. And I became one." He chortles at his own joke.

"I would laugh, but that's not funny, Mr. P. This part of your story makes me really sad. I feel for the twenty-three-year-old guy in this chapter. I just want to hug him and tell him it will be okay."

"I truly felt some miracle would happen the day I got baptized," he repeats. "I believed it with all my heart."

"Where was your baptism?"

"It was on Regent Street, where I went for the meetings."

"He wore a white robe," Mom offers. "We have a photo at home."

"Did anyone come?"

"No. I was baptized alone. I'm afraid this chapter does not have a happy ending," Mr. P sighs. "My life disintegrated after I was baptized. I thought my pact with God would give me the relief I craved. I thought when I went under the water, I would never have homosexual feelings again."

Then Jesus said to His disciples, "If anyone desires to be My disciple, let him deny himself [disregard, lose sight of, and forget himself and his own interests] and take up his cross and follow Me [cleave steadfastly to Me, conform wholly to My example in living and, if need be, in dying, also].

Matthew 16:24 AMP

BUCKLAND IN THE MOOR

Chapter 10

MASTER PENNOCK

Falling for the bait doesn't make you the worst person in the world. You were snared. You were hooked. But you don't have to stay that way. Now is the time to deal with the shackles that keep you enslaved. Today you can leave the prison that sexual immorality has created from your past mistakes.
Craig Groeschel

"It's nearly time to clap!" Mr. P exits the kitchen wielding a stainless-steel pot and long-handled spoon.

"The highlight of his day," Mom laughs trailing him to our tiny balcony. André already leans out our bedroom window, whistling like Babe Ruth just hit a home run.

Our nightly celebration is the noisiest in the neighborhood, where each evening at 8 PM we join all of Spain on balconies and rooftop terraces to applaud and cheer for healthcare workers on the Coronavirus front lines.

Mr. P raises both arms like a Republican presidential candidate greeting the now-familiar faces of our locked-in neighbors. His whole-body waves to three Moroccan-looking Millennials on the roof of the apartment building across the lawn. They enthusiastically wave back. I can see their white teeth without my binoculars.

Mom gently waves in her one-armed way to the round-faced woman who always claps from her kitchen window. The elderly couple upstairs finally appears. She wears her face mask. He blows his plastic whistle, three sharp trills at a time.

"Makes me want to cry, seeing people on their balconies shouting and clapping and waving." Mr. P's compassion is evident in his eyes.

"A little reprieve from the social isolation," agrees Mom. "I don't really think this shelter-in-place thing is good for people, especially those living alone. At least we have each other."

As the clapping dies down, the four of us wave to a spindly woman whose double balcony is just across the parking lot. Each night, she claps and claps in her cherry-colored bathrobe until everyone disappears.

"What shall we do, P's?" I slide the balcony door closed and drag thin white curtains over a metal curtain rod. The curtains don't really keep the darkness out or the light in. But closing them is part of our routine. We clap. We close the curtains. We talk and pray until we are tired.

"Do you feel like talking about what happened after your baptism?"

"Why not?" Mr. P concedes. "What else do we have to do?"

"Not a lot," my husband eavesdrops on his way to the kitchen. "That's why I'm making some popcorn. Anybody else want some?"

"Me!" Mom and I say simultaneously. Mr. P never says yes to popcorn. Unless it's Mom's caramel corn.

"Dear me, we are going back a lot of years," he sighs, settling himself into his chair. "After my baptism I *still* had these awful feelings inside. Nothing had changed. I would pray for hours, pleading with God to set me free. Baptism wasn't enough, I thought, so I decided to do something more—to give up everything. 'If I give up singing forever,' I told myself, 'then surely God will do *something*!'

"I turned down Butlins that summer, even though they promised Sabbaths off. I decided to stop being Steve Parrish and become a pastor."

"A pastor?" André queries from the kitchen. "I never knew you studied theology." My husband sets two bowls of microwave popcorn on the coffee table.

"I only went to Bible college for one year," Mr. P answers. "I roomed with the French teacher and failed French."

"Which is ironic," Mom adds, "considering the fact he later worked for seven years as a nurse in a French-speaking canton of Switzerland."

"Why French and not Greek or Hebrew?" André asks.

"I can't remember. Maybe I had to take a modern foreign language first?"

"Wait, wait, wait!" I say. "I need my laptop. *I* think you just skipped a bunch of details." I transfer my popcorn to the table and open my MacBook.

Ding! The microwave announces André's popcorn is popped. Seconds later he stands in the doorway, holding the bag by one corner. I can tell he is torn between sitting with us and going back to his makeshift office in the bedroom. "I'll be back," he says after a moment. "I just want to finish my chapter."

"We'll still be here. Squeezing out the details," I sigh.

"Mr. P. how did you end up going to seminary?"

"I was absolutely miserable, wanted to get away from everything. I made a plan to become a missionary to foreign lands. That was the idea. Strange, but that was it. The problem was, I couldn't get away from myself."

"So basically overnight you went from singing professionally to studying for the ministry?"

"Yeah, but I had no money. I had to work for about a year to save up for school."

"What work did you do, if you quit singing?" Mom asks. "I've forgotten this part of your story."

"I went to Norway to sell Christian books and magazines door to door. It was awful." He shakes his head from side to side, as if trying to forget the pain of it.

"Big change from pantomimes and record deals." I form my words around a mouth full of popcorn. They come out fuzzy.

"What?" Mr. P asks.

"Never mind."

"I hated every minute of it," he continues. "I rode a bike up and down the streets. I was scared. That was not me—knocking on people's doors. Not me at all.

"I couldn't speak any Norwegian. I learned it off by heart, what I had to say at the door. If I sold something or if I didn't, all I could say was 'Mange takk,' which means 'Many thanks.' That's the only thing I remember."

He picks up his iPad. "Look," he says seconds later, showing us gorgeous images of cerulean sky reflected in water with white-capped mountains in the background. "This is near Ulvik, the village where I stayed. It's on a branch of Hardangerfjord. Every day there I prayed for rain so I wouldn't have to go out and sell those books."

"How were you going to pay for your school if you didn't sell anything?" Mom asks.

"I didn't care. It didn't take a lot of faith to pray for rain there," he laughs. "These photos don't tell the truth. Norway's weather is like England, with loads of rain!"

"So this thing between you and God and the weather has been going on for a long time," I joke.

"I guess so. I used to pray for rain, but now I rebuke it." He pauses. "In all honesty, that did not feel like missionary work to me. If I was truly being like the apostles, I would have said, 'Bring your sick out and let me heal them in Jesus' name,' not sell them a health magazine. I felt guilty selling Christian literature when I knew it had done nothing to help me. A person can read books and pamphlets all their life, but it's the BIBLE that does not come back void. Until a person really reads the Bible to know God for themselves, they will miss the power of the gospel."

Mom reaches for a handful of popcorn. "You must've sold enough literature to pay your college fees."

"No. I didn't. I went back to London and worked at a printing press. I don't remember much about it. I know I lived with a Christian lady who was horrible and worked with an atheist lady who was very kind. The atheist invited me for lunch every Sunday.

"Sometimes I went home on weekends. On Sabbaths I shut myself in my room when my Mum was cooking roast beef and Yorkshire pudding. I thought I needed to isolate myself from my family's 'sins' of working in the kitchen or watching TV on the holy Sabbath day. My strict Sabbath keeping was all about me, not about Jesus. I was absolutely nuts. They must've wondered what had taken hold of me.

"I became a total legalist—trying to obey my way into the heart of God. Legalistic thinking was great for someone like me who truly longed to please God. In the end it became bondage. And it turned everyone around me off. I drove my mother nearly insane with all my can'ts and shouldn'ts and don'ts. I would think she was happy to see me off to college."

"But you were there for only one year?" I ask.

"Yes. There was a write-up in the Dewsbury newspaper when I left. *Geoffrey Pennock gives up singing aspirations to become a minister.* My photo was in it and everything. Dad's deep disappointment cut my heart. I felt it through his silence. Still, I was determined.

"I didn't just want to go for myself. I really *did* want to serve hurting people. I thought mission work was the perfect way to help people and earn a living at the same time. As long as I never had to go door to door again!"

"Did you make friends at seminary? Were you accepted?" I press for more details.

"I suppose I was. And I *did* have some friends. I even stood as best man at one bloke's wedding. But I was still miserable. I would get up early, while the French teacher snored, and go out into the woods to pray. I remember walking and pleading, 'Set me free! Set me free! Set me free!' Oh dear . . ."

"That's heartbreaking, P." Mom dusts popcorn crumbs from her hands and reaches for his.

"It was."

"At what point did you realize it didn't work?" I ask.

"What?"

"When did you realize your baptismal bargain failed?"

"When pretty girls were interested in me, but I only had feelings for men." He cringes like a baby eating broccoli. "I don't like thinking about it now, but that was my life then.

"At college I lived in a men's dormitory. Guys talked about sexual stuff. It wasn't that different from Butlins, really. Except maybe nobody brought girls in to sleep with them."

"They probably did. Even the Vatican has a revolving door," Mom comments. "Remember the secrets that Swiss Guard told you when he was your patient?"

"I certainly do. But if the guys at college brought girls into the dorm, I didn't know about it. And everyone was supposed to be a Christian, so it would have been kept well under wraps. There was even one guy on campus who had the reputation for being the only male on planet earth who had never masturbated."

"How would anyone have known that?" I scoff. "It's not like masturbating is a team sport."

"Obviously you have never lived in a men's dormitory," my husband's voice comes through the thin door that separates our living and sleeping quarters. The door opens. André and his half-eaten bag of popcorn join me at the table.

"I'd like to hear *your* stance on masturbation, Pastor," Mr. P says. "You probably get asked some interesting questions in premarital counseling."

"If a person is asking questions, at least they are aware of a problem," André answers. "If someone addicted to sexual sin is struggling, it is a good sign. A struggle indicates God's Spirit is present. It's when there *isn't* a struggle that a person needs to be concerned. The lack of a struggle indicates someone has given themselves over to the addiction and doesn't care about getting out of it."

"I doubt this is a conversation many men have with their in-laws," I quip. "But seriously—don't we need to address this topic in your book, Mr. P? Aren't sexual fantasies and self-gratification part of the homosexual culture?"

"I think it's just part of our modern culture in general," Mom counters. "My friend recently told her teenage son masturbating is good for him and if he hadn't tried it, he should."

"Oh dear!" exclaims Mr. P. "I can't imagine my mum ever telling *me* something like that."

"Me neither," I agree making eye contact with my mother.

"This conversation reminds me of something funny from my seminary days," Mr. P offers, his face hinting at humor. "Our history professor would take roll at the beginning of each class, but he never used our first names. He would call us by our surnames with 'Master' in front. I was 'Master Pennock.' So each day the teacher would say, "Master Pennock, Master Jones, etc. There was one guy whose last name was Bates. Me and all the future pastors in my class choked back laughter every time the teacher said, 'Master Bates.' Poor guy. He never heard the end of it."

In my mind I'm picturing a scene from *Dead Poets Society*. I envision Robin Williams, with his droll smile as Mr. P's history teacher.

"One therapist I went to years later said, 'Think about God,'" Mr. P continues.

"While masturbating?" André asks.

"Yes. My counselor said, 'If you think about God while you do that, you will get over it. God gave you sexual feelings and you can't deny them. So you think about God and give your orgasm to Him.' That's what the guy said."

"Do you agree?" I ask. "I've heard of pastors who tell alcoholics or addicts to pray whenever they use—like, to invite God into that moment with them, but I never heard that line of thinking applied to self-gratification."

"It does seem a bit strange, doesn't it?" Mr. P replies. "I remember his words because I thought it unusual. He said, 'It isn't best to have that habit, but if you can't stop, think about God and keep surrendering your sexuality to Him.'"

"It *is* strange," I say. "That whole line of thinking somehow takes something God meant for intimacy between *two* married people and makes it only about one person—one person who is thinking about God while they are doing it. Sex was designed to be shared. Isn't it kind of creepy to think about God while masturbating?" I ask. "Especially if you have a problem with fantasizing about men?"

"It's only creepy if you are thinking about God just because someone told you to do so," says my husband. "But it's not creepy if you have a genuine desire for God to give you His gift of victory over the addiction, and you are inviting Him to change your thinking."

"What about what the Bible says about lustful thoughts?" Mr. P asks. "Honestly, can anyone masturbate *and* think about God?"

"If you go into lust-land, then you are really in trouble," Mom adds, quoting one of her favorite scriptures. "2 Corinthians 10:5 says, 'Casting down imaginations, and every high thing that exalts itself against the knowledge of God, and bringing into captivity *every* thought to the obedience of Christ.'"

"True," Mr. P agrees. "A person needs to pray *the moment* that thought enters the mind and use scripture as their weapon against those thoughts."

"Does anyone even *talk* about this stuff?" Mom chuckles. "In all my seventy years, I've never heard Christians talk about it."

"These aren't just homosexual problems. Lustful thoughts lead to actions. What about pornography? That's a similar problem. Do church people talk about *that*?" Mr. P asks. "I read somewhere that 60% of Christian men look at porn."

"Craig Groeschl has a video that pushes it even higher— to 79%," André adds. "I'm not sure how they get those statistics, but either way those percentages are high for Christians."

"What are all these Christians *doing* when they look at porn?" Mom sounds slightly saucy. "Are they just turning the pages of their Bibles?"

Mr. P continues. "It's an embarrassment to Christ's name that most Christian men struggle with this habit, but the temptation to masturbate doesn't just go away when someone becomes a Christian. When I was young, I thought I was the only one. But if we're speaking honestly, I'd say every man in the whole world has masturbated. If someone says they haven't, they are a liar."

"In the 17 years I've been in the ministry," André chews and swallows before finishing his sentence, "we pastors have had *one* book on the dangers of pornography handed to us—with no surrounding conversation. Our ministerial supervisor just said, 'This is a very good book. I encourage you to read it.'"

"After ten years as a pastor's wife, I could tell you many stories of miserable ministers' wives whose husbands are addicted to porn and masturbation," I respond. "This is the elephant in the room among believers. In the area of our sexuality, I think a lot of churchgoers are just doing what the world does."

"Basically the world says it's okay." Mom shrugs. "Everyone says it's okay nowadays. 'Just do what you want.'"

"If we all just do whatever we want, we self-destruct," André argues. "A family physician I know recently shared statistics of young men in their twenties and thirties who can no longer get erections because of pornography and over-stimulation. They *can't* have sex with their wives or girlfriends. They can't masturbate. They become basically nonfunctional because of too much of a good thing. Humans weren't created to have constant sex. Real women can't compete with the fake world of porn. They could never keep up that kind of pace."

"Obviously neither can guys if twenty-year-olds need to go to the doctor because of erectile dysfunction," I say.

"Masturbation isn't only a *man* problem," Mom adds. "All the sex-addicted girls where I used to volunteer promoted it. If someone wanted to sneak out and hook up for sex, another girl would say, 'Why don't you just masturbate? You don't need to go out there and get yourself into trouble.'

"Masturbation wasn't discouraged by the therapists there," she continues. "Maybe they would rather the girls do *that* than be out spreading social diseases or making more babies for the foster care system. I remember one girl bragging, 'My dildo is as good as a penis.'"

"Oh dear!" Mr. P's ears are scarlet.

"She said *that*," Mom continues, "while in the same breath she also said, 'I want a relationship.'"

"That's because it's a counterfeit, right? Anything outside the marriage relationship is a counterfeit for what God has given," André interjects. "We were created for intimacy on all levels—physical, emotional, spiritual."

Mom nods, her ponytail bobbing in agreement. "The devil is behind all this porn and fake sex stuff. What he wants is to destroy deep connection and intimacy. He always comes up with something evil to take the place of everything good God made."

"Humans have become disconnected souls having sex with ourselves. This is so far from God's plan," I comment. "Connection is the antivenin to addiction. I am fully convinced sex addiction is devastating countless couples and families."

"Yes! And single people." Mom agrees. "We forget about those who lose their mate or go through a divorce. They long to be loved. They are used to having sex. They want to have sex."

"Sadly, people are willing to settle for a substitute rather than wait for God's best," I say, reaching into André's almost empty popcorn bag. He pushes it toward me.

"Maybe some think they will be single forever. Like I was." My husband leans back, resting his head on the wall behind his chair. "They lose hope of finding someone. I was fifty-two when we married. That's a long time to wait."

"It's true," Mr. P admits. "Being celibate is extremely difficult. Remember, I was fifty when I married your mother. I'd had to learn to trust God with my sexuality. To believe He knew what was best for me."

"I'm sure she's glad you did," I say. "But imagine if you and André were so addicted to your own ways of satisfying yourselves sexually that you weren't even interested in the real deal when you got it? That's the sad reality many women live with after marrying. I've heard all the stories. Their husbands don't come to bed—they stay up with their computers or phones or whatever. They aren't interested in sex. They can't have an erection without porn. I feel so sorry for people."

"True story," André shares. "I once dated a girl who was divorced. Her ex-husband was gay, and he married her to cover it up. She could not figure out what the problem was—until she realized she was competing with gay porn. He just wasn't interested in his wife. She was very insecure as a result. I've also heard of straight guys getting to the point where they prefer masturbation to real sex with a human being."

"I hate all this virtual reality replacing real relationships!" Mom exclaims. "Now virtual *sexuality* has come into play. During this Coronavirus lock-down, people are more isolated and disconnected than ever. How are they coping?"

"Yeah," I say reaching for the last two kernels in the popcorn bag. "I just read an article about how virtual sex businesses are skyrocketing as more and more people fill their lonely lives with some kind of sexual connection. It's heartbreaking, really."

Mr. P speaks up. "Looking at pornography is so easy for people now, with the internet. We used to have to go special places to buy magazines. They were difficult to get. Switzerland did not allow them. I had to buy them in Italy."

"Mr. P!" Mom teases, covering her mouth with her hand.

"You know all about these things. Things Jesus and I worked out before you became Mrs. P." He grazes her face with the backs of his fingers. "Not to make light of the issue, but the photos in my old magazines seem like children's books compared to what's on television advertisements nowadays."

"Speaking of Italian pornography," Mom recalls, "I remember being visually assaulted in the train station in Naples. I was shocked—lambasted—with everything horrible right in my face! I haven't quite seen anything like that in America. At least they put black covers on the *Playboys* in gas stations and bookstores." She closes her eyes, her teeth crunching un-popped corn kernels. "Where do you think," she pauses then starts again, "Where do you think people learn to be stimulated by things like that?"

"I think it's a natural response," I say. "Our bodies respond to what our eyes see. More and more children, boys *and* girls, are now addicted to porn at young ages because of easy-access on their phones and stuff. And kids masturbate, too. In my early childhood education training, I was taught how to redirect students without shaming or calling attention to them if they masturbated in the school setting. I've had to put that training into practice more than once.

André leans forward, lowering his voice. "Clay McLean says a lot of masturbation happens from separation anxiety."

"Who? Mr. P interrupts.

"Clay McLean. He's a pastor/counselor. I used to listen to his CD's when I began *my* healing journey. Anyway, he says self-stimulation is the pseudo-intimacy a child doesn't get from their parents. Children stumble onto it because they aren't getting affection from the right source. A lot of it starts even in the early years. It's a self-soothing thing."

"So, let's say you are three years old and you're self-soothing like that," Mom says. "It forms a habit. That's your go-to comfort in life. Who is to say that is wrong? What do little kids know?"

"It's a setup," André continues. "Just like they say homosexuality develops early. I know of a boy whose mother didn't want a boy. She used to dress him in girly colors and teach him to knit and sew. He turned out gay. His own mother set him up."

"In this world, we can be set up for just about anything," Mom says. "Neglect, abuse, molestation—all of it leaves children vulnerable, with unmet needs."

"Yeah," I reiterate. "We become vulnerable to whatever the devil decides to offer us as a substitute for genuine love, acceptance and affection. It's awful. Even children are preyed upon by the enemy. Is it their fault they are neglected or molested or traumatized?"

"Of course not!" Mr. P's voice is strong. "Was it my fault my first sexual experience was being abused by a man? NO!"

"I'm sorry, Mr. P," I empathize. "That one experience impacted your whole life. And you were just a kid."

"I think kids and teenagers see things and experience things that set them up for patterns and behaviors that *do* affect them. Our brains can't unsee things when we've been overexposed," Mom adds.

André and I speak at the same time.

"At what point . . ."

"It's true, Mrs. P . . ."

We both stop. He motions for me to continue. I shake my head. "You go. I'll save my question."

He continues, "You're right, Mrs. P. We all have triggers. A man is *created* to respond to the female form. We can see a billboard ad for pantyhose or a woman wearing yoga pants in the Wal-Mart checkout line. Our culture is rigged on all sides with visual stimulation. Sometimes I wish I lived in a Muslim country so I wouldn't have to worry about it. When I was single, it was even more difficult. So, yeah. For any person, married or not married, who wants to be pure in thought, it's very difficult in this modern day and age. You literally have to cast your eyes aside the moment something comes into your peripheral vision.

"What were you going to say, Love?" he nods in my direction.

"I wanted to ask, at what point do we become accountable for our own choices?"

"Many people don't even think any of this is wrong," Mr. P says. "Some will read this book and wonder what we are going on about."

"What does the Bible say?" Mom looks directly at André. "Pastor, what would you tell someone who really wants to know what God says about sexual sin?"

"Mr. P, will you look up 1 Corinthians, chapter 6 in your New Testament?" André asks. "I think there's something right at the end of the chapter that might help answer this."

"Okay. It's the Amplified version, is that alright?" P asks.

"Probably better."

The P's join us at the table where the only light in the room dangles from the ceiling.

Nobody speaks while Mr. P hunts the chapter. I don't know how he can even see the words his Bible is so tiny.

"Maybe this is what you are talking about, André," he says, "Starting with verse eighteen: 'Run away from sexual immorality [in any form, whether thought or behavior, whether visual or written]. Every *other* sin that a man commits is outside the body, but the one who is sexually immoral sins against his own body. Do you not know that your body is a temple of the Holy Spirit who is within you, whom you have [received as a gift] from God, and that you are not your own [property]? You were bought with a price [you were actually purchased with the precious blood of Jesus and made His own]. So then, honor *and* glorify God with your body.'"

"Don't you think that's clear?" my husband asks. "Our bodies don't actually belong to us. What we do with them matters.

"It is," Mom acknowledges. "I was thinking of another verse that lumps most of us together. It says, 'such were some of you.'"

"Yes," Mr. P recalls, running his finger up the highlighted page. "It's just before this section. Verses nine through eleven. Shall I read it?"

"Please."

"'Do you not know that the unrighteous will not inherit *or* have any share in the kingdom of God? Do not be deceived; neither the sexually immoral, nor idolaters, nor adulterers, nor effeminate [by perversion], nor those who participate in homosexuality, nor thieves, nor the greedy, nor drunkards, nor revilers [whose words are used as weapons to abuse, insult, humiliate, intimidate, or slander], nor swindlers will inherit *or* have any share in the kingdom of God. And such were some of you [before you believed]. But you were washed [by the atoning sacrifice of Christ], you were sanctified [set apart for God, and made holy], you were justified [declared free of guilt] in the name of the Lord Jesus Christ and in the [Holy] Spirit of our God [the source of the believer's new life and changed behavior].'"

"These sexual things are not the only things that will keep people out of heaven," Mom says. "But people like to harp on the homosexuals as if their sin is worse than anyone else's."

She takes three glasses and lines them up on the table. "Line up these cups. Sin and perversion is in all the cups. We can't separate them into neat little pockets and say, 'I'll drink from this one, but not from that one.' or 'What's in yours is bad, but mine's okay.' Whatever is inside the cups comes from the same source. 'And such were some of you.'" She points her finger around the table at us. "And me," she says. "Before the blood of Jesus washed us clean."

"You're right, Mom. We love to point fingers at one person's sin. We like to label things. Put them in a box. But when it comes to sexuality, there are a lot of so-called grey areas. For example, there are many married couples—heterosexual couples—where the men like to have anal sex, even among Christians. The wives have told me. They don't like it, but they think they must submit to their husbands, like the Bible says."

"I don't care what men like." Mom sounds feisty. "That's not right. It's not how God made our bodies, and no woman should have to submit to sexual perversion of any kind."

"Most people assume homosexuals are having anal sex," Mr. P says. "I would say that would be the minority when I was young. Now, it probably *is* the norm.

"It's everywhere now," Mom says. "I was in a Christian bookstore and picked up a book on sexual purity for teenage girls. I was shocked to read some girls think they are saving their virginity for marriage by doing lesbian acts or 'only' having alternate kinds of sex with their boyfriends."

"The pornography industry has completely destroyed sexual norms," I add. "People are doing anything and everything with anyone and everyone—trying to emulate what they see in those videos. I recently read an article about pediatricians noting an increase in injuries sustained in young children by older siblings perpetrating on them, trying to do things they see in porn."

Mom winces. "What a hideous, painful world we live in. Those poor children! I ache for all of them, the victims, the perpetrators *and* the people in those porn videos. Most of them are probably hungry and drugged and not wanting to do any of the stuff they are doing. Sometimes they also need medical procedures to repair the damage from those filmed acts."

"It's true," Mr. P says. "When I worked in the hospital, we had patients come in who needed repairs done to their privates. It's awful the stupid things people do. They are looking for something they cannot find."

"Exactly," André agrees. "They cannot find it because they are not looking in God's direction."

"I think many people who act out sexually are searching for something they did not get from their father." Mr. P's voice trembles with compassion as he continues, "I believe that's why many homosexuals are promiscuous. There is an almost desperate longing to be held and loved and affirmed by a man. They are looking for the love they never got—searching for intimacy. They are trying to get it from another human, and it turns sexual. People need to find that intimacy with their heavenly Father."

"I'm with you, Mr. P," I say. "Whether our voids are because of a lack of fathering or some other setup causing us to act out, we all have a God-shaped hole in our souls. We spend our lives trying to fill it with all kinds of things that temporarily make us feel better. Sex or sex substitutes are just some peoples' drug of choice."

"Human beings were created to be spiritual creatures. We are called to live in the spirit, not the flesh."

"You can say that all day long, André, but how does that help someone addicted to sex, porn or masturbation?" I'm not afraid to ask my husband tough questions.

"Yeah," Mom chimes in. "Especially if they've been married and are used to sex and then, suddenly, they don't have it anymore. Or if masturbation is their only source of comfort since childhood."

"Or if they are teenagers," I add.

We all laugh. Then the room falls silent.

"How does a man—or a woman, because women lust, too—how do we transcend the flesh?" André asks before sharing his personal thoughts.

"We transcend the flesh by surrendering ourselves to the infilling of the Holy Spirit and by spending time in God's presence and His Word every day.

"Our sexuality can awaken, and our sexuality can hibernate. It should be awakened when we are in a marriage relationship. When we are out of that context, our sexuality should hibernate. When we have surrendered to Christ, we transcend the flesh and live in the spirit.

"Jesus came to bring us back to that Spirit-filled state. In John 6:63, Christ says the flesh counts for nothing. It is the Spirit that gives life. If we call on the Holy Spirit, drink God's word and are in

His presence, we can transcend the flesh. But if we don't, we will be stimulated a thousand times a day, either visually or from some other source.

"When a person is unmarried, or in a context that does not involve their own spouse, they shouldn't be turned on. When a Christian person chooses a life in the Spirit, but still has sexual expression when they are by themselves, it means that the physical nature is being fed from somewhere."

"So, would Jesus masturbate?" Mr. P softly asks. "I think that's the most important question a Christian can ask on this issue."

"Jesus wouldn't masturbate *or* look at pornography," André says. "I can't see that happening."

"Okay. But does He know our story and have patience with us when we are stuck?" Mom asks then answers her own question. "Yes."

"It's a process," Mr. P continues. "There is a lot of shame involved in sexual sin. It's not something a person can easily stop overnight. We need God and we need accountability to another person with whom we can be completely honest—a friend who understands."

He picks up the empty cup in front of him then sets it down. "How do we break *any* habit?" he asks.

We wait for his answer.

"We must form a new habit. As Christian psychologist Larry Crabb says, we must let *Jesus* become our addiction."

I'm nodding. Mom is nodding. André leans forward, placing both elbows on the table. Mr. P keeps talking.

"If we are self-soothing with sex, there comes a point where we can no longer be self-absorbed. We have to be Christ-absorbed. The more we know Jesus, whatever we were looking at before, wherever we found comfort or satisfaction before, whomever we have been with before—it all disappears."

Mr. P speaks with the conviction of a man whose words are drawn from the well of personal experience.

"In that process of learning to trust God with our sexuality, if we fail—and we do, because the Bible says, 'all have come short of the glory of God', we keep moving forward with God. We don't get discouraged and give up, because His Word also says, "If we confess your sins, He is faithful and just to forgive our sins and cleanse us." He repeats himself, "If a person fails and falls, they can start over again."

The tears glistening in Mr. P's eyes are contagious. He has tasted the fruit of victory over Satan's lies, but his hard-won wisdom is not without its battle scars.

"Have we exhausted the subject?" I ask.

"I think so," Mr. P responds. "Tea anyone?"

Dear Reader,

We prayed for you following that conversation. Without knowing your particular struggle, we know you are reading these pages for a reason. May our loving heavenly Father give you hope through Mr. P's testimony. He who began a good work in each of us promises to carry it forth to completion (Philippians 1:6). Be kind to yourself. You were bought with a price. As Art Thomas says, "Jesus deserves what He paid for." You are so loved.

Blessed are the pure in heart, for they shall see God.

Matthew 5:8 NKJV

VENICE

Chapter 11

BIG PROBLEM, SMALL GOD

Your thoughts of God are too human.
Martin Luther

Jesus did not die at the hands of muggers, rapists, or thugs. He fell into the well-scrubbed hands of deeply religious people, society's most respected members.
Brennan Manning

"I got up so late I missed lunch." Mrs. P shuffles sleepily into the living room, her scarlet kaftan wrapped around her like a silk blanket.

"I was beginning to wonder," I answer, looking up from my laptop.

My mother was born in the wrong century, the wrong country, and into the wrong family. She quite possibly is a direct descendant of some royal princess somewhere. No wonder Mr. P sometimes calls her "Principessa." She is elegant even with pillow marks imprinting the soft cheek where she slept hard until well past noon.

"20,000 deaths in England. More than 22,000 in Spain." Mr. P announces looking up from his iPad. He's been scrolling for half an hour, reading all the pandemic updates while I sit at the table slurping sliced Valencia oranges and posting images on Instagram.

"Please don't greet me with awful statistics P. I couldn't sleep last night for thinking of poor old people, abandoned in that Madrid nursing home. And the thousands of funerals nobody can even attend. And what Edward Snowden said on YouTube about the government using COVID-19 as one more excuse to remove our freedoms. This world isn't somewhere I want to be today."

I push my plate of oranges toward Mom. She salts a slice before popping it into her mouth. This is probably the only habit convincing me she is her mother's daughter. Grandma salted everything. Even oranges.

"I hate to be morbid, P's," but since you're both talking about death today, would you like to discuss Jennifer? It's where I am in Mr. P's story."

"I don't think that child should have died," Mom blurts. "It's a horrible story."

"Papa," she asks, "are you up for talking about your little sister?"

"You tell it," Mr. P answers. "If I may speak Yorkshire for a moment, I feel quite blethered."

"Why are you exhausted?"

"Because I had to go out and walk and sing and pray by the sea, didn't I? And I don't care if the police say something. I can't just sit in this building. I will go mad!" He squawks nearly as loudly as the neighbor's scarlet macaw.

"One P again went out alone from the pod?" Mom asks. "Does a P go out alone? No! Ever since the P's became the P's they go out together."

Mom's bottom lip protrudes in a perfect seventy-year-old princess pout as she approaches her husband. "For two months now, P, you have sneaked out alone. We always go out together. We hold hands. I'm tired of this. I feel stuck. I need to go out, too."

"The internet says we can hold hands this Sunday," Mr. P drolly replies reaching out his arms for her. "Spain is lifting the lock-down in stages. Today children are allowed to go for a walk with their parents. We're advancing to "Phase 1," which means couples can soon go out for a one kilometer walk together for one hour between ten and noon. Maybe we can go to the ice cream shop."

"Sounds very controlling," says Mom. "I'm not used to being told when I can hold my husband's hand and for how long we can walk together."

I'm wondering if I should just stick with Instagram and forget about writing today. The P's are definitely in interesting moods. Not that I blame them. Weeks and weeks of lock-down have made us all a little cuckoo. I browse my photos from seven years ago, mentally reliving our Venice trip with the Peasies. My Honey and I only had three married years under our belts then. Each photograph conjures precious memories of less terrifying times. Today San Marco Square stands empty as Italians continue to live quarantined lives.

Venice is the city where the P's fell in love back in 1990, when they were still just "Geoff" and "Susan." For them, our 2013 trip was a second honeymoon. Nostalgia hung over those two lovebirds like a morning mist blanketing the Grand Canal. I stalked The P's like the Paparazzi, photographing them walking hand in hand down narrow streets and kissing in the gondola.

I'm secretly stalking them now. Mom has plopped herself onto his lap.

"Oww!" He jumps.

"Am I hurting you?"

"No."

"Then why are you saying, 'Oww?'"

"I don't know."

Mom looks at me. I dare not look up from my keyboard as I feel her eyes boring holes through my pretense of being otherwise occupied—although I am typing every word they say.

"I don't trust that girl over there at the typewriter," she whispers loudly behind her cupped hand into Mr. P's ear. "We must be very careful what we do or say."

I try to stop my mouth from curving into the smile I know will give me away, but I can't help it.

"She's writing everything! That's wrong!"

Mom points at my cheesy cat grin, her arm extended like she's about to banish me from her kingdom.

Ignoring the threat of exile, I keep keying her words.

"Juliet! Erase that! Get that out! That's not going in your book!"

Laughter rumbles way down deep. I hold my breath in an effort to prevent its escape. My eyes water. I know it's cheeky to get the giggles when the atmosphere reeks of death and drama. I suppose we all respond to stress in different ways. Since this is the first pandemic of *my* lifetime, I'm uncertain of the social norms for handling the fact that this virus and the fear surrounding it has utterly crippled our planet. All I know is in the middle of a discussion about death tolls and conspiracy theories, I'm laughing so hard I have to excuse myself to the bathroom.

"Now, where were we?" I return three minutes later with what I hope is a straight face.

"What did you type?" Mom is standing too near my laptop. "I do not trust you. And I never shall again—writing everything we do."

"Mother . . ." I wrap my arms around her. "I'm just taking notes for future chapters. I need authentic dialogue to surround the subjects we cover in each section. It's almost like I'm writing two books—one in the past and one in present."

"I know, but you're a bad kitty. You write everything I say." Mom's arms are limp at her sides. I hug her, but not too tight. She feels frail beneath the thin fabric of her kaftan.

"That's because you are funny, and you lighten the mood when topics get too heavy."

"Well I don't feel very funny today," she says, sitting once more at the table.

"It's okay. Today's topic is not funny. Mr. P loses someone dear to his heart. There's nothing funny about that."

"Jennifer worked at a bank, right P?" Mom asks as she pulls a chair from under the table.

"Yes." He looks up. "She was sixteen. She was in pain at work. That was the beginning."

"Right," Mom continues. "So she goes to the doctor. He misdiagnoses her. It's medical neglect, honestly. If this happened today in America, there would surely be a lawsuit."

"Well, that was 1965 in Dewsbury. Nobody was suing anybody," Mr. P says. "Jennifer went back to the bank after the doctor told her she was just having stomach upset."

"It's an awful story. She ended up in the hospital with excruciating pain. But it was too late. By that time peritonitis had set in."

"What is that?" I ask.

"It's inflammation in the abdomen that can cause sepsis. Her appendix had ruptured," Mom explains. "She was in agony and nobody took it seriously."

"Until it was too late," Mr. P adds, joining us at the table with a small bag of 85% dark chocolates.

"Would you like a chocolate?" He offers.

Mom and I decline.

"I think I'll have one," he says more to himself than to us.

We watch Mr. P unwrap a square and pop the whole thing into his mouth. He starts speaking before the chocolate is completely chewed.

"I'm in French class . . ."

Mom hands him a napkin.

". . . when the department director, Pastor Corbyn calls me out to tell me my sister has died, and I need to go home.

He swallows hard. His fingers roll the wrapper into a tight little foil ball.

"I pack a rucksack and stand beside the road with my thumb out. Within minutes a guy stops. Thumbing a lift wasn't unusual in those days. I expected to piece the 200 miles between school and

Dewsbury together with several different rides. This guy could have been an angel. He drops me within a mile of my home.

"Jennifer is in a wooden box in our living room. That's how they did things then. Mum is kneeling next to her, touching her face, kissing her, weeping and weeping for days."

"Oh, P." My mother's eyes fill with tears as she reaches for his arm. "This is making me cry."

"I haven't thought of it like this," he says, using the napkin to wipe his eyes. "It was quite a shock. And I was a believer in divine healing, even then. But there was nothing I could do for my sister. I was devastated. No more letters. No more jokes. No more late-night chats about the end of the world. She was just gone. That was it. I didn't get to say goodbye."

"I'm so sorry." My fingers stop typing as I think about Mr. P's loss. "Your whole family must have suffered terribly."

"To the end of his mother's life, if anyone mentioned Jennifer, she would cry," Mom recalls. "It absolutely broke her heart. She never got over it. A mother can't."

"Nor could my dad," Mr. P remembers. "Jen's death made him bitter. Just before she died there were some tent meetings going on in Dewsbury. Mum and Dad went together every night. My mum was so pleased, after years of sitting in the pew at our Methodist church without him. After Jennifer died, Dad said, 'I can't believe in a God who would let your sister die.' And that was it. He never went again—to any kind of church."

Both P's wipe tears from their eyes.

"I've never seen you become emotional when talking about your sister's death," Mom says.

"That's because I don't. It was so long ago. Today we are discussing it more than usual, aren't we?"

"I met Jennifer's only boyfriend, Richard one holiday. Do you remember?" she asks him.

"Richard? Of course you would have met him. He dropped off a gift and visited with my mum every Christmas for forty years or more."

Mom looks at me. "Richard never forgot Jennifer, even though he did marry someone else. In fact, his son and Jean's sons were best friends growing up."

"That's how small Dewsbury was," Mr. P jokes. "Everybody knew everybody."

"So, what happened after Jennifer's death," I ask. "Did you return to seminary?"

"Yes, but I didn't do well. I couldn't concentrate on my studies. I flunked French. I was in agony over my sister's death and the death of my dreams of becoming a singer. I felt I gave up everything and God did nothing except let my sister die and break my parents' hearts. I still struggled with the fact that I was not interested in girls and had feelings for guys that I dared not express.

"I hadn't mentioned my broken sexuality to the pastor who baptized me. Or to anyone since that doctor in Sheffield. After years of silence, I could no longer take the internal torment. I finally decided to speak with someone again, thinking it might be different, baring my soul to a Christian person. I went to the highest spiritual authority on campus, having convinced myself he would have the answer.

"Terrified yet hopeful, I found Pastor Corbyn's office and knocked on the door. A few minutes later I walked out, wanting to die. I will never forget his easy and obvious solution for my problem." Mr. P's tone is sarcastic. "Why hadn't I thought of it before?

"'Just forget about it,' the pastor said. 'Find a hobby and forget about it.'

"How cruel is that? After someone has been in anguish for years—to simply dismiss them with a trite answer. No genuine care or concern for my wellbeing. No prayer. No hope. No follow up—nothing! His lack of compassion was insane!"

"What did you say?"

"Nothing. What could I say? He was the headmaster. He was the religious bigwig. Who was I to say anything to him?

"But now? Now I *would* say something, wouldn't I? I would start by saying, 'Your God is too small.' That was from a book I'd read by J.B. Philips. I might even say, 'Why don't you get a job worthy of your religion—at McDonald's, serving up hamburgers. Because that's the only thing you *could* serve! You certainly aren't serving God with an answer like that. If only transforming my sexuality were as easy as 'getting a hobby and forgetting about it!'

"Of course I didn't say any of those things. Instead I hung my head in utter shame and shut his door behind me."

Mom puts words to something I'm thinking. "That man was not a shepherd of God's flock."

"No, he wasn't," agrees Mr. P. "Like that verse in Ezekiel chapter 3, he did not strengthen the weak or bind up the injured. He didn't search for the lost. He just let me walk away. I had no one to shepherd me and I became exactly what the verse says—food for the wild animals.

"I felt deeply disappointed to discover the God I sacrificed my dreams for was apparently too small for my big problem. Although I kept up the pretenses of religion, my faith that God could heal me wavered. I still believed in Him, I just questioned whether He could deliver me from the bondage of my feelings."

I reach for a chocolate. Mr. P continues his story.

"I packed my bags and left the seminary. I had flickering faith and zero respect for pastors. How could I become one? Still bent on serving in some mission capacity, I set my sights on nursing. I went home to Dewsbury and applied for nursing school in York. I think my father was secretly pleased, although he said nothing.

"Home was not the same without Jennifer. My family felt broken. Dad worked and watched television. I hated him for sitting there, ignoring everyone. Ignoring me. Mum went to church. Jean was dating Michael, her future husband. I was happy to receive a letter of acceptance and move to York. It was only about thirty miles north, but it took an hour and a half by bus.

"In York I stayed with Ms. Hansen, a sweet elderly spinster lady. I can see her now, in one of those old-fashioned pinafores that goes over everything. She wore it always.

"Ms. Hansen lived just across the road from the city walls. To get to my classes at the hospital, I had to walk past York Minster. Each morning I went inside to pray. Nowadays you'd have to pay about ten pounds to walk in the door."

"Actually, you couldn't walk in the door at all," I remind him. "York Minster is closed, just like the rest of the churches, due to Covid-19.

"Wicked virus!" Mom declares.

"Anyway, that's what I did," Mr. P continues. "In that magnificent edifice to God's glory, I sought my Savior.

"I have visited most of the famous cathedrals in England. They are all beautiful with their stained glass and spires, but there is something special about York Minster. Like me, it survived the German Blitz of World War II."

Mr. P smiles at his own dry joke before continuing. "With planes bombing 9,000 York buildings in one day, it's quite amazing nothing touched the Minster. It has endured a lot in 600 some years. Only in the 1980's, did catastrophe happen. When a pastor said something blasphemous about Jesus, immediately lightning struck the Minster. There was no storm or anything."

Mom sets a cup of tea in front of him.

"Thank you. How did you know I wanted tea?"

"How long have I known you, Peedy P?"

"Long enough to know me."

"Do you want one, Ju?"

"Chamomile please."

"I quite enjoyed living in York." Mr. P pauses his story to stir exactly one-half teaspoon of honey into his ginger tea. "York is not at all like its namesake, New York. It has a medieval feel. Did you know it was a Viking city?"

"No."

"It was! Some streets have really strange names. The Shambles is one old street; so narrow, a person could shake hands with the neighbors across the street through the upstairs windows. The smallest street is called Whip-ma-whop-ma-gate. That means 'neither one thing nor the other.' Isn't that ridiculous?" He chuckles and wipes crumbs from his mustache.

"My favorite place in York is Bettys Tea Shop," Mom says. "Mmmmm. Clotted cream and strawberry jam!"

"Bettys is famous for a wonderful Yorkshire cream tea," Mr. P smiles. "I wish I had a scone with strawberry jam right now."

"You are making me hungry," I laugh. "What can I eat with *my* tea?"

"How about some of these Spanish digestive biscuits?" Mom suggests. "They are made with spelt flour and zero sugar."

"Hmmm. Sounds a lot less tasty than scones and clotted cream, but okay."

While I dip tasteless biscuits into my tea, Mr. P bravely carries on with his story.

"I made a couple of friends in York. There was this guy, Mark, from church. I was attracted to him. Of course he never knew it.

"Mark played the guitar. When he found out I could sing, we quickly became chums. He taught me some Christian songs like, 'In the Heart of Jesus.' We often sang together at church. Being able to sing again was an encouragement to me. Having a close friend felt good, also. I had been lonely for a long time.

"Mark was a nice kid. I was best man at his wedding."

"Seems to be a theme here; you being best man," I deduce.

"Yeah. In those days, I could never picture myself as the groom. I could only picture myself *with* the groom. I was jealous of Mark's girlfriend. She was a bit snobby—a real upper crust from the south of England. Mark and I were from the north. People from the south looked down their noses at people like us—folks from Yorkshire and Dewsbury. I don't know how Mark landed her, but he did.

"On the night before their marriage, Mark and I had to spend the night in a hotel. In the same bed. Is that not cruel? For me it was brutal.

"Why did you have to be in bed with him?"

"Because we had to go to another town and get a hotel. That was all he could afford. I don't know about now, but back then guys would do things like that. Sleeping together in close quarters was no big deal. Unless you were me."

Mr. P glances at my mother.

"You know this story."

She nods.

"Mark was twenty-four and a virgin. In those days, virgins really existed!"

Mom laughs.

"He asked me, in bed with him on the eve of his wedding, about my sexual experiences with girls. He wanted me to give him some advice. He didn't know anything about anything. But then, neither did I."

"What did you say?"

"I told him the truth. I had never been with a girl. I felt stupid, didn't I?"

Mr. P sips his tea. He stares at me. "Write some emotions down."

"Like what?"

"Torture."

"Torture! That's strong."

"That's how someone like the me I was feels when a very close friend finds a girlfriend or gets married. To lose them nearly feels like the death of a loved one. I had already experienced the death of my sister. When Mark got married, I experienced the death of our friendship."

"Oh, P." Mom has tears in her eyes. "I'm making some connections I've never made before. You really suffered some heavy losses within a short time frame—your dreams, your career, your sister, your friendship . . ." Her voice trails. I can see deep thoughts brewing behind Mom's eyes. I finish my tea. Finally she says, "I think you experienced compounded grief. It's a wonder you didn't just give up on life."

"Oh, I wanted to. In my heart I had no peace. All of those losses were hard and made even more difficult because of the constant inner turmoil with my sexuality. I spent my days off fasting and pleading for God to set me free, to no avail."

"I'm feeling such compassion for you, Mr. P. With each chapter we write, I'm appreciating you more and more."

A smile turns up the corners of his mouth. "I'm okay," he says. "Some of these things are difficult to remember. If they can help someone in some way, it will be worth it.

"I did have another friend in York," he recalls. "A woman from nursing school, June. June and I became real good friends. Something clicked between us. Years later, I found out she was a lesbian."

"Like attracts like," Mom quips.

"Pain attracts pain," I counter. "June probably felt safe with him and he with her. There was no sexual tension. Unlike his relationship with that other girl . . . What was her name?"

"Diana," both P's remind me in unison.

"Yes. Unlike that one-sided thing he had with Diana, Mr. P and June could just be friends with no expectations. Even if they never mentioned their sexuality, their souls knew. At least that's my take."

"Perhaps you are right," Mr. P affirms. "Poor Diana. She married someone very quickly after I went away to seminary. I didn't keep up with her after that.

"June was a bit different. She was a deep-thinking Christian, also searching for something more from God. She invited me to a series of meetings. In one meeting we heard Corrie ten Boom preach on forgiveness.

"Ms. ten Boom was old, maybe in her seventies at that time. As she spoke of coming face to face with the Ravensbrück concentration camp guard responsible for starving and murdering thousands of women, my heartbeat hard inside my chest. I will never forget the way she told her story. I could see that guard. I could understand Corrie's flashback years after the war was finished, as he greeted her after hearing her speak on forgiveness in Germany. When that Nazi offered his hand and asked Corrie's forgiveness for the atrocities he committed, she hesitated.

"I understood her hesitation. A wicked thing had also been done to me. Like Corrie, I had tucked it away and carried on with my life. I did not care to remember it, nor forgive the person who did it. When she explained that forgiveness is a decision, not a feeling, something clicked inside my head. I realized there is a difference between acting on feeling and acting on faith.

"After Ms. ten Boom made the decision to follow God's command to forgive, she acted on faith and offered her hand to the abuser. Only then did the *feeling* of forgiveness and the release it brings flood over her whole body like an electrical current.

"Listening to Corrie strengthened my faith that God could heal me. She said something about God that has always stuck with me. She said, 'There is no pit so deep that He is not deeper still.' Her words gave me something to hold on to as my pit grew deeper over the next years."

"What a powerful testimony her life was," I say. "I remember reading *The Hiding Place* when I was around ten. Thank you for this reminder of the difference between faith and feeling. It's so easy to let feelings lead and expect faith to follow. As a witness to your life for much of my adult life, I have consistently seen you practice putting faith first. Thank you for your example."

A rosy flush creeps up Mr. P's cheeks. He doesn't like accolades. Rather than acknowledge my compliment, he continues his story.

"June and I also heard Richard Wurmbrand who wrote *Tortured for Christ*. That was a very famous book."

"I've been to the place where he lived in Romania," Mom interjects. "When I was doing mission work after the accident."

"I haven't heard of him," I admit.

"I'm surprised. But, then you're young."

I can't tell whether Mr. P is being sarcastic or not. He starts talking again before I can ask.

"Wurmbrand risked death to serve the underground church in Communist Romania in the 1940's. It was just after the end of the war. Bold enough to preach on the streets, he was imprisoned for a total of fourteen years. If I remember right, he spent three years in solitary confinement.

"People will have heard of him. He founded The Voice of the Martyrs. They still help persecuted Christians all over the world."

"Oh, okay. I have heard of Voice of the Martyrs. They rescue Christian victims of ISIS."

"Yes. Well, Richard Wurmbrand started that ministry. The story I most remember from hearing his testimony was when he was in a cell by himself for, I don't know how long. He was tortured, starved and kept in the dark. A loudspeaker repeated, 'God is dead. God is dead.' Twenty-four hours a day, nonstop. Richard's mind was so wacko he couldn't think, couldn't remember any verse from Scripture. All he could recall is 'Jesus Christ is the resurrection from the dead.' He repeated that phrase out loud in rebuke of the loudspeaker's repeated lie. That makes me cry."

Tears immediately pool in the blue-grey eyes behind Mr. P's glasses. He sniffs loudly, wiping his nose with a napkin.

"I identified with Richard Wurmbrand's story," he says, "because I also felt like I was in solitary confinement. I didn't have physical wounds to show for the internal torture I had endured for years, but I understood how torture could drive a person to the brink of madness. I was in solitary confinement because I could speak with no one about my struggle, not even my best friend, Mark. And we were *close* before he got married.

"I had some good friends through the years, but I was always living a lie. It must be awful . . ." Mr. P snickers because he is speaking as if he is speaking about someone else. He corrects himself, "It *was* awful. Awful—when you think you're friends with people for years and they don't really know you."

"You had on a mask," Mom empathizes. "A Venetian mask."

There is a moment of quiet before Principessa P speaks a different thought completely, "I would like to wear one when we go for a walk this weekend. Not one of those ugly flimsy blue and white things. A Venetian mask would be so pretty." She smiles a tiny princess smile. "I'm going to order one online."

"I don't think that will keep the Coronavirus away, but it would be much more glamorous, wouldn't it?" Mr. P agrees. He knows he is married to royalty.

"Actually," Mom looks at me, "Venetian masks were invented to protect people from breathing the air during the plague. Did you know that?"

I shake my head.

Mom continues. "Yes, a shopkeeper in Venice told me the whole story. I asked him why certain masks had such long-pointed noses. I always thought they were some demonic thing, but the shopkeeper explained the noses were packed with herbs to keep away the Black Plague."

"Maybe you *should* get one then," I tease.

"Yes," says Mr. P, "We can all get one and wear them to the ice cream shop on Sunday."

We laugh together. Sometimes humor is the thing that keeps us sane through things we cannot explain—like pandemics and pedophiles.

"On that other topic," he says, "I'm thinking of how liberating it was to finally be myself with Walter and my friends in Switzerland."

"According to the life timeline you gave me, you are getting way ahead of yourself Mr. P. We are still in York. You've got about fourteen years before you meet those friends."

"Oh, dear!" he exclaims. "I don't even want to talk about what happened during those fourteen years."

"Well, we don't have to talk about all of it today, but if you don't mind, I'd love to get you through nursing school in this chapter."

"Alright, but can we sit somewhere else?" he concedes. "My bum hurts sitting in the same spot."

While Mr. P settles himself in his corner chair, I check in on my husband. André is clicking away on his laptop. I blow him a kiss and close the door. Returning to the living room I find Mr. P with two slippered feet on the coffee table. Eyes closed; he basks in a small patch of sunlight filtering through the sliding glass door. I hear Mom running water in the kitchen. Tonight is pasta night. I hope she's making her fabulous mushroom cream sauce.

Mr. P looks so serene I almost don't want to disturb him. But I disturb him. We have a deadline. Our travel agent has finally been able to confirm our tickets out of Spain. We have three weeks left to write together here and two weeks at home in self-quarantine. My goal is to complete this manuscript before we return to normal life—whatever that will look like in the aftermath of a pandemic.

"Mr. P."

Silence.

I lie on the sofa next to his chair, bend my knees and prop my laptop on my stomach. *Why didn't I think to write like this before?*

"Mr. P, can you hear me?"

"Yes."

"Do you want me to leave you alone?"

"Yes and no."

"I'll do whatever you want. We can work on this later."

"It's just really hard to talk about what happens next," he sighs.

"We can wait."

"We might as well get on with it."

"I only stayed in York for a year," he begins with a loud exhale, "because I hardly had any money. I couldn't survive financially.

"My last semester was awful. I was miserable and depressed. Finally I broke down and went to see a psychiatrist. He would be the *third* person I told about my struggle. No hobby was going to fix what was going on inside of me. I was desperate for help. It was awful, but I told him everything. Even more than I had shared with the doctor in Sheffield or the pastor at seminary. My dad was right. I *was* becoming a fruit and nutcase.

"The psychiatrist was not a Christian. He advised me to date girls, which I tried. This caused a bigger problem as some got attached to me and I was never interested.

"Another part of his treatment plan was what they used to call 'aversion therapy.' He gave me two electrodes, which I had to attach to my wrist. I was supposed to imagine having sex with a man and give myself a shock at the same time.

'Turn it up until you can hardly bear it,' my psychiatrist said."

I stop typing and peek around my screen at Mr. P's face. His eyes are closed, his forehead creased. His words painful to hear.

"I took the electric shock thing home. Each day I followed his prescription to shock myself with increased levels of electricity as I had these sexual thoughts—in order to create an association between sex with a man and pain."

"How horrifying! No wonder you didn't want to talk about this."

"It *was* quite shocking."

His lips are closed but I can hear him laughing inside himself, little puffs of air bursting from his nostrils.

"Mr. P! This isn't funny."

"No. It isn't. It wasn't. I was mortified."

"Then why are you laughing?"

"I don't know. It all seems so ridiculous now—me sitting in some spinster's spare bedroom thinking strange thoughts and shocking myself . . . Ms. Hansen in her pinafore listening outside the door."

I glance toward the kitchen. My mother is standing in the doorway holding her wooden spoon like a scepter. I don't know how long she's been listening.

"But P," she says sympathetically. "It wasn't ridiculous then. It was your reality."

"Yes, but it was bizarre because I hadn't *done* anything to think about. My sexual experience was confined to the one and only time I was violated . . ."

He pauses. My fingers also pause on the keys of my keyboard. I wait.

". . .violated by that man in his car more than 10 years earlier. Since that was my only point of reference, the electric shock procedure seemed crazy.

"I hadn't had any sexual adventures with men. I didn't know of *anyone* who lived that lifestyle. I hadn't even viewed pornography yet. I didn't know homosexuality was a thing. It would still be illegal in England for a couple more years. I wondered if I was alone on the planet with my feelings of attraction for the same sex—a freak of some kind.

"After a few months I discarded any idea of shocking myself while imagining things I knew nothing about. That type of therapy seemed less than helpful. Broke and broken, I returned home to Dewsbury at the end of the term so I could live with my parents and complete my degree."

Mrs. P crosses the room in two seconds, wraps one arm around her husband's neck and kisses him firmly on the forehead. The spoon she holds in her other hand, just above my head smells like sautéed mushrooms.

"You are *not* a freak," Mom proclaims. "You're my Mr. P."

You have not strengthened the weak or healed the sick or bound up the injured. You have not brought back the strays or searched for the lost. You have ruled them harshly and brutally. So they were scattered because there was no shepherd, and when they were scattered they became food for all the wild animals.

Ezekiel 3:4-5

YORK MINSTER

Chapter 12

NEW YORK, NEW YORK!

No pit is so deep that He is not deeper still;
with Jesus even in our darkest moments,
the best remains and the very best is yet to be.
Corrie ten Boom

"It increases sexual desire, does dark chocolate. I'm ready to go eat the whole lot!"

"Okay Abraham! I'll be like Sarah and laugh if anything happens."

"I *already* call you 'The Mother of Many Nations,' don't I?" he teases.

I'm eavesdropping on the P's as they chat in the living room following their first walk outside together in exactly seven weeks. Just before this weekend, Spanish authorities approved a strict age-based exercise schedule for everyone to follow after the lock-down. The P's counted down the hours to when they would be permitted to walk hand-in-hand in the sunshine by the sea. Now they are completely giddy!

Excited about my own opportunity to get out with My Honey, I'm lacing my sneakers by the front door. Because André and I are in a different age grouping from the P's, our walk-window is an hour after theirs. I can see the P's, but they don't see me. Like a sneaky kid, I'm trying not to giggle as I overhear their conversation about sex and chocolate.

"How many chocolates are left?" he asks holding out his hand.

"A few," Mom answers. "I think these 72% darks taste better than the 85% ones, don't they?"

"They do! So let's buy a lot and get with it!" I hear mischief in Mr. P's voice.

"Geoffrey Pennock! I haven't heard you talk like this in ten years! What's wrong with you?"

"I don't know."

"I don't either."

Mom hands him another square of chocolate. He unwraps it, shoving the whole thing in his mouth at once.

Gesturing toward a glass my mother filled with springtime blooms from their walk, Mr. P declares through his mouthful of chocolate, "Those flowers are lovely."

"I love camellias," Mom sighs. "Remember when I carried some—roots and all, on the plane from England and planted them in our garden?"

He nods, gathering discarded chocolate wrappers into his hand.

"They look a bit like a rose." She touches a bloom's soft pinkness.

"In Lugano there were whole camellia trees," Mr. P recalls. "That's one thing I really miss about living in Europe—all of the beautiful gardens and the smells of blooming trees in springtime."

Mom takes the wrappers from his hand, crinkling them into a ball on her way to the trash. Unfortunately, my hiding place is also on the way to the trash and the jig is up—she sees me squatting in the entryway, guilt written all over my face.

Mom's expression is a concoction of surprise and censure as she declares, "Mr. P! We have a spy among us!"

For a second I am eight years old getting 'found' in a game of hide-and-seek, laughing until my sides ache.

"Be careful! We never know what she will do." Mom shakes her finger at me, "You ARE a bad kitty. There better not be *anything* in that book we don't approve of!"

"André! Let's go for our walk," I holler to my husband. "I'm getting in trouble!"

Ninety minutes later, I have been peacefully pardoned and allowed back into Principessa's castle. The P's and I sit around the table with mixed drinks of grapefruit juice and sparkling water. Today we will pick Mr. P's brain about his life from 1967-1970.

After a bit of background research on that era, I now know in 1967 the UK passed 'The Sexual Offences Act' which, according to Wikipedia, "legalized consensual homosexual acts between consenting males above the age of twenty-one." That was the year Mr. P turned twenty-six. That was also the year he returned home and became a student at the Dewsbury School of Nursing.

"At what point did you realize there were other people who had similar same-sex attraction feelings to yours?" I ask.

"I heard some other nursing students gossiping about the 'gays' and 'queers' who hung out at a hotel bar in Leeds. That information planted a seed of curiosity."

"England had just legalized homosexuality, so you overhearing a conversation like that would make sense. For the first time in your country gay people might feel free to be visible in a public place."

"I never realized *when* it became legal," he explains. "Nobody marched in the streets or anything. There was just a rumor about a certain corner in a quite posh hotel near the railway station with two or three gay people hanging out at the bar. Not like a gay bar now. People were very discreet. But they had to be in those days, didn't they?"

Mr. P is quiet, twirling his glass between his fingers.

"'Queer' was a sniggering word," he continues. "If someone was openly homosexual back then, people would snigger. It was like saying you're poop, wasn't it? Not like now."

"I don't remember this part of your story, P." My mother's pale face is freckled from her walk in the sunshine. Her eyes sparkle with interest.

"This is during my nursing studies—when I lived with my parents for three years. At some point I got invited to sing at church. My voice was a bit rusty, so I went for singing lessons in

Leeds. That high class hotel happened to be across the road from my lessons."

"Ah-ha!" Mom declares. "I doubt *that* was a coincidence. The ole devil was always trying to set you up."

"Going to the pub is an English thing. It's been the life of every village since Shakespeare's day. Even the vicar would go to the pub," he explains. "So one day I casually popped in after my lesson. That's when I met Dan."

Mr. P looks at Mrs. P.

"You know Dan."

"Is it Dan as in Thomas and Dan who came to our wedding?"

"Yes. Dan invited me for a shandy at the bar."

"'I don't drink,' I told him—still super strict about not drinking alcohol or eating pork. I thought abstaining would get me points with God somehow. My religion was all about me."

"So what happened with Dan?" I ask.

"Nothing happened. I ordered a Bitter Lemon and we talked. It's easy to talk to someone in a bar isn't it? Not like at church. An English pub is much more friendly than church—where a person comes and goes and never really talks with anyone."

"I can see that," I consent.

He continues. "Francis Chan tells the story of a former gang member who goes to church. Afterwards the guy says. 'I thought church would be more friendly than being in a gang. In the end, gang members are friendlier than church members.'"

"I wonder why it's like that?" Mom asks

"Maybe because at the bar nobody is pretending to be something they aren't," I reply shaking salt into my grapefruit juice.

Mr. P shakes his head. "You are like your mother, salting the strangest things." He finishes his juice before offering his opinion. "A person at a bar can be their authentic self. A person at church feels pressure to conform.

"Dan introduced me to some of his friends. Meeting them was my first realization there were other guys like me."

"That's huge!" I declare.

"It *is* huge, but all the guilt and all the everything did not go away just because I discovered there were other men attracted to men."

"Did Dan like you?" I ask.

"Noooo! Dan had a lover. Thomas. They are still together—married for as long as it's been legal. We all remain friends fifty-some years later."

"We've stayed in their home," Mom says. "It's lovely. They are very wealthy, *very* interesting people."

"Dan and I had the common interest of singing," Mr. P adds. "He was in a famous British choir and even sang in the Royal Albert Hall!

"Another male friend of Dan's also became a friend of mine. Oliver was a nurse—gay, but not my lover, just a friend. On days off I would meet him in Leeds. We went around the stores together or to lunch.

"Those were the first gay people I ever met. I could go to the bar after singing lessons and have camaraderie with the guys and my parents wouldn't know anything would they?

"I feel strange talking about all of this actually. It feels like a whole other life."

"Would you ever talk about your feelings with these guys at the bar?" Mom asks.

"Of course I would."

"Were they Christians?"

Mr. P responds with a touch of cynicism. "Well, nearly everyone is a Christian if you ask, aren't they?"

He pauses.

"The Gospel was never preached in the church I grew up in. The pastor smoked his cigarettes outside after the service and downed his toddies like everyone else. The people talked about getting back to their soaps as they came out the door after service. 'Christianity' meant going to church once a week. It didn't interfere with our

British way of life. There wasn't much difference between the Christians and the atheists from what I could tell."

"Not so different from modern churches," Mom ventures. "Remember our refugee son who stopped attending because the guys always talked about ball games in the foyer and he didn't understand how that fit with the sermon? Moses had no reference point for American sports and couldn't comprehend why football games were the usual after church conversation topic."

"I understand," I chime in. "I've often said my church wasn't relevant to the hell I was living when I was still married to Jon and he was strung out on cocaine all the time. I think the church, for the most part, has sacrificed its mission for tradition."

"I'm trying to change that," André quips as he passes through on his way to the kitchen."

"Are you spying on us Pastor André?"

My husband puts a hand on Mr. P's shoulder. "No. I just happened to catch that last sentence. Sounds like your book is beating the same drum as mine."

"Actually, we've strayed off topic a bit, haven't we P's?" I laugh. "Where were we?"

"Talking about my first gay friends," Mr. P answers.

"Right. So—you didn't bring your new friends home to meet your family?"

"Never. I kept them separate from my other relationships. I had different sets of friends. At work I was very close to Keith, a hetero nurse at the hospital. He still writes to my sister at Christmas. Keith was my friend for a very long time, but he knew nothing about me. Sometimes I still went dancing with a group I kept up with from the Operatic Society. On Sabbaths, I hung out with people from church. Actually, Pastor Rielly and his wife became quite good friends of mine. Of course I didn't tell *them* anything about anything; at least not at the beginning.

"I hid my gay friends from my Christian friends, but I didn't hide my Christianity from my gay friends. Does that make sense?"

Mr. P asks the question but doesn't pause to wait for an answer. "Dan was also a churchgoer. He and Thomas always *have* been—singing in the choir every Sunday. Somehow, they were able to be okay with their homosexuality and never let their lifestyle keep them away from church.

"Even having those friends didn't ease the torment on the inside of me. I still felt like an outcast. I still couldn't explain to anyone that I just couldn't accept it. My feelings did not reconcile with what I read in my Bible. No matter what I did I remained miserable on the inside, constantly searching for answers. It's almost like I was two different people, the outside and the inside. Once a week I went to the bar with the gays and then to the Christian bookstore to try and find out what was wrong with me."

"Oh, Peedy. It's awful the struggle you went through." Mom strokes his arm as it rests on the table.

"This is only the beginning," he replies, forging ahead.

"I read as many books on healing as I could get my hands on. I was especially interested in the ministry of Katherine Kuhlman, the American healer. I later attended her meetings in Toronto, Canada.

"A ray of hope finally came after I read *The Cross and the Switchblade* by David Wilkerson, founder of the Teen Challenge Center in Brooklyn, New York. In Wilkerson's book, he wrote of homosexuals being changed at his center. Nothing else I ever read or heard gave me as much hope as the testimony in that book. I believed one hundred percent if I had the faith to go the Teen Challenge Center, God would change me, too. I begged God to get me to New York City."

Mr. P scoots his chair away from the table. "I've got to move."

We play musical chairs and resettle ourselves in the lesser of the evils, he in his chair, Mom and I on the sofa.

"Let me tell you a funny story," Mr. P says.

André sets his water on the table. "Can I hear?"

"Of course!" Mr. P's eyes laugh with the memory. "Just before I finished nursing school, I got to know a good-looking student doctor from India. We often exchanged longer-than-normal glances. Now that I knew there were other people like me, I was aware he was flirting.

"The doctor was leaving to go back to India and the medical staff were having his farewell party. He had a room in the hospital. During the festivities, he and I ended up in his bed."

Mr. P turns his palms up and shrugs his shoulders as his hands punctuate each word. "Why. are. gay. people. so. promiscuous?"

"I don't think it's just gay people," André answers. "Its all people. People without the Holy Spirit will do anything to fill the void, won't they?"

We all nod in agreement.

"Straight away," Mr. P continues, "there was knocking on the Indian doctor's door. We could hear female nurses laughing and screaming, 'We *know* you have a woman in there! Who is it? We are waiting right here until she comes out!'

"Immediately, the doctor pushed me into his wardrobe and locked it with a key. Then he went to the door saying, 'I feel unwell and need to rest. No one is here.'

"The girls jiggled the door handle. It wasn't locked. They barged into the room shouting, 'She's in here! She's in here!' They even shook the wardrobe!

"Nobody at the hospital knew anything about what was going on inside of *me*, so it would have been very strange had they discovered it wasn't a girl he was hiding, but Geoffrey Pennock!

"I stayed in there a long, long time until the doctor released me. I was so nervous with being discovered; I went straight home. Absolutely nothing happened between us.

"My workmates asked the next day, 'What happened to you last night? You just vanished!'

"I felt sick and went home, I said to them. Nobody knew the truth." Mr. P laughs. "Oh, dear. What a carry on."

"Well, Mr. P," I joke. "I wasn't expecting you to literally come out of the closet in this chapter, but here you are!"

"I was twenty-nine."

"And look how God still protected you by sending those nurses," Mom adds. "He didn't want you going down that painful path."

"I don't suppose He did," Mr. P agrees. "But we all have the power of choice, don't we?"

His question hangs in the air, waiting for the rest of his thoughts to follow.

"In my heart, I was glad nothing happened with the doctor. I was ashamed for being curious and weak in that moment. I made a deeper resolve to hold on to God and seek His healing.

"After graduation, I noticed advertisements inviting nurses to practice abroad. I could have gone to Oman, or Lebanon to American hospitals, or to Saint Thomas, Ontario. My only thought was *Ontario is a lot closer to Brooklyn than England is!*

"In my mind, the Teen Challenge Center was the Promised Land. All I had to do was cross the Atlantic and I was one step closer to freedom. The *only* reason I applied for a job in Canada was the prospect of one day going to New York to Teen Challenge."

"Why does this make me want to cry?" I ask.

"Because it's absolutely heart-wrenching," Mom says. "You can feel his desperation."

André doesn't say a word. He doesn't have to. Compassion is written all over his face.

"Within weeks I had a plane ticket to Canada," Mr. P resumes. "I kissed my mum and my sister goodbye and flew 3,000 miles on a prayer. I can't remember anything about my dad as I was preparing to go.

"I also can't recall how many months I worked in St. Thomas before transferring to a Christian hospital in Toronto. I do know I was thirty years old in 1971 when I finally had the money, time and courage to buy a bus ticket to Brooklyn."

"How long did that trip take?" I ask, patting the cushion next to me so My Honey might move to the sofa.

"I spent nine hours on the Greyhound. We stopped at Niagara Falls on the way. You know me, always looking for an adventure. I had plans to go up the Empire State building and all these touristy things after I was freed from my constant headache and inner torment. I was one hundred percent sure if I could just get someone at Teen Challenge to pray for me something would change inside. The Teen Challenge Center was my Pool of Bethesda."

André leans forward to catch Mr. P's eye. "I must say—you had a lot more courage than I ever would, going to Brooklyn by yourself."

"Who was going to go with me? Sure I was friendly with a few people from work, but nobody had a clue what I was suffering. I felt it was something just between God and me. I *knew* He was going to do something big for me in Brooklyn.

"The Teen Challenge place was in a part of the city where the gangs and drugs were. At that time, it was the most dangerous place in New York for a white person to go alone. I felt trepidation."

Mr. P chuckles. "Trepidation. I don't normally use such big words, do I?"

"Go on P." Mom says what I'm thinking. I've got a movie playing in my mind and he's just pushed pause.

He continues. "I never saw another white person in that dingy broken-down drug infested area. Mr. P from Dewsbury had never been *anywhere* like that before. I got a room at the YMCA and locked myself in for the night. In the morning I would meet someone who would change my life forever.

"I stopped at a little café the next morning where a dark-haired waitress served me breakfast before my appointment to tour the Teen Challenge Center and meet with a minister for prayer. My stomach was in knots with nerves.

"At the center one particular pastor invited me into a room and listened to my story. Afterward he told me to undress and stand before God in my nakedness, as when I was born. I felt strange taking off my underwear in front of a man I'd just met but I'd come such a long way I was willing to do whatever it took to get free.

"The pastor laid hands on me and spoke in tongues for what felt like an eternity. Afterward he said, 'Now you are heterosexual and whole. Hallelujah!'

"Praise God! Hallelujah! I got dressed and jumped for joy as I sang praises walking down the street.

"On my way back to the YMCA I stopped at the same café where I'd eaten earlier. I looked at the pretty waitress, wondering if I had any masculine feelings I hadn't had earlier in the day. *Had I changed?* I didn't notice any particular attraction toward her. But I did notice a good-looking guy standing at the bar.

"*Is he looking at me because I now look like an angel after all that prayer?* I thought. *Or is he looking at me the way I shouldn't be looking at him? Did I get the Holy Spirit or an evil spirit from the strange pastor who had me get naked for prayer?*"

Mr. P stops talking. Mom, André, and I perch on the edge of the sofa like birds on a wire, waiting for his next words. André reaches for my hand. Mr. P reaches for Mom's. He swallows hard. For a pregnant minute nobody says anything. Finally Mr. P continues.

"When that handsome Italian on holiday from Rome left my room the next morning, I knew I *was* changed. Was going to New York to spend the night with an Italian guy the culmination of all my dreams and prayers?" Mr. P's voice raises and cracks with contempt for what he'd done.

"I was gutted. Yes. My life *did* change—to a love/hate lifestyle I was never meant to know and a love/hate relationship with the God I thought I knew.

"My mind was numb as I took the lift to the top of the Empire State Building. I had fought for years against my feelings and when I finally felt I met God face-to-face, He spit in mine.

"I stood in that little observatory on the hundred and second floor wishing there was some way I could throw myself off. Teen Challenge was my last hope. An utter failure. Looking out over

New York City I said to God, 'I have tried *everything* I know for *years* and You have not changed me. You, God, can go to hell.'"

Dear Reader,

A few weeks later, Mom and I discover the actual letter Mr. P wrote home to England from the bus station on his way back from Brooklyn. Of course his lighthearted descriptions of New York City in the seventies don't honestly reflect the discouragement and utter hopelessness he carries in his heart as he returns from Teen Challenge Center, but his words do give some additional insight into some of what he was exposed to while visiting 'The Big Apple.'

Dear All,

I am sat at the bus station in Buffalo (I should say 'depot' here.) and have traveled overnight from New York. I left at 10:30 pm and should be in St. Thomas at about 1:30. It's a 500-mile journey. I got in at 6:30 and have to wait until 8 for a bus, which isn't too bad. Buffalo is the border town. (I hope they don't confiscate my marijuana and pornographic books.) Ha!

I've slept quite a bit off and on. Even though the seats go back like in a plane, it's not so comfortable. I was sat with a young chap from London, England. He has a three-month runaround ticked for all of the U.S. and Canada. He'd been all over the U.S. for two months and was now on his way to Canada before going home. He had all his maps out and bus timetables. I had to laugh to myself as it reminded me so much of me. I admire somebody with a bit of adventure in them. The Canadians have none at all.

Hardly anyone has been to New York. They all seem to go fairly local for their holidays.

In the waiting room there are about a dozen chairs with their own little TV attached, and you put money in a slot. What a good idea when folks have a long wait for a bus!

I've just had a peep outside the bus station and it's very scruffy here. Just like Dewsbury's approach to Leeds before it got pulled down.

When you got off the main street in New York, it was pretty bad, too. On our way back we came through the town where the killings at the jail have been. You are forever hearing the police siren going in New York and it makes you wonder what's happening, as the place is crawling with drug addicts and the like.

A friend of mine was stopped by two blokes one day and had his money pinched. I've never seen as many seedy looking characters around. Three folks stopped me and asked me if I could give them some money. If you can imagine Piccadilly Circus on a ten times bigger scale, then this is the Times Square area of New York.

There's a street with eleven cinemas side by side and all but one was showing some sex film. Everywhere are pornographic book shops. Father would die if he looked in the windows. I've never seen anything like it. But can't help but look when you're passing. I don't think I'm naive, but when you walk past a shop and see a magazine in a window of a couple making love and showing all they've got, it certainly shocks you. I'm sure things like this were not allowed in England. My friend was saying all these cinemas show this sort of thing. (I wonder how he knows!) Ha. No wonder there is a sign outside them all saying—'Warning, unless you are very unshockable and broad-minded about sex, don't come inside.' I quite honestly have never seen anything like it. Everywhere are strip clubs and bars with topless waitresses. You can see them from the outside. It's too far for your holidays father, I'm sorry.

The tubes are not a patch on London. It's really filthy down there. In fact, London, England is a much cleaner city altogether and a nicer one. You don't need to go around for your souvenirs, you can get all the black Spanish lamps in Woolworths here. There was also a Greek shop with loads of stuff in it. I bought a couple of things that said 'New York' on them. I might give someone them at Christmas.

It's nearly time for my bus, so I'll close.

All my love, Geoff

Awake, Lord! Why do you sleep? Rouse yourself! Do not reject us forever. Why do you hide your face and forget our misery and oppression?

Psalm 44:23-24 NIV

THE PENNOCKS AND VAN HEERDENS, SPAIN 2020

PROVENCE

Chapter 13

DOUBLE LIFE

God buries our sins in the depths of the sea
and then puts up a sign that reads, 'No fishing.'
Corrie ten Boom

"Only one hundred twenty-three Coronavirus deaths in Spain yesterday! That's the lowest we've had in six weeks, on a day. The people in the little empanada shop got a paper this morning, with the tip. Pray for them. They just opened back up. I told the man I'm going to put his business card in my Bible and pray for his business every day."

Mr. P speaks ninety miles an hour behind his flimsy blue mask, his face flushed red from sunshine and the special brand of excitement he always exudes after making contacts for the Kingdom.

Our section of Spain has finally moved to "Phase One" and he's been out and about early, before anyone else stirred. Mrs. P meets him at the door with a bottle of hand sanitizer and helps him remove his shoes. At seventy-nine he walks really well, but bending is something altogether different.

When my mother sees Mr. P's holey, hairy socks she says, "Hand them over."

"What?"

"Give me those socks."

Mr. P removes his mask and sits on the sofa. Mom grabs a plastic bag and holds it open in front of him. He doesn't move. She sets the bag on the floor and reaches for his foot.

"My soooooocks," he cries as she peels his socks off, dropping them in the bag. "I think we should have a funeral for them. I've worn them every day for ten weeks."

"I think we should have a funeral for a few things," my mother says with disdain.

"I hope not me," he teases.

Mom laughs as she ties a double knot in the grocery bag containing Mr. P's well-worn socks. The back-story is he came to Spain with two pairs of socks and a plan to buy more from a cheap vendor on the Spanish market. The day after we arrived in Malaga, COVID-19 struck fear in everyone and there have been no open-air markets or anywhere else to buy clothing.

"This week some stores will finally open. Maybe you can get some new socks," I shout from the balcony where I'm enjoying my corn flakes in the sunshine.

"What are you going to do with those?" he asks, looking up at my mother with a mischievous grin. Sometimes the boy on the inside of him causes me to forget the graying hair and wrinkles on the outside of him. I can easily imagine Mr. P as his much-younger self—handsome and jovial. I wish he'd met my mother before New York happened, before anything in this chapter happened, before he had to suffer like he did.

"I'm sorry we have to throw them in the trash," he moans as Mom silently stuffs his socks in with the rest of the garbage by the door. "Too bad we can't give them to the rag and bone man."

"Who on earth is the rag and bone man?" she quizzes.

"He used to come house to house with a horse and cart. When I was a kid. He collected bones from the meat we ate and sold them to factories for making different things, like glue. We saved our plate scrapings for the pigs and our bones for the rag and bone man."

"What does this have to do with your socks?" Mom's face is a puzzle.

I'm leaning toward the P's, trying not to miss a word. This is a Mr. P tidbit I've not heard before.

"Well, he also collected rags, which must have been shredded somehow to make uniforms for the soldiers in the war. I don't know how they would do that. But the same guy picked up the rags and the bones. They called him 'the rag and bone man.'"

"Now *that's* an interesting piece of history," she says. "I wonder if Spain recycles socks?"

I take my empty cereal bowl to the kitchen.

"You heard Mr. P's story?" Mom asks.

"Yes. I like it. And I think we need a rag and bone man for a few of my things as well. I'm sick of wearing the same clothes day after day.

I sit next to Mr. P.

"You've had an interesting life," I say.

"Oh dear."

"For real. Not everyone has a rag and bone man story up their sleeve."

"My dad liked when the rag and bone man came by because the man would shovel all the poop from his horse into our garden."

"I'm glad you mention your dad because I've been wondering how you communicated with your parents when you were in Canada. Did you only write letters, or did they have a phone by the 1970's?"

"We never had a phone."

"Never?"

"Only when I lived in Switzerland did my mum get a phone. Before that, she used to go to our neighbor to talk to me. My dad never did. Only Mum."

Mrs. P hands him a glass of water. He takes one sip and keeps talking.

"In Toronto I still wrote letters home, but not as often as before."

"Drink all of that," Mom says. "You've walked in the heat for a long time."

"Well, I stopped at the croissant shop and had something to drink," he replies. "The girl there will also get a paper. Now that we can go out, we have work to do, Mrs. P."

"You *are* a little missionary, aren't you?" she says. "Give me a kiss. I'm proud of you."

"Well, it's what we came here to do you know. If we can't go to Morocco, we may as well share Jesus here. Maybe we can go out together this evening," he suggests.

"Okay. I'm a bit nervous after weeks of not going to stores. Let's see how the day goes. I think Juju wants to work with you on the book."

Mr. P turns toward me.

"Do you want to talk about Toronto?" I ask. "It's been a few days since you were suicidal in New York at the end of the last chapter."

"Okay. It's just difficult speaking of these things after all these years."

Mr. P moves to his chair in the corner. My mother stands in the doorway. I can tell she wants to say something.

"What is it, Mom?"

"All the things that make you the you you are . . ." she pauses, sits on the sofa next to me. Tries again.

"When you know someone . . ." Again her voice trails.

"What are you saying?" I ask.

"What I'm trying to say is when someone is your husband, they tell you stories. And the reasons they tell you their stories, well that's what makes your marriage ***your*** marriage. It's your private life."

"Yes," agrees Mr. P. "I think you will have to change all the names in this book. I could be Fred Blogs. *The Life and Times of Fred Blogs*. Now *that's* a title."

"So it's starting to feel too painful?" I ask. "Too personal?"

"Sometimes I feel harassed about it. It's *my* husband. It's his story. It's OUR story. It's OUR life. I feel uncomfortable at moments with putting it all out there."

"I understand. Brené Brown calls it a 'vulnerability hangover.' I've had a few. Sharing your story takes a lot of courage."

"It's quite a good story," Mr. P jokes. "I might buy the book myself and read this tale about Fred Blogs."

"Sharing your story is a sacrifice to the Lord," I remind them. "After we've been delivered from bondage, we must do what Jesus told the Gadarene man to do, 'Tell how much God has done for you.' We can't just keep our stories to ourselves."

"Yes," says Mom, "but there's a difference between sharing with a few friends or even telling your testimony in church and writing a whole book about the intimate details of your life. But if I end up in some mass grave in Spain, it won't matter."

"Mother!"

"Susan!"

Mr. P and I shout simultaneously.

"How can you say something so awful?" he asks.

"Well," she says with tears in her voice, "this wicked virus is killing off all the old people. If I go out there, I'm vulnerable. I don't like it. And if it gets me, it won't matter if our personal lives get splattered all over the world."

"Oh, Mom." I put my arms around her.

"By the time this book is ever done, Jesus may have come back anyway."

"Good. He can be the first to read it."

"I want you to change the names," Mr. P says matter-of-factly. "I don't want my wife to be upset. Call us Mr. and Mrs. Pippit."

"P's, I know this is hard for you. I know you are private people. You can veto anything I write. I want you to be comfortable. If you want to skip today, we can. André and I can go down to the sea or something."

"No, it's okay," Mom sniffles. "I know it's important. If it helps even one person not to suffer the things my husband has suffered, it will be worth it."

We're here. We might as well get on with it," Mr. P agrees. "Maybe I can have a cup of tea and a biscuit while we talk about Toronto."

While Mom makes the tea, I pray for Mr. P. "Dear God, please cover this conversation with Your peace. Give Mr. P courage to share what may be helpful to others for Your glory. Give me wisdom to write in a way that helps but doesn't hinder anyone along this healing path to the heart of our true Father. In Jesus' name, amen."

"God didn't heal me in New York," he begins. "I believed one hundred percent He would. Psychologically, this left me thinking *God hates gays.*

"I hated myself. For years I felt I couldn't be my authentic self because I felt different. I felt an anguish inside, which never went away. My friends had girlfriends. I was good looking and could have had any girl. But I didn't want any girls. I wanted something that I couldn't name. I became something I didn't want to be, a legalistic hypocrite."

"What do you mean?"

"I worked at a Christian hospital where I prayed with my patients. We had religious discussions. I went to church. All my life I went to church. Even when I succumbed to the gay lifestyle, I never gave up my relationship with God. I visited churches of every denomination imaginable in my search for freedom. I never really heard the true Gospel that could transform me, until I was forty years old."

"I think you had faith even before you learned how to really wrestle with God," Mom says setting his hot tea on a coaster. "Which biscuits do you want?"

"Thank you. I'd like those ginger ones I got from the health food shop," he replies before continuing.

"I somehow always had some kind of faith. Even after I told God where to go in New York. Even though for the year I worked in Canada, I spent most of my days and nights off up in Toronto and doing all the things that had been pent-up inside me. God was still with me as I frantically lived out the darkest excesses the city's gay scene could provide.

"I had a room at the home of the hospital's administrator, Mrs. Graystone. She was from Yorkshire and often invited me for a meal of roast beef and Yorkshire pudding, which I really looked forward to.

"I worked on the urology floor. My degree was not accepted in Canada and I was only paid as a nurse's assistant. The winter was freezing. My nostrils just about froze up. Mrs. Graystone's home was across the road from the hospital and I went there for most of my meals. In the winter, even this seemed a painful trek.

"Week after week, I went to church. My mind was so confused I didn't know who I was worshipping anymore, as even in church I was thinking of who I could meet in downtown Toronto.

"For some time I was seeing a sensitive young oriental guy. Our romantic trysts were in my room at Mrs. Graystone's with Dionne Warwick's *I know I'll Never Fall in Love Again* playing full blast. Sometimes, even in the midst of sin, I would say to myself, '*This is not who I am or who I want to be.*' I was devastated when my new and first love returned to Thailand to look after his ailing mother.

"God knows you are not happy, and this is not really the life you want. He knows you are searching. You reach out to Him, even in the sin and misery and He doesn't abandon you."

Mom brings two more cups of tea to the coffee table and sits down between me and Mr. P. She brushes crumbs off the arm of his chair and pats his hand as it rests there.

He looks at her and explains, "It's because you are searching for the love of a father that you never got, and it turns sexual. It's a desperate searching for something you never got."

I notice it is easier for him to say, "you" than "I."

"Psych people write against that father-figure theory in books now Papa, but I agree with you. Maybe, if a person is in that lifestyle—even if they *had* a good father or didn't grow up with a father at all, they are looking for unconditional love. It's a deep search for an unmet need."

"In Toronto, I was acting out something I had suppressed for all those years. Somehow, I still held a deep belief that God hadn't shown up yet, but one day He would. I *never* gave up on that.

"During that time I also went to all sorts of Charismatic meetings, searching for the Holy Spirit. Before I left England, I'd read Katherine Kuhlman's books *I Believe in Miracles* and *God Can Do It Again.* I was thrilled to learn she was coming to Toronto. *Maybe I will get a miracle,* I thought. I took a day off and went to her healing service. Thousands of us queued in the hot sun for five hours to get in. A lady next to me gave me a sandwich as I'd forgotten to bring food and wasn't about to leave the line to find some. She'd come from Montreal, six hundred miles away, to be healed.

"When we finally got inside, I got a seat not too far from the front. Every seat was taken, and some people even sat on the stage. Ms. Kuhlman spoke about the work of the Holy Spirit and about Christ being the same yesterday, today, and forever. She looked radiantly happy and seemed very different from the ordinary kind of person. After a short prayer, the healing began. An elderly lady who had hobbled up the entrance stairs with a stick ran to the stage to testify. There were people crying with joy as they walked forward carrying and waving braces they'd worn all their lives. A lady who had cancer of the breast and was awaiting an operation said the pain and the lump had just vanished. It was marvelous to see the power of God before my eyes. Even two physicians, who attended as skeptics, were healed of physical ailments.

"Ever since then, I've always believed this kind of thing should be happening among believers all the time, not just at big meetings with well-known names.

"After that experience I began attending one group to learn to speak in tongues. It never worked."

"I never knew this!" Mom interjects.

"Yes. In most of the books I'd read on healing, someone spoke in tongues. I thought God might heal me if received that gift."

"Even after your awful experience at Teen Challenge, you still wanted to speak in tongues?" I ask.

"Well, some preachers are false, and some are true, aren't they? Some tongue-speakers are true, and some are false. There is always a counterfeit for everything good God has for us."

"I see. You really persevered, didn't you?'

"I did. But it was all confusing."

"Why?"

"Because of Genavié."

"Genavié?"

"Yes. I met her and her female lover at one of the meetings. Genavié was studying to be a pastor. She was lovely. We became good friends, actually. Sometimes I went out for lamb at the Jewish restaurant with her and her girlfriend. After some time, I confided in Genavié. She was easy to talk to.

"She told me to read a book by a Roman Catholic priest. It was called, *Time for Consent*—probably the first Christian book condoning homosexuality among believers. Genavié said, 'You have tried everything to change. Now you must accept who you are and believe that God accepts you as you are.' She encouraged me to believe that being gay was okay and that God would accept me that way. I only had to meet the right person and have a monogamous relationship.

"I yearned for this, but deep down I knew this line of reasoning was not Biblical. However difficult and frustrating it may seem, apart from the bonds of marriage between a man and a woman, Jesus said, 'Deny yourself.'

"Several months into my new double life, I discovered Pastor Henderson, who had baptized me in London was now working in

Toronto. I met with him and found courage to open up about my lifestyle. He anointed me with oil. Years later he admitted he never expected anything to change when he prayed for me that day.

"My life consisted of work, charismatic meetings with Genavié, searching for the baptism of the Holy Spirit and searching for men in gay places."

"What a combination, Mr. P!" I exclaim.

"It sounds like a lot of confusion," Mom empathizes.

"I could cry and get very upset right now," he says. "It's bringing back a lot of emotions. How can someone work at a Christian hospital, constantly talk about Jesus, and live a life of uttermost filth? That was Mr. P. I had a demon of depravity!"

"P . . ." Mom's voice is soft, "all that filth is gone forever, just like your dirty socks."

"It's true," he agrees. "Corrie ten Boom wrote something I've always remembered—'When God throws our sins in the bottom of the sea, He says, 'No fishing.'"

Mr. P looks into his wife's face. "In God's eyes," he says, "all of that is forgotten. Dead. Forgotten—as if I never did any of it. I hated that life! Hated it. Telling this story is bringing out anger but also the truth that even living in the depths of hell, I never gave up on the hope heaven."

But God demonstrates His own love toward us, in that while we were still sinners, Christ died for us.

Romans 5:8 NKJV

PIAZZA DELLA SIGNORIA, FLORENCE

Chapter 14

LOVERS, LAUSANNE, & LUGANO

When you decide to follow Jesus,
all that He promises you is Jesus.
Francis Chan

"Face mask, passport, money, keys." He pats four pockets and repeats it again. "Face mask, passport, money, keys."

The P's are going out this evening. Spain is now in Phase Two of the government's four-phase deescalation of lock-down restrictions. Andalusia, the region where we stay enforces strict rules about face masks and social distancing with fines of up to 600 Euros for noncompliance.

"Oops! I forgot my mask!" Mrs. P returns to their bedroom for her flimsy blue and white face mask.

"I don't need my sunglasses this time of day, do I?" she asks her ready-and-waiting-by-the-door husband.

"No. Unless you want to be a diva."

"Well, I like diva stuff," she responds squatting to primp in the rectangular mirror on the buffet near the dining table.

"Don't forget your pamphlets, Ms. Diva," I remind her as I slide a stack of neatly folded papers from the coffee table. Mom tucks them into her handbag.

"Did I tell you what I said to the spinach pie man this morning?" Mr. P asks.

When Mom and I answer, "No," we sound like the same person.

"I've been in there several times, you know. Today was the day for him to have a paper. I said, 'I used to sing in nightclubs. I was not a Christian. This verse changed my life. I'd like to give you this paper to remind you that you are loved as much as God loves Jesus.'

"The man had tears in his eyes as I gave him the paper and told him, 'I promise you I will pray for you and your business each day. God is going to bless your business. And I would like to help Him get started by ordering four spinach pies for tomorrow."

"What a precious story," Mom says as she slips on her sparkly Spanish sandals. "I think people's hearts are receptive right now because they are struggling after being shut down and locked in for so long."

"Telling someone God loves them as much as He loves Jesus is something really powerful. I didn't know that for one hundred years," Mr. P exaggerates. "I had the impression God hated me until I was at least in my forties."

"I'm proud of you P's," I say. "You never just go out thinking of yourselves. It's always about advancing the Kingdom."

"As weak and sinful as we are, God uses us," Mr. P acknowledges. "Talking with the spinach pie man in his little shop made me think of the Pope's lawyer's sister who said to me, 'Jesus came into my negozio today.'"

Mom's face lights up with the memory, "Who goes into a shop and prays?" she asks. "We *are* a bit unusual. Do you know this story, Ju?"

"I do, but I've forgotten."

"Her dog died. She was so upset she couldn't hide it," Mom remembers. "We went into her Italian art shop looking for souvenirs, but we ended up empathizing and praying with her. Our compassion really touched her. Afterward she put us in contact with her brother, who was in charge of Italy's refugees.

"That's when we were trying to help that first wave of asylum-seekers from Africa in 2006. We wanted to rent an apartment and put refugees in there with us. Her lawyer-brother was freaking out. You can't do things sometimes because of the culture. The villagers wouldn't stand for it. We didn't understand their fear of black people."

"I remember now. You P's have done some radical missionary work."

"It's true. But who will do this work if we don't? Who else is going to tell the spinach pie man what John 15:9 says about him?" Mr. P's voice is strong with emotion.

"The Bible is right. The harvest is ripe, but the workers are few," Mom agrees. Her words become a prayer. "Who is crying today, Lord? Someone out there is crying."

Mr. P adds, "All of India is crying. The people in the refugee camps coming from Syria are crying. They don't know Jesus. It's overwhelming to think about. What I saw on the Internet this morning broke *my* heart.

"Thousands of migrant workers are hungry and desolate because COVID-19 shut down their jobs in India's cities. They are walking hundreds of kilometers back to their villages. The photographs made me cry. When you've been to a country you feel more for the people. What can we do? All we can do is pray for them and do our part to share the Gospel wherever we are."

Mr. P opens the door.

Our neighborhood scarlet macaw screeches repetitively at the top of his angry-caged-bird lungs.

"If that bird knew the Gospel," Mom jokes, "this whole area would know the Gospel. If only he would squawk out some Jesus!"

With that she dons her diva sunglasses and prances into the hallway.

"Goodbye P's. Have a nice time."

I'll be working on this chapter alone. Mr. P loathes this part of his testimony. The other day he grabbed a pen and paper saying, "I need to write something." He then sat for a long time in his chair, writing, writing, writing. Hours later he hands me a stack of pages covered in blue ink. "Keep these out of the way then. I feel embarrassed."

I understand. Of course Satan wants to cover him with a shame blanket—even after all these years. I could see writing the last chapter unsettled him. Mr. P wants to live the life he has now, with the wife God gave him. He doesn't want to dwell on the lifestyle he practiced forty-some years ago.

I sit down with my laptop and those blue-ink pages.

Here is this chapter of Mr. P's story in his own words, with a few of mine added for clarification.

In 1972, I left Canada and went back to England. I talked with Pastor Rielly about my double life in Toronto. Without any counsel, without any talk with me or with a committee, he scratched my name off the church register—threw me out because I said I couldn't believe homosexuality was wrong because God hadn't changed me. For the next twelve years I went headlong into the gay scene.

I worked in a hospital in Bournemouth for about a year. There I made several gay friends. One died of AIDS years later. When I think back, I know that could have been me. I thank God it wasn't.

One day I learned there was a possibility of going to Lausanne, in the French-speaking part of Switzerland. I'd always wanted to travel abroad. To earn really good money for my move to the most expensive country in the world, I worked for a few weeks in a private hospital. Then I took an intensive French course in London (this time I passed) and packed my bags for Switzerland.

Lausanne is on Lake Geneva. I rented an apartment twenty minutes walk uphill from the hospital. The first thing I did was wallpaper the bedroom. Hanging paper was another thing I learned to do with my father. I also bought furniture for the first time. It was rustic kind of furniture, brown wood and a rattan chair with bamboo end tables.

The view from my window was of the town and the lake with the mountains and France on the other side. It was half an hour by boat to the opposite shore. There was a path to the hospital behind some apartments through the woods. This was my prayer closet as I walked to work each day.

Around the corner from my apartment lived an older workmate, Madame Francini. She treated me like a son and often invited me for delicious Italian meals.

Also near home was a wonderful boulangerie (cake shop). There I learned my love of croissants. The only place French croissants have neared the mark in the United States are the ones at Whole Foods bakeries. French bakery shops are a dream.

I remember a funny story from a few years ago. We were on holiday in Nice with Juliet and André. He went to the bakery to buy treats for breakfast and came back with two large boxes full of small desserts. "I didn't know which ones to choose, so I bought one of each," he said. We all laughed and laughed and ate French pastries until we were stuffed!

At the hospital I worked with many girls from Holland. They were very friendly. On my days off I would often go out with one of them up into the surrounding mountains. The Dutch are very openly friendly to gays and I had no problem telling them. This made it more relaxing for me at work. The girls included me in their conversations, twittering about handsome patients, "We've just got a good-looking guy in bed number four."

There were three other male nurses. My gayness (I don't know what you call it) made no difference to our good friendships, either.

Three girls I worked with were from England. In my department there were more foreigners than Swiss, all speaking French with bizarre accents. I would work half a day and go for French lessons the other half and still get full pay. The Swiss love their weekends off to go skiing in the Alps. That's why there was an influx of foreign workers at the hospital—foreigners didn't complain about working weekends.

One girl, Jane, was a particular friend. She became known in all my stories as the 'lesbian birdwatcher.' In Switzerland, there is a daily routine of kissing one's workmates on each cheek. It got to be quite exhausting, especially when there were sixteen of them to kiss. I told the girls, "I kissed you all this morning. I'm not kissing you goodbye as well."

Jane always flinched when I kissed her. I knew something was seriously wrong. She later confided her story of being gang-raped. She was terrified of men, so she found her consolation in women.

Not fully understanding the language for the first few months in a foreign country is nerve wracking. At first, I didn't know if my patients were operated on last year, today, or would be operated on next week. The patients were lucky to have some English nurses around who had worked there longer than I had!

I loved Switzerland and my days out from Lausanne. In springtime, the hillsides are covered with narcissi. I often visited Gruyeres, a nearby fairytale village famous for the cheese used to make Swiss fondue. Gruyeres cows also produce a very thick cream, which is eaten with raspberries. How wonderful it was to walk in the crisp air of the mountains above the village, the only sound being the large bells around the necks of the cows.

Many years later I brought my wife back to walk those same trails with me. She especially loved the end of the season festival. Every summer in Switzerland, farmers take their cows up into the high meadows to eat alpine clover and bellflower and everything that makes the milk and cheese taste so good. When summer is over the villagers make a festival to celebrate the end of the season. The local people dress in Swiss alpine ethnic clothing and parade the cows through the streets. The cows seem to proudly wear their tall headdresses made of flowers and decorative collars carrying giant bells.

I was paid very well and spent all my spare cash on travel. Europe was at my fingertips. I was able to visit places most people only dream of, but I was alone. I did most of my traveling alone. I made plans for my trips as soon as the thought came into my head. Switzerland's highest mountains—Eiger, Monch, and Jungfrau were a short ride away. I often wondered if anywhere in this world could be more majestic and beautiful?

I was definitely in the thrall of travel addiction. My adventurous spirit took me on the overnight train to Venice where I woke up to a dream from another world. Other long trips took me to Prague and Budapest. This was during the days of communism. My train chugged through high barbed wire fences. Each piece of luggage was searched by police with large dogs.

The three and a half years I lived in Lausanne was the only time in my life I didn't regularly attend church. The French Swiss are not the friendliest of people. I tried to go to church a few times. The people would say, "Bon jour" when I arrived and "Aurevoir" when I left. Nothing else. I felt invisible.

Jesus' last prayer before the crucifixion in John 17:22 says the main reason people will know He is the Messiah is that Christians will love each other and have the same relationship He has with His Father. Twice Jesus repeats this before He is lead away to be crucified. I believe a lack of unifying love among followers of Christ contributes to the fact that after two thousand years, two thirds of the world remains non-Christian.

In general, people who go to church are not much different than the people in the world. As I often say, "People in an English pub are more friendly than the average church." I doubt whether a church having the unity described John 17:22 exists, even though many denominations profess to have 'the truth.' The Bible says, "Come behind in no gift," but in my experience, most churches are behind in most gifts.

After a couple of years in Lausanne I attracted a male friend. Marceau lived out of town and we saw each other only once a week. I am a very stick-in-the-mud person for restaurants and food. I don't change. I only want to eat the same food. Invariably, we had fondue at the same place each week. The Swiss say the best thing to digest all that cheese is white wine. This would be the only time I drank a little.

Marceau always called me "Monsieur Pennock." The Swiss are quite formal. It is very unusual for them to use a person's first name unless they know you very well. A first name would never be used for anything official like at the bank or on a phone call. Strangely, I liked that. I liked being called Monsieur or Signore Pennock in Switzerland.

I started having another love affair at this time—with the Italian-speaking part of Switzerland, five hours away by train. Often, I would go and spend the night there. I went to Locarno on Lago Maggiore. This area was part of Italy until 1803. Switzerland has four distinctive areas and languages: German, French, Italian, and Romansh. Ticino is the Italian-speaking area, so different from the rest of Switzerland. The climate is mild, with palm trees by Lake Lugano. There is much more sitting out at cafés. I loved to sit at Café Munger, near the main square having a coffee, a piece of rhubarb tart and watching the people walk by. On a Sunday, Italian signorinas from Milan would often waltz past in their black Gucci and Versace dresses. I fell in love with Ticino at the same time Marceau fell out of love with me.

My codependence with Marceau was so sick I was devastated when he went to live with his new friend, about four doors down the road from my apartment. I always feared I would see them together, although I never did. I felt I couldn't bear to live without him. I needed a person in my life and my person found someone else. I had to get away. That's why I left Lausanne and moved to Lugano.

I put an advert in the paper requesting Italian lessons with a family. A Sicilian family promptly replied. After a few lessons, they invited me to have a meal with them. From then on, we had our lessons talking over a meal. If you have never eaten at an Italian table, you have missed out on one of life's greatest pleasures. I was hooked! Aurevoir Lausanne! Bon giorno, Lugano!

My rattan chair and I moved to Lugano, where we lived for the next twenty-one years. Of anywhere in the world, the lakeside tourist town feels most like home to me. Lugano had about 50,000 inhabitants when I arrived in the spring of 1979.

Switzerland is not simply a country full of cute chalets, but one as modern as any in the world, with the highest standards of cleanliness and service. The Swiss are very precise. If a train is more than three minutes late, the driver will be fined. All Swiss men must serve in the military and keep their rifles in their homes for all their lives. Switzerland has one of the lowest violent crime rates in the world. I always felt safe to walk Lugano's streets after dark.

Ticino was and still is predominantly Roman Catholic. Ospedale Civico, where I was hired to work on the surgical floor was an ancient building. It was an old-fashioned hospital run by nuns who lived on the premises. The head of each nursing department was a nun. Our main boss, Sister Angela would come downstairs every night before going to bed and check what was happening on the floor. In Lausanne, I felt somewhat free at work—everyone knew I was gay. In Lugano hospital I went back into the closet, as all my bosses had vowed poverty, chastity, and obedience.

Sister Angela doted on me and the other male nurse like we were her special pets. She was one of the loveliest people you could ever wish to meet, beautiful and round with the most sweet, innocent face. She radiated Jesus.

I never heard her speak badly of anyone, apart from one patient. He was a young gay guy who came in for an anal repair. I was shocked to hear Sister Angela exclaim, "What a dirty pig!" Although I had not tried anal sex and she had no idea I was gay, I felt she was saying the same about me. Her words stung as if I'd been slapped in the face.

A few weeks after I was hired, Lugano's new hospital opened. It was located on one of the highest streets in town. If I remember correctly, twelve floors were above ground, with equally as many below to use in a state of emergency. All the floors had every single thing in the exact same place, just in case a nurse needed to work on a different floor.

After we moved to the new building, my first shift was the night-shift. I had just one patient. Despite my inner pain, I wore a smile and served with compassion and love for all my years as a nurse there—even when my wife and her daughter became my patients after the accident. Our hospital had an excellent reputation. Wealthy people from other countries sometimes came for treatment. One patient I remember was the owner of Barilla Pasta, who came up from Italy. We also had a Swiss guard from the Vatican, who told me stories about the priests that could make anyone's hair curl.

My apartment was on the fourth floor of a building just across from the hospital. Like the patients from their windows, I had a commanding view of Lake Lugano and the surrounding mountains from mine.

Most of my workmates came from Italy, which was only four miles away. Italian workers daily crossed the border because Swiss wages were higher, but the cost of living in Italy, much lower.

I loved being so near to Italy. Even now, forty years and nearly forty countries later, Italy remains my favorite. Before I had a car, I traveled by train to Como's outdoor markets. I thought I'd gone to heaven. The cheeses, olives, dried tomatoes, and fruit were well worth the half hour commute. Lake Como is spectacular with lakeside villas and world-famous spas. No wonder George Clooney lives there. If I had his money, so would I!

On one visit a shopkeeper insisted I was German. We argued loudly in Italian. He finally believed me when I told him I only knew three German words for basic communication with my patients: Schlafen? Schmerzen? Stuhlgang? (Sleep? Pain? Bowel movement?). How funny!

Italians are some of the best-dressed people in the world. I love beautiful clothes. Back then, Florence was the place to buy them. Going to Firenze became one of my downfalls. I often took the three-and-a-half-hour train ride, my carnal mind dreaming of meeting a beautiful Italian guy and living happily ever after.

I'd book a room at the Pensione Roberta, near the railway station—cheap in price and also in décor. I hoped after visiting the Tabasco Night Club, I would not have to spend the night alone in my chintzy room. Tabasco, an underground gay bar, is on the corner of the Piazza della Signoria, one of Florence's most beautiful squares, which has a copy of Michelangelo's famous statue of David standing in front of the Palazzo Vecchio.

I lived a life, which the hedonistic part of me wanted so much and the spiritual part of me hated so much. Even with anything I wanted at the tips of my fingers, I was never happy. There was always an empty void inside, a void I didn't know at the time only Christ could fill—the real Christ, not the spirit of religion. In all my searching for a man, no man would ever be the right man, unless that Man was Jesus. But I did not yet realize Jesus was enough. I thought I needed an Italian. In the back of my mind I was always searching for one.

Even in the depths of my now-addiction I continually hoped and prayed for a way out. A female work friend was going to Israel and invited me to travel with her. 'This is my chance,' I said to myself for the umpteenth time. If I walk where Jesus walked, maybe He will help me.

Denise and I toured around for a week, then I was to have a few days alone to meet Jesus.

One of our trip highlights was visiting Mt. Sinai. We crossed the desert by Jeep and over the border into Egypt, spending the night at St. Catherine's Monastery at the foot of the mountain. We were awakened at 4:30 AM for breakfast. We had to leave early otherwise it would have been too hot in the daytime for the two-and-a-half-hour trek on the camel path up the mountain.

A young Arab boy with a lamp went ahead of us. When we reached the summit, I soaked in the view. There was only desert and mountains. It was quite awe-inspiring. I thought about the Israelites wandering around here for decades. I did not envy them, but I understood how they felt, as I'd been wandering in circles in my own wilderness for most of my life.

A day or two after Sinai, Denise left, and I was alone to spend time with Jesus. I again visited some of the usual Biblical sites. The most inspiring and memorable moments were praying in the Garden of Gethsemane and on the Mt. of Beatitudes.

My mind was in the usual state of torment and condemnation. Even as I contemplated the Bible scenes in the place where they had taken place, I couldn't find the perfect peace Jesus talks about. Even as 'I walked today where Jesus walked' by the Sea of Galilee.

My mind was in turmoil in Jerusalem because I had gone to Israel in desperate hope that like Naaman, I might go home without my leprous spots, but though I had spent two weeks walking on holy ground—nothing changed. I didn't know the gospel and I desperately needed the deliverance Jesus modeled to his disciples.

Because I believed in the Sabbath, you can imagine me, in Israel, on the Sabbath. Spending a Sabbath day as Jesus had could have been the highlight of my trip. Instead, it was insanity. Satan knew he could get to me. I had a real struggle about whether or not to even write about this, but I think it is important to share what happened on 'holy ground' because readers need to know when we are seeking Christ, the roaring lion comes after us with fury. I didn't understand the principles of spiritual warfare at that time. I was too weak to be alone, even in a spiritual place like the Holy Land.

Many people go to the Holy Land, have this marvelous spiritual experience and come back with something special. I longed for something special, too. I didn't just want to go home with some olive-wood trinket the vendors outside Gethsemane's gates were selling.

Those trinkets are probably made somewhere in China. They cannot really be crafted with a piece of the cross of Christ, yet we buy them. We take them home. We wear them around our necks. But it's a lie. And what Satan tells us about ourselves and about Jesus is also a lie we buy into. I knew I wanted Jesus, but I didn't know how to resist the overwhelming urge to act out my sinful nature. My spirit was willing, but my flesh was weak.

The day before I left, I walked past a gay bar in Jerusalem. You see, The Holy Land is not so holy these days. Tel Aviv has the largest LGBT festival in the Middle East. In 2019, there were 250,000 participants. That seems unbelievable. Tourists go to The Holy Land for something spiritual, but they also go for other things.

I did not know how to resist the overwhelming temptation to go into that bar. I turned around just as another guy was coming out. He held the door for me, and I went inside where immediately I met someone interesting.

Hours later I walked with my newfound friend through the ultra orthodox Mea Shearim district. All the men we saw were dressed in somber black clothes and had ringlets of hair hanging down on either side of their faces. A plaque on the wall of one of the buildings had quotations from the Torah and a list of "do's and don'ts" for this special area, like wearing modest clothing in the neighborhood.

I wondered if at any moment, I might be stoned—because of all the Torah's restrictions and rules. And because of what I was.

That day I learned firsthand that Jews take off their kippah caps in bed. The irony was not lost on me when my new friend turned Diana Ross down low, as loud music would be offensive on the Sabbath. I didn't disagree, as I understood legalism all too well.

Afterwards I couldn't cope with my conflicting emotions. I was insane! Absolutely insane. I had an almost uncontrollable urge to simultaneously scream and laugh in insanity and madness. I needed to let out my emotions, but I didn't know what to do. In repentance and despair I went and swam in the Sea of Galilee, hoping I might drown. Because of where I was, I think out of all the years of hating myself this was the moment I hated myself the most. This memory makes me want to cry.

How does a person recover from that? I went home to Lugano consumed by guilt and shame.

One of my good friends in Lugano was my barber Matteo. For years we would go out for a meal after he cut my hair. He was always depressed. Like a lot of gay people, he was mentally tormented, but didn't know where to go. In the end he set himself free by taking his own life. I understood how he could get to such a desperate place, but I didn't yet know the way out.

It was through Matteo I finally met 'my Italian.'

This is difficult to write. I feel stupid. I was stupid, but I didn't know what to do about it.

Luca was the third love of my life. How he got into the gay lifestyle helped me to understand, some years later, how I could get out of it.

Near Locarno, where Luca lived, was an area of the river where gays used to go and sunbathe. This was a well-known fact. Luca knew about this place and one day was tempted to go there, even though he had never had any inclination towards men a day in his life. He was married, with two kids and had recently left his wife, but that one exposure lured him into the gay lifestyle.

Luca and I saw each other for around six months. When we were together, he would always say, "Mi fa impaziere!" (You drive me crazy!) Our affair was one of turmoil. One day he said, "It's finished. I have decided to go back to my wife and kids."

That day, I said to God, "If You give me Luca back, I'll give You an hour of my time each day." As Jacob who wrestled with the angel, I said, "I will not accept no for an answer. I will not let You go unless you bless me." How's that for crazy theology? I was still bargaining with God, "If I do something for You, You do something for me."

Right around this time, my old Pastor Rielly sent me a letter. He said he'd heard about someone in America who found freedom from homosexuality. I wrote him back straight away. "I tried everything for years. This freedom thing is a load of dung. I don't believe it!"

Without Luca, I felt I no longer wanted to live. My sexuality was all about trying to find my identity in someone else. That's why the emotions were so strong and demonic. Romans 4:18 says, "Against all hope, Abraham in hope believed." That was me. Against all hope, I believed for an entire year Luca would return to me. Even though I never saw a shred of evidence he would. I kept praising God for something I could not see, even though I had moments of despair and doubt.

Because I wanted Luca back so badly, I faithfully kept my side of the bargain. Every day I spent an hour reading my Bible and talking to God. On my days off I visited the Valle Verzasca, my majestic prayer closet in the mountains where I walked for hours singing and praying and praising God for what He would do for me. In my mind I refused to accept Luca would never come back. He never did.

One verse I read over and over was Deuteronomy 31:6, "Be strong and courageous. Do not be afraid or terrified because of them, for the LORD your God goes with you; he will never leave you nor forsake you." Even though I felt abandoned by every man who had ever been in my life, I began to believe my heavenly Father would never abandon me.

After many months of communing with God each morning my life was gradually changing without me consciously thinking about it. I stopped going into any gay places. Off and on I went to church again. And some evenings, I helped out in a handicapped children's home, talking to the kids about Jesus.

November 13th was a Sabbath. I woke up that morning and said to God, "For one and a half years I have led a fairly decent Christian life. I have spent a lot of time with You, even whole days praying and singing in our valley. I am a different person, yet You haven't given me my Luca back. I cannot trust You anymore. I'm done trying." For the second time in my life, I told God where He could go. In a spirit of rebellion I also said, "I'm not going to church today. I'm going to Club Tabasco."

Before packing my bag for Florence I walked down to my mailbox. Inside was another letter from Pastor Rielly. I think he felt guilty for kicking me out of the church and for failing to have faith when he anointed me for healing. Through the years he would reach out to me once in a while, but I had not heard from him for eighteen months—not since I'd told him what I thought about his American 'freedom from homosexuality' story. That's why the timing of his letter that day was miraculous.

I opened the envelope and a magazine clipping dropped to the ground. I picked it up and started to read. The words I read resonated so deeply in my soul that I reversed my rebellious plans. I had heard from God. He answered my prayer in a different way than I expected, but He answered none-the-less.

"For my thoughts are not your thoughts, neither are your ways my ways," declares the Lord.

Isaiah 55:8 NIV

GANDRIA, LAKE LUGANO

Chapter 15

COMING OUT

It's time to get healed. It's time to confess ... Hear your Father's voice call out to you above the noisy clamor of our culture. He says, "I love you. You're free to go now. Sexual sin has no hold on you."
Craig Groeschel

"Yesterday was the first day I've been in a store for two months! It was weird. I was chemicaled. They spray you with chemicals!"

Mom is on WhatsApp with her friend Connie in Switzerland, comparing notes on their lock-down experiences. Although Mom is in her bedroom with the door closed, her every word wafts through the open windows.

"Walking along the beach was like a boardwalk nursing home with old people in masks hunched and hobbling along. It was like walking with a bunch of crabby oxygen-deprived zombies. I hated it. Really!"

Although I can't make out her words, Connie's sing-song Swiss-German voice sounds empathetic.

"It *is* depressing," Mom agrees. "We are only allowed to walk down there at certain times, only with the other old people. I don't like my slot. I don't like all that weirdness—to segregate humanity like that. They act like they are trying to protect us, but they are trying to kill us. Forcing us to wear masks walking by the sea . . . It's ridiculous! How is putting a bunch of elderly, vulnerable people together a good idea? I'm not going down there anymore. I don't like it. Marginalized, categorized, and segregated. Those are my words!"

I'm on the balcony sipping grapefruit juice and checking my email. Mr. P and André have gone for a walk together, even though they are in different age-categories and this is not Mr. P's time slot for the elderly. Today they are breaking the rules because tomorrow My Honey is leaving us. He finally got a roundabout flight to America and must return home to work. The P's and I will remain in Spain until a more direct flight opens up. Sleeping in airports is no longer on their can-do list.

My mother appears in the balcony doorway, her brown eyes sparking.

"Connie tells me they even have to wear masks in the forest in Switzerland. This entire COVID thing is of the devil. Why is the Coronavirus in the woods? Why is it down there by the beach where I need to breathe? This. Makes. Me. SO. Mad." She punctuates each word by banging an empty water bottle on the door frame. "The control and the strangeness through this whole lock-down makes me feel like going home and being in my garden. I could tell all those controllers, "Leave me alone. You've made me not be social and now I feel like I don't *want* to be social. I don't care."

Mrs. P plops into Mr. P's chair and laughs at herself.

"I think I'll sit here and be quiet a minute. Which is quite unusual."

After her temper cools, Mom mentions something else her friend said. She joins me at our tiny balcony table, stretching her pale legs into a small patch of sunshine.

"Connie remembers when Geoff gave his testimony at Lugano church thirty-some years ago. She and Heinz were crying and whispered to each other, 'If he can come out of *that*, God can get *us* through anything.'"

"We aren't to the testimony part in the book yet, but we are very close. At the end of chapter fourteen Mr. P gets that life-changing letter in his mailbox. That's where we are."

Just now our husbands' voices come around the corner seconds before they do. Deep in conversation, their eyes do not raise to see two blondes eavesdropping from our balcony vantage point.

"I fought the urges with the Word of God," Mr. P declares. "That's how Jesus fought the devil."

"I don't feel like I'm as bold with the Word as you are," André admits.

"I haven't always been. There were periods when I said, "To heck with it all."

"Why was that?"

Their voices disappear into our apartment building's downstairs entryway.

"Sounds like they are discussing the details," I say.

When Mr. P's key jiggles in the door, he is still talking. "Even though I went downhill for quite a few years I always had a relationship with God."

"What was your breakthrough?" André asks, slipping off his sneakers and hanging his face mask on a hook by the door.

"It started with an article I received in the mail."

Mr. P sits on a dining chair to untie his shoes. His back is toward us. Mom and I remain quiet, half-hidden by the blowing curtains, not wanting to disrupt their conversation. I switch screens on my MacBook and frantically type Mr. P's words in a new document, knowing I will need them later.

"Tell me about your breakthrough," André prompts. He brings three bottles of water to his usual spot at the table, two for him, one for Mr. P.

"The article came at just the right time. It gave me hope that kept me from relapsing into my sexual addiction—after a year and a half of doing nothing but praying and praising God for something seemingly impossible that I could not see."

"What did it say?"

"It's been a lot of years since then, but I still remember what caught my attention. The article spoke about the power of praise. More specifically praising God for something you can't see or feel with your emotions. Praising God that you are created heterosexual and whole because deep down, that is your true identity.

"Because I had already been praising God for eighteen months that this guy, Luca would come back, I understood the biblical concept of praising Him for something you don't see or feel, like Paul and Silas did in jail. Yes, I misapplied the scriptures because I was asking for something that goes against the Bible, but I had created a habit of spending time with God and praising Him with faith and thanksgiving. God used my own experience and the ideas expressed in the article my former pastor sent to give me hope that God's Word really did hold the keys to my freedom. The system was the same. Something clicked that day. I believed what I read one hundred percent. If I had gotten the article on any other day, it would have been thrown in the trash.

"Wow, Mr. P! That is truly incredible," André exclaims. "I've heard praise and thanksgiving called 'weapons.' You certainly learned how to use them."

Mom glances at me and gives a double thumbs-up. She's glad I'm typing this conversation. I wish I were a stenographer. It's hard to keep up.

Mr. P takes two sips of water before replying. "The way to freedom was not pleading to be set free (like I had always done), but against my feelings to the contrary—to praise God that I was now free in Christ and heterosexual and whole because of what Christ had already done, not what He would do in the future. That thought just gave me hope that it's NOT about me anymore. In my mind Jesus became a different person. I could trust in Him.

"From my Sunday school years I'd always believed, *If you're not a good boy, Jesus won't love you.* But that's a lie. 'All have sinned and come short of the glory of God,' so there is not one 'good boy' in all the world."

Mom leans toward me whispering behind her hand, "Romans Chapter 3. He realized Jesus took his place. This started Mr. P on his justification walk."

I nod.

Mr. P continues, "Until I was nearly forty years old, until the Holy Spirit spoke to me through the book of Romans, I could never measure up enough for God to love me. I felt hopeless—until the truth clicked in my mind that it was one hundred percent the faith of Jesus that counted, and not my weak faith at all. I always thought my salvation depended on me, *my* obedience, *my* faith, *my* good works. The incredible truth dawned on me that my sozo (the Greek word for salvation, which includes forgiveness, healing, *and* deliverance) depended solely upon Jesus and *His* completed work at the cross. He accepted even my weakest offering of faith. 'Abraham believed God and it counted as righteousness.'"

"Romans four verse three." André adds the text.

"Very good, Pastor! Romans holds a key to unlocking righteousness by faith."

"Realizing God no longer charged my sinful feelings and urges against me was incredible news. That's from Romans eight. I'm not sure of the exact verse. I began to understand as long as I clung to Christ, even though I still struggled with sin, I was treated as righteous."

"Right," André interjects. "Romans 5:8 and 10, "While we were yet sinners, Christ died for us. While we were enemies, we were reconciled."

"Exactly. And Ephesians chapter two where it says even when I was 'dead in my trespasses and sins God made me alive with Christ and saved me by His grace.' I had been under the influence of the powers of darkness for decades, but I learned for the first time that Christ reins over the powers of darkness because of His victory on the cross. He is sovereign over all that happens in our lives. If God is for us, who can be against us!"

Mr. P's voice carries strong to the balcony and beyond. If our neighbors understood English, they might be shouting, "Amen!" from their courtyard below.

"Preach it Mr. P!" André cheers. "I need to get you on the preaching schedule at my church, you even quote Greek!"

"I'm no preacher," Mr. P chuckles, "but I do get very excited about these verses. They changed my life. Until then, I was always afraid. Always. In my mind, my salvation hung on my every move. If I acted out my sinful thoughts, or even if I had sinful thoughts, I was afraid I was lost in that moment. I always thought I was complete dung, even when I *wasn't* doing anything. I did not serve a God of grace, understanding, or mercy. I thought it was all up to me. Now I knew I didn't have to do something for Him in order for Him to do something for me. My bargaining theology went out the window."

"This is beautiful Mr. P. Many people do not understand the gospel like this," André affirms. "I never got it when I was younger, even *with* a theology degree."

"As I began to study more," Mr. P continues, "it was as if a light turned on inside my head. When I discovered John 15:9, I was forever changed. To think that God loves me as much as He loves His own son, Jesus—me, a miserable boy from Dewsbury, England who had spent his whole life searching for the love of a father. I no longer needed to search. I had been found from the foundations of the earth."

I can only see the back of Mr. P's head, but I know he is weeping as he wipes his eyes with one hand.

"Then I learned some other verses," he continues. "Forgive me if I don't remember where they are found, but these are the ideas: God did not give me that spirit of fear and I did not need to be a slave to it. 'Keep your mind on the things above.' 'I can do all things through Christ.' I know that one is found in Ephesians 3:20. 'Greater is He who is in me than He who is in the world.'

"John 4:5," André adds.

"I found a powerful promise in Psalms that says, 'The Lord will accomplish that which concerns me.' It was liberating to recognize it was God's work and *He* would do it. I didn't need to strive. When I got this part of the Gospel, the weight I had inside for as many years as I can remember left me! At forty years of age I finally felt free to be the person God intended me to be. This was life saving. It changed the way I thought about everything."

"It was a total paradigm shift for you."

"Yes. With that paradigm shift and the unconditional love, prayer, and fellowship I finally found within my faith community in Lugano, I began my path to healing. Nothing was instantaneous. I still had a battle—to keep close to Jesus and fight the lies of Satan armed with the truth. I had to use my new armor of God against the old thinking."

"That's the sanctification part."

"Yes, Pastor. But I didn't know the big words. I was just learning there was a big God who loved me as much as he loved Jesus and who did not condemn me but was 'faithful and just to cleanse me from all unrighteousness.' First John one, right?"

"Yes. Verse 9. I'd really like to learn from you, Mr. P. I spend time in the Word of God at the beginning of the day, but then I seem to lose it, especially when it comes to dealing with my kids. The word of God is like a reprogramming of the mind, right?"

"Yes, because we want the mind of Christ, don't we? It took years of work to undo my years of twisted thinking. Healing takes time. I learned that as a nurse. Only after I met Susan did I begin to understand that Jesus actually took on my nature and won my victory because of His dependence on His Father. She showed me things about spiritual warfare and the nature of Christ that helped me understand the other half of the Gospel. That's when I got truly free and stayed free."

"How did you meet her?"

"It's a long, long story. Dear me. The first time I met Susan I felt like I'd never felt before about anybody. She seemed so different from anyone else. I sent her a Christmas card for years. It was just a friendship thing. She'd been divorced for about six years before we got together."

"And then you had that horrible accident. Did you claim a lot of scriptures through that experience?"

"Yeah, I did. After I told God to f-off. That was the third time in my life I really lost it with Him. The accident nearly destroyed my faith. After everything I'd been through to get my wife and then to have her brain damaged and her body ruined. After I had learned all the sexual things that please a woman and then it was lost. Her brain didn't have any emotions at all. She couldn't even feel that I was her husband!"

I squint at my mother through the sun's rays. She doesn't have on her diva sunglasses. I can tell she wants to say something, but she dares not interrupt their conversation. She squeezes my arm, points to her head and nods in agreement with what her husband was saying.

I blindly type their every word—the sun on my computer screen making it impossible to see what I'm doing.

"Can you see God's hand in all of that?" André asks.

"No. The only good thing that came out of the accident is the orphan school in Romania my wife built with her settlement money. Not much else."

"But the fact she wasn't killed was miracle. And my wife, too."

"Susan was reading something spiritual when it happened. I feel it was a direct attack from the devil against our marriage. I've never understood why God allowed it."

"This topic will have to be a sit-down with God in heaven to puzzle things out," André empathizes. "You know, even if what God promises isn't visible, the fact that we are in His Word and the fact that we trust Him is still a great comfort, irrespective of what happens to us. When you know God is with you, even though his Word is not being fulfilled in a tangible way, just by holding onto His promises, you actually get His presence with you. And you have an inner strength and a peace that can carry you through anything."

"In the end," Mr. P adds, "a person can understand different kinds of people—what they go through. I think suffering gives people a depth of character we wouldn't learn anywhere else. You can't learn these lessons in theology school."

"Yeah," André agrees, "when I think of my dad's death . . . I was only four years old. We can't see any sense in these tragedies."

"And *my* sister Jennifer dying when she was sixteen," Mr. P remembers.

André chugs the last of his water. Crunches the plastic bottles flat. Rolls them into rectangles. Then screws the caps back tight. "If you think about it," he finally says. "Death is actually a merciful thing. It's the loved ones left behind who suffer." Silence hangs in the space created by his words.

Mr. P breaks the pause. "All we can say is God's grace is sufficient. But it does shake a person's faith, doesn't it? Because there are so many promises in the Bible where God says, 'I will protect you.'"

"I guess we must choose to be like Job and say, 'Though He slay me, I will trust Him.' I don't know what I would do if something like that happened to Juliet now. I don't want to think of it. Like you, I also waited until I was older to get married. I was fifty-two."

"Of course. You understand how it feels to pray a long time for a wife. I was fifty when I finally married Susan."

"You have really inspired me to be bolder with God's Word, Mr. P. I think the enemy tries to keep us from the Bible because we don't realize how powerful it is. The same word that created the universe is between those covers. I think the Word of God healed both you *and* Mrs. P. When I look at the two of you, I am amazed to know the story of where you came from. The confidence you have had to rise above everything is incredible."

"My wife is down today, André." Mr. P's voice is soft.

"She's down?"

"Yes. She's really down."

Mom pulls her legs in, leaning forward to catch every syllable, which is difficult now because the macaw across the way is revving up its volume.

"She is," Mr. P continues. "I don't like seeing her like that. I still have codependent tendencies. It affects me."

"I wonder why she's down?"

"I don't know. Who can understand a woman?"

They chuckle together like men do when they think their wives aren't listening.

Then Mr. P says, "I think it's because everything is really strange now after the lock-down."

"Let's pray together Mr. P. Let's thank God for our wives and pray for them."

After 'Amen' Mr. P abruptly stands. "I think I'll go see if she's awake."

"I'm awake P!" Mom is already halfway across the room, her arms stretched toward him. His worried face softens, and he hugs her for several seconds. "How are you Mrs. P?" he whispers into the ponytail nestled under his chin.

"I'm alright. I'm better. I talked it all out with Connie. It's not just Spain that's insane. The whole world's gone mad, even Switzerland."

André comes out to the balcony and rubs my shoulders. "My wife the super-spy," he jokes. "How's it going?"

"I'm glad for the things Mr. P shared with you because they fit in perfectly with where we are in his story," I explain. "I needed that Bible part. These are the scriptures that make him so bold in his faith. His testimony can help anyone, not just someone struggling with same-sex attraction."

"It's true," My Honey agrees. "He's got a good grip on how to practically apply the Gospel. What are you going to do now?"

"I hope Mr. P still feels like talking because I'd like to finish this chapter today."

I pick up my laptop and move indoors. My husband gives me a firm peck on the lips before disappearing into his writing den. The P's are nowhere to be found. I tap three times on their bedroom door.

"Come in," they chorus.

I open the door. The Peasies are lying on their backs in bed. Or should I say 'beds' as there are only tiny twin beds in this apartment—definitely one of the downfalls of our Spanish lock-down experience. Like us, the P's have pushed theirs together to form an almost-queen-sized bed.

"You can come in," Mom repeats, patting the mattress beside her. "We're just resting and talking."

"Do you want to talk about your friends in Switzerland? Because those friendships were key in Mr. P's healing journey and they would fit in nicely right here."

"Sure," Mom says scooting to the middle.

"The crack will be uncomfortable," I say handing her a blanket to pad the gap with.

I lie down next to my mother and prop my laptop on my bent knees, silently wondering how long this writing arrangement will last.

"Mr. P, we are at the part of your story where you begin to grasp the Gospel and begin your transformation journey."

"I wish I could tell you from then on my struggles were over, but that was far from the case. One thing I knew was that what God started He would finish. That's His promise in Philippians 1:6. Another thing I knew I needed was a support group. Coming out of a gay lifestyle was too difficult to go through cold turkey and alone."

"Here's where Walter and Connie and Heinz come in," Mom says. "I'm so glad he had such lovely Christian friends because they've been my friends too, for all these years. Connie has checked on us more during this pandemic than anyone else."

"One counselor said I needed a group of praying male friends I could relate to in a nonsexual way," Mr. P explains. "God gave me Walter, Heinz, Gustavo, Daniel, and Massimo. That's a lot all at once. Two of them, were young and exceptionally good-looking. I knew the Holy Spirit was talking to them as they gave me something I really needed—genuine love and acceptance. These men prayed with me, listened to my frustrations and cried with me, sometimes for hours. I think that's incredible."

"They were just being good buddies to you, in a natural way. That naturalness produced the healing," Mom says.

"It's true," he agrees. "True to their Mediterranean culture, they often walked or sat with an arm around me, demonstrating the non-erotic kind of love I never had with a man before. I marveled that they were not afraid of me. That was unusual in my experience with heterosexual males. The way my new friends treated me made me think of Jesus—not flinching when John laid his head on His chest. That would be frowned upon in today's world, wouldn't it?"

Mom reaches for his hand. "They *were* like Jesus, P. They really were your Jesus in flesh. Italian men often walk around with their arms around their friends." Mom hesitates, then adds, "Well, maybe not so much now that COVID-19 has wiped out so many Italian lives. Fear might disrupt their culture of physical connection."

"Maybe this is why I fell in love with Italy," Mr. P agrees. "I enjoyed the warmth and natural camaraderie after growing up in a culture where men were as cold as the North Sea. The only time my dad visited Italy he quickly noticed all the Italian men walking arm-in-arm. Dad leaned over and loudly observed, 'Italy sure does have a lot of gays, doesn't it?'

"I believe homosexuality has a lot to do with stunted emotional growth. It was 10 long years of ups and downs before I felt I was ready to get married. Through those years, Walter and Bronia's and Heinz and Connie's homes were always open to me, as if I lived there. I was welcome to just show up without an appointment and they would love me, feed me and pray with me. That's how Walter was with everybody. It was strange. Very strange. And wonderful. And new—to have real Christian friends who accepted me, even with all my struggles. I told them who I was and where I'd been, and they loved me anyway. This is rare.

"One of the friends, Massimo, after weeks of prayer and sharing together said, 'I know Jesus on a deeper level because of my friendship with you.' His compliment made me feel something deep. I felt useful for God. I knew I had not yet arrived, but my new life with my new understanding of Jesus had started. The good work He began in me, He would finish."

The twin mattresses have split, and Mom is not-so-slowly sinking into the crack. Mr. P pulls her toward him and keeps talking.

"Walter especially became the best Christian friend I ever had. We both loved pizza with Gorgonzola, Mascarpone and Rucola and often had a pizza date."

"I'm so glad you had pizza dates with Walter!" Mom kicks her leg up twirling her ankle in the air. "I *love* Walter."

"Walter was younger, but he was like a mother and a father and a sister and brother to me, all rolled up into one wide man with a wonderful laugh and a ponytail. When I read that verse in the Bible where God is portrayed as a hen gathering His chicks under His wings, I always think of Walter. That's how he was like God."

"Walter *was* wonderful," Mrs. P agrees. "I remember the first time I saw him. His silhouette was framed in their shuttered bedroom window. It was my first visit to Switzerland, and I was flouncing down the steep steps to Walter and Bronia's home. I remember exactly what I was wearing that day—a square-necked dress with a soft pattern of green leaves and tiny flowers on a cream background. Walter stared holes through me with his Swiss blue eyes. Then he smiled and nodded ever-so-slightly. In that moment

I knew he approved of the woman Geoffrey Pennock would marry one day."

"Well, when you get the approval nod from your future husband's 'mother,' you know you're in," I tease.

"You know what Walter was like," Mom says. "He was everybody's mother. He and Bronia took in stray chicks from all over Europe until the day he died."

Someone is sniffling on the other side of our makeshift double bed. I sit up just in time to see a tear roll from the corner of Mr. P's right eye down into his ear. Mom is also teary-eyed. It's only been a couple of years since a blood clot snuffed out the liveliest light in their friends' group. The grief feels fresh.

"My friends in Lugano were much more than family," Mr. P laments. "They were a heaven-sent family. They knew me inside out. Some things my blood family doesn't know to this day. Unless maybe they are reading this book," he jokes. "I always say I had the best friends anyone could have.

"Walter was like an AA sponsor. He would sit for hours with his arm around me. God told him I needed nonsexual touch from a man. Because a boy has a void in his life from an absent father, he might turn to another male for attention or affection. We often cannibalize what we can't have. Or what we haven't had. What every hurting boy needs is a Walter."

For a few moments the only sound in the room is the erratic squawking of that miserable macaw. Mr. P interrupts the bird to say, "Walter probably wasn't any further along spiritually than I was when we first met. He never treated me like he was some spiritual authority and I needed to sit at his feet."

"Your friends realized their sins were no more sinful than yours. They never acted superior or treated you like you were a weirdo," Mom agrees.

"Unlike other church people who deify some sins and demonize others. In my past experiences with so-called Christians, especially pastors, I felt so shameful, I dared not bring up my personal problems. What I learned through my experience with my friends in Lugano is healing takes place in community. Real community. Not pseudo-community, like so many churches."

Mr. P quickly changes the subject. "Early in the Spring of 1983 I attended some Christian meetings in America."

"Oh! Here comes the fun part!" Mom claps her hands and squeals like a preteen girl. "I'd been shopping and came to the same meetings in my new red hat."

"At the conference I learned deeper spiritual points about my identity in Christ. For the first time I grasped the concept that I am never who I think I am, but I am always who God says I am."

"You sure took *that* thought to a new level," Mom singsongs.

"What do you mean?"

"What did YOU mean, kissing me like that?"

"Mr. P! You kissed her at the Christian conference?" I tease.

"I had that red hat on, and he just leaned in and kissed me right on the mouth! Right there! Right in the seminar! I'd never had an experience like that!"

"I not only noticed your mother because of her red hat. I noticed her because she was beautiful. I wasn't used to looking at a woman twice. But I did a double take because of her beauty, not just her red hat," he repeats. And yes, I kissed her—full on the mouth!"

"You had fat cheeks and great legs in Swiss hiking boots. I thought you were very cute—and fascinating because you were foreign."

I can tell Mr. P is smiling, even if I can't see his face.

"What on earth were you doing?" Mom banters.

"I don't know,"

"Had you ever kissed anyone like that before?"

"No."

"Of course not! You weren't used to kissing women on the mouth. That's not the Swiss custom. Nor the Italian custom or even the French custom! You kiss *me* and you start writing to *me*."

Then he looked at those seated in a circle around him and said, "Here are my mother and my brothers! Whoever does God's will is my brother and sister and mother."

Mark 3:34-35 NIV

SONOGNO, VALLE VERZASCA

Chapter 16

UNHOLY TIES THAT BIND

Grace is the first ingredient necessary for growing up in the image of God. Grace is unbroken, uninterrupted, unearned, accepting relationship...Grace, then, is the relational aspect of God's character.
Henry Cloud

"I need to peck something."

Mom and I hear Mr. P's voice from the kitchen. "You need to what?" she asks.

"I'm peckish."

"Is it time for a snack already?" She glances at the clock above the television.

"It's time for something," I say from the sofa where I'm texting back and forth with Carlo, our travel agent.

"Time to say goodbye . . ." Mom's soprano voice bursts into song.

"Watch out Sarah Brightman. Here comes Mrs. P."

Mom laughs from the balcony where she's pinning wet socks and underwear on the clothesline. After her solo she hollers into the kitchen, "What you eating Mr. P?"

"Turkey. I'm going cold turkey. Ha! Ha! Ha!"

Two minutes later he ambles out with a loaf of bread in one hand and a jar of peanut butter in the other.

"You know, I hardly ever eat peanut butter at home, but here the peanut butter is so good! It comes from Holland."

"It probably doesn't have as many mouse turds in it," Mom quips.

"Why do you say that? Does peanut butter in America have mouse turds?"

Mom laughs like a naughty kid.

The P's are in rare form today. I would say they are actually giddy. Finally, we're going home! Carlo confirmed our tickets three days ago and just ordered our beds at the Transit Hotel in Zürich Airport. It will be a horrific trip through five airports, but it's the best CBY Travel can do for us.

André left two weeks ago. We were hoping for a less-stressful itinerary than his, but no luck during a pandemic that has basically shut down air travel completely. At this point we are thankful for anything we can get.

"One thing I am really going to miss about Spain is going shopping," Mr. P says between bites. "I love Benalmádena's little shops. Every day I go in for our fruits and vegetables and say 'hello' to the shopkeeper. For me that is a more normal way of life than driving around the Walmart parking lot looking for a space."

He picks up his iPad and starts scrolling to see what the weather will be for our final days in Spain and whether any new stores or restaurants will reopen before we leave. Mom still wants to go to Zara in Malaga. She's a shopper of a different kind—dresses, scarves and perfume!

"King James the First had three male lovers," Mr. P declares without context.

"What in the world Pennock?" Mom asks as she passes through with a pile of dry towels from the line.

"I just read it on Wikipedia." His face is droll.

"Isn't that the guy who translated the Bible?" I ask.

"He sponsored the translation," Mom corrects. "And he just did that for political reasons. From what I've read he was a bit of a scoundrel."

"Speaking of male lovers," I say setting my phone down and looking at Mr. P, "would you like to work on the next section of your very dramatic life?"

"Male lovers!" Mom exclaims.

"Squaaawk!" the macaw-across-the-way echoes.

"I thought we were done with male lovers and on to the Red Hat Lady," she says planting a smooch on Mr. P's cheek. "Didn't you get the Gospel in the last chapter?"

He swallows a mouthful of peanut-buttery bread while nodding the affirmative. "Yes, I did. But I didn't fully understand how to apply it. And I didn't understand codependency. And . . ." he pauses ". . . I was still missing the rest of the warfare part."

"Well, hurry up!" she huffs dramatically, "I'm ready for you to take me to the South of France and call me Principessa."

"I'm ready too," he agrees. "But first I have to slay a couple of giants in the name of Jesus."

"I'll be in the bedroom talking to Connie then," Mom says. "I've heard some of these stories enough for one lifetime."

Even though my mother knows all of Mr. P's history, it may be as difficult for her to hear certain stories as it is for him to tell them. I watch her disappear into their room with her phone.

Mr. P asks, "Where are we?"

"You had just met Mom for the first time," I remind him. I reach for my laptop as he abandons the peanut butter and moves toward his chair.

"Right. Well, something *really* dramatic happens on my way home from America after meeting my wife who I didn't yet know would become my wife."

He stretches long suntanned legs onto the coffee table, crossing them at the ankles. His daily produce runs have made him as brown as a local.

"Life for me really began in my early forties. I returned from America feeling the true reality of who I am in Christ—a prince seated in heavenly places. My security, significance, and self-worth were no longer like a ship blown about on the ocean of my successes as a singer, a nurse, or a son—or my failures, which were too many to name. What a change this revelation made in my psyche. When I got off the airplane in Zürich I felt light on the inside, excited and hopeful."

Mr. P pauses as I type his last sentence.

"Here's the dramatic part," he repeats. "It's like a movie. I can't believe it's my life. I arrive at Zürich station from the airport to catch my train to Lugano. Guess who is standing on the platform waiting for the same train?"

"Who?"

"Luca."

"The guy you prayed for a year and a half to have back in your life?"

"Yes. Now tell me *that* wasn't a setup from Satan."

"Wow. What did you do?"

"What *could* I do? We were both going to Bellinzona station. I felt trapped by the culture and trapped by the past. I couldn't just pretend he wasn't there. He was Italian—of course he greeted me with a kiss. Six months earlier, I would have embraced him and thanked God for answering my prayer. Instead, I felt his kiss as dangerous as the one Judas gave Jesus in the Garden. My mind raced like crazy as I prayed for an escape."

"You were right, Mr. P. This *is* like a movie."

"He followed me to my compartment. No one else was around. We sat opposite each other and started chatting. He said the very words he'd said before. The words I'd held onto for all those months I was praying and praising God Luca would return to me.

"You know how people flatter with words, right? And when we are empty, the empty words of others seem to fill a void. But now, when Luca said, 'I've never met anyone like you in all my life,' I wasn't empty. I was full of the Word of God after spending all that time with Him. I didn't respond to Luca's comment.

"I wanted to stretch my legs out like they are now, but I dared not give any suggestion of entering his physical space. Not after he just told me he was back in the gay lifestyle. After a while Luca said, 'Let's turn off the light and pull the seats out to sleep.'

"It was nighttime. In European train cars, this wouldn't be unusual. The ticket collector would not be around again for two hours."

"Oh, Mr. P! I'm nervous for you in this story right now," I say.

"Not as nervous as I was in this story back then," he replies. "There we were, two big men side-by-side in the sleeping compartment with the curtains drawn. I knew if I didn't touch Luca nothing would happen. He was an insecure person. He wouldn't risk rejection by initiating anything.

"Satan was at work on my mind as in no moment before or since. I had craved for the person beside me for months and months and here he was.

"I could not sleep the whole two hours to Bellinzona. Against all contrary feelings and emotions, I put my hands together in prayer and said over and over again '*In Jesus I am heterosexual and whole, and I don't need Luca anymore.*'

"That night Luca and all the thoughts about him went out of my life forever!"

"Wheeew!" I let my breath out long and slow. "That was too close for comfort. I was getting nervous."

"I tell you," Mr. P nods his head in agreement, "that experience was my first glimpse of the unseen world of warfare. In the days before cell phones, there was no communication between Luca and me for two years. It was definitely the opposite of a 'God thing' that he *happened* to be on the same station at the same time on the same day as my return from learning about freedom in Christ and meeting your mother.

"I returned home to beautiful Switzerland and for the first time I could enjoy the mountains, trees, flowers, and birds without one ounce of the constant heavy weight I'd carried inside my soul for a long as I could remember. All nature seemed to tell me I was truly alive.

"Someone gave me the book *Dynamite in Praise* by Merlin Carothers. I learned to claim God's promise in Romans 8:28. 'And we know . . ."

I join him in reciting the verse.

". . . that all things work together for the good of those who love God and are called according to His purpose."

"Praise is the most powerful tool in the face of Satan," Mr. P continues. "I praised God in every situation, even the things that didn't seem like blessings. For example, I did date girls once in a while. I'd be sitting in a restaurant with a girl and I'd see a good-looking guy. My emotions would tell me I'd rather be with him than with the girl. At that moment, I praised God that He had made the good-looking guy, but in Christ I was whole and heterosexual and my emotions were an illusion. In that moment, a negative situation became a positive situation.

"We cannot trust our emotions. We must trust what the word of God says, and act on that truth, rather than our feelings. That kind of battle went on many times in many situations until those emotions gradually diminished. Psalm 22:3 became my reality, 'God inhabits the praises of His people.' I felt close to Him as never before.

"Soon after my visit to America I purchased my first car, a hatchback Renault. I was forty-three and very pleased to be the first person in my family to own a vehicle. A great joy in my life was driving to my favorite place in the mountains near Lugano. It is the Verzasca Valley, near Locarno, which I've always called 'My Valley.'

"The magnificent Valle Verzasca became my church. On my days off from work I would sing and pray as I hiked alone to Sonogno, the village at the end, loudly affirming the new man I was in Christ.

"I claimed by faith I was heterosexual. This was a different kind of prayer than all the years before when I would plead from the depths of despair for the Lord to set me free. Now I *was* free, and I could praise God for it until my emotions gradually *felt* that I was free. Does that make sense?"

"Yes. That's faith—the substance of things hoped for and the evidence of things not seen," I reply, quoting Hebrews 11:1.

"Exactly. But the difference for me was my new understanding that it is the faith *of* Jesus, not just *my* faith *in* Jesus that holds the power. Like a child, I place my trust in *His* faith. Some modern translations have the words switched around from that verse in Romans 3:22 or the one in Galatians chapter 2 that says, *'Man is not justified by the works of the law but by the faith of Jesus Christ.'*

"In the Geneva Bible or the old King James Bible (even though King James was as messed up as I was), the translation is correct. It's the faith of my Savior Jesus that makes the difference for me. When I am in Him, *His faith* is mighty to move the mountains and slay the giants."

"It's amazing the difference one word can make, isn't it?" I ask.

"Yes. When I think of all the years I went to church and missed the meaning of righteousness by faith, I feel sad. My life might have been completely different."

"You might not have met Mrs. P, though, if you weren't on a spiritual journey that led you to America."

"That's true. And I wouldn't trade her for anything. I just wish we had met earlier, before all the garbage."

"Do you want to keep telling stories?" I probe as I slide the balcony door closed. "That squawking bird is driving me crazy! You say you will miss the food markets when we go home. What I will *not* miss is that angry macaw! I can barely hear you over his incessant noise. Do you think he's gotten worse since we've been here, or are my nerves just shot?"

"I don't know. I can't hear him so well," Mr. P admits. "I guess that's one advantage of being almost eighty." He laughs. "If you want to keep going, I'm up for the next part. It's the last embarrassing bit and I prefer to tell it when my wife is not around. I wonder what she's doing?"

"Well, my ears *are* really good, and I can hear my sister's voice in your bedroom, so they must be FaceTiming."

"Good," he says. "Let's go on then."

He leans back in his chair and closes his eyes. This is difficult for him, I know. *Who reveals their innermost life struggles to their stepdaughter* (and the rest of the world by proxy)? I don't say anything. I just pray as I wait quietly for him to begin.

"Since my move to Switzerland, Mum was the one who always came to visit me. Year after year she came over without Dad. Of course I enjoyed showing her all the beautiful places, but I secretly wished I could take someone other than my mother to Wengen, Menton, Eze, and Provence.

"On a rare visit to England after about a year of my new walk of faith, someone came into my life whom I call 'The Last Giant.' We met at one of those 'conversion therapy' organization's programs in Sussex, in the town of Battle. The irony is not lost on me that the place renowned for one of the most recognized battles in British history was the place I began a lengthy battle of my own.

"Do tell, Mr. P."

He stalls. Detours. Delays dishing his personal history my direction by sharing mini lesson about William the Conqueror. I wait.

"Every child in Britain knows in the year 1066 the town of Battle, in Sussex was where William the Conqueror killed King Harold of England by shooting an arrow through his eye. As a result the south of England came under French control."

"I don't remember that story."

"You wouldn't. You're American."

I wince, but I know he's right. I slept through European history class. So did a generation of my peers.

"Recently," Mr. P continues, "my nephew Tim did one of those family tree things. He discovered we are direct descendants of William the Conqueror."

"That's interesting," I acknowledge, still rubbing my ego after the American comment.

"God knew I needed some warrior genes to battle the giant that came into my life at that conversion therapy conference," he half jokes.

"Somewhere I'd learned of this ministry that supported people coming out of homosexuality. A lot of these organizations that want to change gay people, they make it about sexual orientation. That's not it at all. It's about becoming like Jesus. Apparently, I wasn't the only one who left disappointed after a series of meetings though, because the organization is now defunct.

"I don't know if it's true or not, but I heard somewhere the leadership went back to their gay ways. I feel very bad for them and everyone else who wanted out but didn't have all the keys. I didn't get anything from their meetings except for a few years of purgatory in a sick codependent relationship."

I punctuate my, "Oh, no!" with a Simon Cowell-style facepalm.

"Oh, yes. And I think I need a cup of tea."

He starts to stand up.

"Don't move, Mr. P. I'll get it."

I make two cups of ginger tea with lemon and honey and grab some shortbread biscuits from the buffet. I normally don't drink ginger tea but feel I might need something stronger than chamomile to get through these next few paragraphs. While I admire his tenacity, sometimes I weep with disappointment for the young Mr. P in this story. After fifteen chapters I am *so* ready for him to walk out his victory. But here we go again, down another rabbit trail that leads to nowhere but heartache. In my own experience I've taken similar detours under different circumstances, but still I have to ask: *Why do we do these things to ourselves?*

"On the first evening of the program," Mr. P begins, "I look around the room. Out of forty young men and a few women, I only notice one guy—Asger, a handsome Swedish medical student with perfect teeth. Later, Asger said he'd surveyed the room and noticed only me. There was an instant unholy connection.

"Oh, Mr. P . . ."

"It was ridiculous," he says. "Like when two drug dealers meet at one of those Anonymous meetings. The demonic attraction was so strong, but it was masked behind a façade of spirituality. Now I can recognize it for what it was—evil spirits, but then all I knew in that moment was nothing and no one else mattered.

"After the keynote speaker finished presenting, Asger came back to my room. We talked into the wee hours about spiritual things and prayed together. I think Satan unleashed everything he could on me. I felt as if I'd found the man I was looking for all my life. I forgot to remember I was no longer looking for a human man; that I was heterosexual and whole."

Mr. P sips his tea, eats a biscuit, and sips his tea again before saying the one sentence we both dreaded.

"Asger spent the night."

"Noooooo!" I shout.

"What's wrong?" Mom hollers from the bedroom.

"Nothing!" Mr. P and I reply in unison.

"When the meetings ended, I numbed with my drugs of choice—travel and photography. I escaped to the village of Chilham in Kent, where the bluebell woods bloomed, and the beauty of the village took my mind off the guilt and shame that would follow me home.

"Asger and I were both believers longing to be free from the emotional bondage of homosexuality. That first night together was the one and only time we crossed physical boundaries. The overwhelming problem was I became more emotionally involved with him than anyone before in my life. For me, it was agonizing to be around him, and agonizing not to be around him. I had never heard the term ‘codependent’, but our relationship was the epitome of *excessive emotional and psychological reliance on another person*—to the detriment of my own wellbeing.

“After our indiscretion, we both repented of our physical sin, but instead of parting ways we continued to communicate on a deep spiritual level. It seems strange now in the days of WhatsApp and the internet, but my relationship with Asger was kept alive by cassette tapes and letters. We recorded ourselves talking and mailed the cassettes. These were mostly spiritual conversations, trying to build each other up by sharing scriptures and spiritual insights.

“A few months later, I visited Asger in Stockholm, where he was studying to become a doctor. When I left him at the station I felt as if all the demons in hell were on my tail, nagging me to throw myself under the train and end it all. After such wonderful, deep conversations and laughs over coffee and cream buns I could not see myself going home alone to my empty apartment.

“For the next five years I was caught up in a codependent relationship with Asger while at the same time growing spiritually as never before. I decided I would add something to my prayers that I’d dared not ask in the past. For the first time in my life, I praised God for the wife I didn’t yet have.

“Whenever I could, I drove the hour-and-a-quarter to the Valle Verzasca, singing praises all the way with the Maranatha Singers in my cassette player. Even though I was emotionally mixed up with a man, I began prayer-walking My Valley thanking God in advance for the wife He would give me.

“During that period Asger came to Switzerland at least twice a year for a couple of weeks at a time. We visited all my favorite places together. I was so emotionally dependent I would get anxious about him leaving even before he came to see me. After he left all I seemed to think about or talk about was Asger.

“I had picture postcards of places we’d been piled up at my door. Every couple of days for years I sent him a postcard with a Bible text or spiritual quote. Somehow, I took it upon myself to be his

Jesus and became obsessed with helping him get free from homosexuality.

"Eventually, I realized codependency was making me sick. Seeking understanding, I saw a psychologist in Lugano for quite some time, specifically about my emotional attachment to Asger. I thought of Asger as my giant—the Goliath I could never slay."

"I understand Mr. P," I respond. "In my Celebrate Recovery group people often say, 'codependency kills.' I'm sure you remember what codependency did to *me* in my first marriage to a husband with a substance use disorder. My addiction to rescuing, controlling, and enabling Jon was as debilitating to me as his addiction to cocaine was to him."

"Exactly. Of course I remember. Your mother and I were very concerned about you."

"Yes, we were!" Mom enters the room in the crux of our conversation. She stands hesitantly near the hallway door.

"Should I leave?" she asks.

"You can stay if you want," replies Mr. P. "We're discussing Asger."

"Oh, the one person in my life I'm sorry I was ever nice to." My mother is smiling, but I know she's telling the truth.

"You know all about Asger from the beginning to the end," Mr. P says reaching for his wife as she approaches his chair.

"I was addicted to Asger," Mr. P cautiously continues as Mom sits between us. "His words of affirmation were like a drug. He would say in his letters how much he loved me. 'There is no one I care for more," he often wrote."

"Oh, brother," Mom sighs.

"In my unhealed insecurity," he explains, "I latched on to Asger's lies as if they were truth. I didn't understand soul ties can be formed through words. I longed for a David and Jonathan kind of friendship. The Bible says *their* souls were knit together."

She leans forward to catch his eye. "You honestly didn't recognize the danger in your relationship with Asger, did you P?"

"Not at first. But my true friends did try to warn me something wasn't right. Once, when I was depressed after Asger visited, Heinz told me, 'That guy needs to go.'"

Mrs. P cheers, "Go, Heinz!" Then she says something profound.

"It doesn't matter if you are having a lot of spiritual conversations or not, if you become more fascinated with the person you are talking to than the Jesus you are talking about, you are on dangerous ground. I've been there. I know.

"And, Mr. P," she continues, "the difference between Jonathan and David and you two is *their* relationship was pure. Despite what gay Christians on the Internet say, there is nothing in the Bible that proves otherwise. No doorways had been opened to the devil through ungodly sexual contact. You and Asger, on the other hand . . ." her voice trails.

"I could never understand why my emotions were so strong with him. It wasn't the same as with my other male friends. Walter and I were very close, but I didn't have the extreme highs and lows I experienced with Asger. Only when he started trying to sabotage *our* relationship did I begin to realize there was something sinister going on."

"It was demons," Mom blurts. "Demons from the doorways you opened that first night you met him *and* seductive spirits that had access to you because of your lack of boundaries. This can happen to anyone, straight or otherwise. A person in a counseling situation or even a deep friendship has to be careful because too much emotional intimacy can lead to unhealthy soul ties. The enemy will try to get in wherever. This is how emotional affairs get started. First, people lose their minds and then their marriages."

"Wait," I say. "Asger sabotaged your relationship with Mrs. P? I didn't realize there was an overlap."

"You met him at our wedding," Mom reminds me.

"Yeah, but I didn't know the back story. You had a lot of gay people at your wedding."

Mom glances sideways at her husband. Shaking her finger like a scolding schoolmarm she chides, "Two of them should *not* have been there. We didn't have a good boundary on that situation."

Turning to me Mom explains, "Our compassion caused us to allow Asger back into our lives even after we were married. We felt sorry for him because his lover burned to death inside a car just before our wedding. He was a wreck and we tried to minister to him."

"So he gave up walking the straight and narrow and went back to male lovers?" I ask.

Mr. P nods. "He did. He lost it. When I first knew him, he was quite spiritual. Ours was a friendship that became sick." He pauses. "But I got better, and he went the other way. It's a shame, really. I had to cut him off when he disrespected my relationship with Susan."

"How did he try to sabotage your relationship?" I ask.

"It's a long story," Mr. P says.

"I have all day. But I'm kind of disappointed because I was hoping to write about your first date before we wrote about someone sabotaging your relationship."

"We can talk about our first date, right P?" Mom asks. "I'll happily take a break from the Asger thing."

"Of course," he agrees.

"Do you remember what I wore on our first date? It's okay if you don't."

"No."

"Do you remember where we went?"

"No."

They laugh.

"We're not doing so well with this story, are we? We went to a Mexican kind of restaurant," she reminds him.

"Dear!" he exclaims. (Mr. P notoriously does not care for Mexican food.)

"We each had a big tortilla thing that's like a bowl," Mom recalls.

Now it's my turn to laugh. "It's called a taco salad," I said.

"That's exactly what we had," she confirms. "We got on like a house on fire."

Mr. P's wit fires back a reply, "Since then the house burnt down."

"Don't describe our honeymoon yet," Mom jokes. "This is just our first date."

He laughs. "I *do* remember our first date was four years after I started sending Christmas cards to the lovely girl in the red hat. Why did we wait so long Mrs. P?"

"You were too far away."

"Yes. And what was I going to do with an American divorcee?"

"I guess you figured that out, didn't you?"

"What were you doing in America?" I ask.

"I was on holiday and seeing some Christian friends. On the last day of my visit I got up courage to ask Susan out for a meal. As we ate together it seemed all we talked about was Jesus. It was evident she loved Him as much as I did. Again, I felt those attraction kinds of feelings, just like when I'd first met her. I'd never experienced anything like that with a woman before."

"Maybe that's why you can't remember what you ate," I joke.

"I never remember Mexican food. You know that."

He turns toward my mother and takes her cheeks in both hands. "What touched me about Mrs. P before she was Mrs. P was her compassion, which she still has to this day."

Mom's cheeks flush pink.

"Thank you, Peedy. It's a gift Jesus gave to both of us. I guess we recognized it in each other. Is that why you told me everything on our first date?"

"I couldn't help myself, could I?"

They hold hands as he tells me the rest.

"As we talked and talked, I realized Susan understood people like me because of her own personal experience with her ex, a codependent friendship, and the deliverance ministry she was involved in. I told her my story and from that moment we started communicating constantly."

"Did you send *her* cassette tapes?" I asked.

"I phoned," Mr. P remembers. "I know because for about three years—until we got married—I used to spend loads of money on the phone bill."

"We mostly wrote to each other," Mom reminds him. "Piles of letters and postcards from foreign places I'd only dreamed about came into my mailbox when I lived in the little house by the stream. My girls didn't know because they were away at school. I kept my Mr. P a secret for a long time.

"Now we are back to the Asger story," she says. "I've forgiven him. But I wasn't impressed with his antics. When Geoff started writing to *me*, Asger stepped up his game and started hassling and sending *him* a lot of cards. Mr. P felt uncomfortable with the sudden extra attention from Asger when he and I had started a relationship. He would forward Asger's postcards to me and talk about the situation because it was bugging him."

"That wasn't right, was it?" Mr. P says. "I felt Asger didn't want me to move on and walk out the healing God was giving me. It seemed like he wanted me to remain stuck and codependent with him somehow."

"I agree," Mom says. "You thought he was your friend, but he didn't have your best interest at heart."

She continues, "People think getting free is all about will power. They ignore the demonic forces. They agree with the lies of the devil and believe them. I'm not one of those people and neither is my Juju." Mom's voice is adamant.

"My daughters were raised in a home where spiritual warfare constantly raged because of the ministry I was involved in. I know what I'm about to say is unpopular in today's culture, but our prayer team ministered to many people who manifested spirits of homosexuality and were delivered by the name and power of Jesus Christ. I knew Mr. P was not battling Asger's flesh and blood, but against principalities and powers and rulers of darkness, as Ephesians 6:12 says."

"I remember a few times when harassing spirits left me," Mr. P recalls. "Your mother taught me not to back down until they let go in Jesus' name. These were things I never heard in churches. I'd learned about the Holy Spirit, but before I met Susan, I knew very little of how to deal with the evil spirits that tormented me for all of my life."

"I remember when I started really battling for you about Asger. It was wintertime and you'd sent me a fat stack of Asger's postcards to pray with you about. I was so mad at the devil for trying to destroy what God was doing. I stoked up my pot-bellied stove down in the basement and started rebuking the devil. I showed him what was going to eventually happen to him as I shredded each card and threw it in the fire.

"One by one I tossed those cards and told the demons to get out of our relationship and out of Mr. P's life in the name of Jesus. I had that fire so hot I thought I was going to burn the blooming house down. I had to wear an oven mitt to even open the stove doors. Satan was not going to have *my* Mr. P!"

For we do not wrestle against flesh and blood,
but against principalities, against powers, against
the rulers of the darkness of this age, against spiritual
hosts of wickedness in the heavenly places.

Ephesians 6:12 NKJV

SAINT PAUL DE VENCE

Chapter 17

HEALING THE FATHER WOUND

Church is too often a place of pretense and therefore a place without hope. When brokenness is disdained, where the real story is never told, the power of God is not felt. Where brokenness is invited and received with grace, the Gospel comes alive with hope.
Larry Crabb

"These are awful! They are bloody awful!"

Mom and I giggle as Mr. P's face contorts after tasting one bite of vegan meatballs from Walmart.

"They aren't so bad," Mom counters.

"Yes, they are. They are the worst thing I've ever eaten in my life!"

The P's are home-sweet-home after our grueling two-day trip from Spain via Zürich, Frankfurt, Chicago, and Pittsburg. Mom dug up some dregs from the freezer for lunch. Apparently, Mr. P is not impressed.

We are exhausted, but grateful to have made it home without incident, which is remarkable given the current chaos in our country. Circulating social media is the viral video of George Floyd repeating, "I can't breathe" for eight minutes as a police officer's knee presses into his neck until Mr. Floyd is forever silenced.

Between rising outbreaks of COVID-19 and escalating violence across every city in America, tensions are at an all-time high in the land of the free and the home of the brave. Our United States is definitely divided over how quickly America should re-open after the pandemic lockdown and if systemic racism is at the root of what is broken. It all seemed surreal as we watched CNN from Spain, but when our white driver told us a black man in a truck pulled a gun on him en route to the airport, things got way too close for comfort.

"I think I'll go up and lie down for a bit," Mr. P announces after lunch.

"Me, too," Mom agrees. "I want to trim my rose bushes, but I'm hurting after yesterday. My bags were too heavy for my crooked little arm to carry through all those airports."

"Are you going to sleep or just rest?" I ask.

"Why?" Mr. P questions as he starts up the stairs.

"Because I want to start writing the next chapter. We need to finish this manuscript during our two weeks of self-isolation. I need to go home to my family as soon as I know I haven't picked up *'Rona'* anywhere."

"How are you beginning the chapter?" Mom asks from the stairwell.

"I was thinking about telling the story of Mr. P forgiving his father," I say to the back of her floral housedress as she trails her tired husband.

"I can . . . *something, something, something* . . ." Mr. P's voice doesn't carry down to where I'm standing at the bottom of the stairs.

"What?"

"He says he can tell that story," Mom interprets. "Come on up."

We settle in their guest room, Mom and I on the bed, Mr. P stretched out on the tiny divan. His legs stick past the end, but he looks comfortable anyway. Better than yesterday's cramped airplane naps.

"Somewhere along the way I realized I must get my relationship with my father in order," Mr. P begins. "The Bible says, '*For if you forgive men their trespasses, your heavenly Father will also forgive you.*'

"I hated my dad all my life. We had nothing in common. He was a footballer. He got medals for football. I cared nothing about ball. It was always me and my mother doing things together. If we went out to the Yorkshire Dales, it was me and my mum," he singsongs. "Never my dad. I've told you these things before," he sighs.

"On the day of my civil wedding to Susan, my mum was crying. Do you remember this Mrs. P?" He continues without waiting for an answer. "When I asked her what was wrong, Mum confessed to weeping because she was emotionally closer to me than to my father and felt she was losing me. That was sick, really sick."

"I do remember. She was jealous of me. She warmed up in the years before she died, but there was always this unseen thing between us. After all you'd gone through, I would have thought your mum might be more pleased you finally had a wife."

"So, I hated my father," Mr. P repeats. "And my mother might have hated him as well, I don't know for sure. She always had to beg him for money to feed the kids and for clothes because he gambled it on dog fights. I think I told you this before."

"Yes."

"My father never came to Switzerland. '*I don't need to go to Switzerland. I've seen the postcards,*' he always said. And for about ten years he never came to visit me. Only my mother did. I'd see him once a year when I would go home for the holidays.

"I don't know if he said this every time, but I certainly remember one incident. I hadn't seen my dad since the last Christmas. I walked in the door. He was in front of the TV watching *Fawlty Towers*. Dad said, '*Don't disturb me now. This is my favorite television program.*'

"I felt that as rejection. I felt very angry. Ignored. Worthless. Of course! I felt like he couldn't give a hoot about me. You don't see your son for an entire year, and you can't even look up from your television program! What is that? I absolutely hated him. I hated him!"

Mr. P's voice chokes with emotion.

"Bitterness toward my father was affecting my spiritual growth. As God broke me free from one spiritual stronghold, I couldn't hold onto another. A Christian counselor said to me, *'You have got to forgive and love your father before he drops dead. You have got to do it. Even if you don't feel it, you have to do it. Love is an act, a decision, not emotion.'*

"Although I did not feel *any* changed emotions, I chose to act on principle and not on feeling. I went home just after Christmas, as always. My dad had gone to bed when I arrived. Although I had no positive emotional feelings toward him in my whole being, I went upstairs to his room. 'Dad,' I said, kissing my father on his bald head, 'I really, really love you Dad, and I wish you would come to Switzerland.'

"He jumped straight out of bed. He pulled two new shirts out of the cupboard and said, 'Your mum has just bought these at Marks & Spencer. Would these look nice in Switzerland?'"

"I wonder what your dad was feeling?" Mom asks.

"I don't know, but he certainly changed. This was the start of a relationship with my dad.

"The following summer, he came with Mum to Switzerland. I took them everywhere—to all my favorite places. In Wengen the Alps are awe-inspiring. Dad was so emotionally touched, he cried going up in the funicular from Lauterbrunnen to Muren. *'I've seen all the photographs of Switzerland,'* he said, *'but I never could have dreamt it were so beautiful.'* No postcard could ever have replaced that moment or induced such a response to natural beauty."

Nostalgia creeps onto Mr. P's face, turning up the corners of his mouth. He draws a long, slow breath before his next sentence hurls my mother into France.

"One of my travel addictions was Menton on the French Riviera."

"Menton! I love Menton!" Mom bursts into the conversation. "Croissants, lemon tarts, the nearby villages," she pauses, "and the *incredible* smell of French fragrances wafting through the air."

"For years," Mr. P continues, "I strung my days off together and went to Menton four days each month. I would leave Lugano by car at 5 AM to miss the heavy traffic around Milan and would be swimming in the sea by 8 AM. I stayed at the same hotel each trip. If they were full, the proprietor put a board and a mattress over the bathtub in an unused bathroom for me to sleep on.

"Historically, Menton was a refined place where the British royalty and Queen Victoria used to go," Mr. P explains. "Later, Charles Spurgeon went there to recuperate from gout. I also used to go to Menton to recuperate—from mental agony.

"I loved walking and praying by the sea. During the year and a half I waited for God to do something about Luca, I chose to go to Menton to pray rather than to go to Florence and be gay."

Geoffrey Pennock cracks himself up. Mom just looks at me and shakes her head. "He's nearly eighty," she whispers. "What can I do? His humor has always been a bit special."

He keeps talking. "Years down the road, I walked by the seaside praying for a wife, but of course I didn't know it would be Susan. When Dad and Mum came to visit, I booked the best hotel on the seafront in Menton. The same hotel *we* stayed in on our honeymoon, Mrs. P."

His eyes sparkle.

"Dad and I would leave my Mum and go walking on the beach. We would sit together by ourselves and have a coffee or an ice cream. This was like a miracle—something I *never* thought I would do with my dad.

"All that joy resulted from my simple choice to forgive, without having any feeling or emotion that I wanted to. I did it for my own sake, really. But after I did, a beautiful relationship developed and continued until Dad died.

"This is the funny part now." His face lights with amusement. "Near Menton is a medieval village, Eze. At the top of the village are some castle ruins and a cactus garden. Dad was tired. Mum and I walked further up the hill to the castle, leaving him to rest on a bench beside the garden gate. My dad put his straw hat on his knee. Tourists thought he was begging and dropped coins in his hat. Always thrifty, Dad never said a word and was quite pleased with the result!

"All this happened when we stayed in Menton. So many happy memories happened in Menton. That's why I love taking my Principessa there."

Mr. P smiles at Mom.

"Oh, I'm Principessa again, am I?"

"You are always my Principessa, P."

"I'm sorry to interrupt your mushiness, but was that the end of your story?" I inquire.

"There's a bit more. Not long after his visit my father had a stroke and was in hospital—dying. I must've taken holiday time to go back to England to care for him. He was unconscious when I arrived. I washed him. Shaved him. Read the Bible to him. I was so glad I was able to do that for my dad.

"I'm thankful I made things right with Dad after hating him for so long. A dear friend, Nicolo had a bad relationship with his father and it was never reconciled. He had a nervous breakdown when his dad died. For me, doing something I did not feel like doing at all really broke hatred's hold and paved the way for me to love *my* father. That was a fairly good story, wasn't it?" Mr. P concludes.

"Yes. Powerful. Thank you."

I save the file and start to close my laptop when he adds something significant.

"People have got to know they need to make things right. If we are trying to get things right with God, we need to get it right with people."

Quickly I reopen the document and type his weighty words. "Forgiveness does not always mean reconciliation or relationship, but it does mean acknowledging someone hurt us and choosing to let go and forgive."

Mrs. P adds her insight. "The Bible says to love our enemies and do good to those who persecute us. I think that means choosing to do something—be it writing a letter, giving a gift, or kissing someone on their bald head. God will show us what is necessary for our situation. Making that choice *does* release forgiveness. It opens the way for the angels and the Holy Spirit to work and breaks the stronghold of the enemy. Bitterness, unforgiveness, and resentment keep us bound to a person in the spiritual realm. When we release them from that bondage, regardless of their response, we are set free."

"I'm proud of you, Mr. P," I affirm.

"That was a long time ago," he says, deflecting compliments as always.

The room falls silent except for the faint tink, tink, tink of the ceiling fan chain against the light. I close my eyes and think about forgiveness. *One thing I find strange is God wants us to ask Him for forgiveness, but we must forgive others, even if they don't ask.*

An hour later Mr. P opens his eyes and reaches for his glasses. They are nestled in a furry footstool next to the divan. Mom is still beside me, sending hilarious Bitmojis to her grandkids from her iPhone. I'm editing previous chapters and thinking about where to go next.

"Ciao, P." Mom waves from across the room.

"Hello."

"When did you get baptized?"

"How do I know?" he answers. "It was a hundred years ago."

"Did you get baptized before or after you made things right with your father?" she persists.

"I thought you got baptized in your twenties," I say.

"I did."

"How many times have you been baptized?" I ask the question simultaneous to opening a new Word document. This may be our next section in Chapter 17.

"Twice. And sprinkled once as a Methodist baby."

"The Methodist's sprinkle?

"Mhmmm."

"I didn't realize that."

"A lot of things in religion don't make sense," he says. "What did I know as an infant?"

"Not a lot," Mom states the obvious.

"What did I know in my twenties when Pastor Henderson baptized me?"

"Didn't you know Jesus?" I ask.

"I wanted to. I mean I knew *something* about Jesus. But mostly I knew about do's and don'ts. I didn't know how much I was loved. I wasn't assured of my salvation. Christianity is the only religion where we can be assured of salvation. John 6:47 says *right now* we can be sure of eternal life. I love this verse in the Amplified Bible. Just a minute. I will read it to you."

He disappears briefly into their bedroom, returning with his tiny New Testament. "'*I assure you,*'" Mr. P reads, "'*and most solemnly say to you, he who believes [in Me as Savior—whoever adheres to, trusts in, relies on, and has faith in Me—already] has eternal life [that is, now possesses it].*'

"What could be more clear or more encouraging than that?" he asks. "Back then I was still trying to manipulate my way to heaven. Obviously, I failed because Pastor Rielly threw me out for saying I couldn't believe being gay was wrong, because God hadn't changed me.

"I spent ages trying to prove the pastor right for crossing my name off the church books. But that whole situation was wrong. I haven't been very impressed with pastors, to be honest. The redemptive thing is, years later he was the pastor who baptized me for the second time."

"The same pastor who threw you out baptized you again?" I question.

"Yes. But what did it all mean? Through all my garbage, I always had some kind of relationship and ongoing conversation with God. When I needed pastoral and church support the most, I was condemned and abandoned."

"Legalism is a really hard one to unravel," Mom says. "Being in your situation was hard to unravel. The healing with your dad was huge. Don't you think you were rebaptized *after* your father passed away?"

"It must have been after that." Mr. P sits up, using both hands to punctuate his words. "I was really seeking God after my father died—God and a wife. My praise and prayer walks in the Valle Verzasca were filled with faith affirmation that God would move the mountain of codependency out of my life and create in me a clean heart. I praised Him for renewing my mind and focusing my thoughts on Him. Sometimes I literally screamed at God to remove every impure thought and to give me the mind of Christ so I would be able to truly love a woman and be a man worthy of a woman's love. Then I praised Him that he had already given me the desire of my heart."

"I remember when you first took me way back into your valley," Mom adds. "No one could ever have a more beautiful prayer closet. May I describe it?"

"Of course."

"We drove as far as possible. Then we walked. That's where I saw a hoopoe bird for the first time. Majestic mountains go straight up into high, high peaks like church steeples on either side of the narrow road."

Mom's hands draw Alps in the air as she talks.

"The raging river on the left is full of rocks and waterfalls and swirling whirlpools. The color of the cold clear water is a light aqua blue."

Mom's word picture jogs Mr. P's memory. "The road trickles into a cart track where I used to walk," he adds. "I never saw anybody back there except for the mountain goats with bells on. At the beginning of my walk with God in My Valley I would scream, 'Set me freeeeee!' After I understood Jesus already set me free when He died on the cross and won victory over my sinful nature, my agonizing prayers changed to praise that echoed off the Alps.

"You shouted to show me," Mom reminds him. "When we went back there together you yelled in that valley so loudly it echoed off the mountains. Your voice came back to us like three times. Hearing your echo was an amazing experience."

"Where can you go to truly get alone with God in this world?" he asks. With tears threatening, Mr. P declares, "In *My* Valley, alone with *my* God is where He transformed my mind. It wasn't anything external. I wasn't instantly changed. But my personal wrestling and sacrifice of praise at the top of my lungs brought lasting transformation.

"Like little David facing Goliath I thought to myself, *God helped me kill the lion of lust and the bear of same sex attraction. Those victories give me faith to kill the Goliath of my codependent relationship with Asger.* I thought like that, you know. You've got to remember what God did in the past. It helps you know what God will do in the future.

"I got the idea to be re-baptized and to make a fresh start in church. Acts Chapter 17 has a verse about how God winks at past sins but calls us to repentance. Let me find it."

He adjusts his glasses and flips pages in his Bible until he finds what he's looking for.

"Verse thirty, *'Therefore God overlooked and disregarded the former ages of ignorance; but now He commands all people everywhere to repent [that is, to change their old way of thinking, to regret their past sins, and to seek God's purpose for their lives].'*

"After all my messing about I was repentant and regretful of the past. I wanted my sins to be washed away in front of witnesses."

"Do you remember who was there?" Mom asks.

"I think my mum might have been there. I was rebaptized in England."

He pauses.

"Dear me! I gave my testimony. Dear me! I think my mother must've lost her false teeth. I was really brave. I think Mum was quite shocked and disgusted with me."

"But didn't you talk with her first? Did she know anything about your struggle?" I ask.

"I don't remember. That was ridiculous. I would not give my testimony anywhere now."

"You sure will." Mom points her thumb toward me. "She's writing a whole book about you!"

"Oh."

There is ten seconds of silence before Mr. P stands and says, "I might have my last shortcake biscuit with a bit of milk."

"Milk?" Mom asks. "Since when do you drink milk?"

"I never do."

"I thought not. What's happening?"

"I don't know."

"Do you need a hug?"

"Maybe."

"I'm proud of you, Peedy P."

Mrs. P puts her arms around her husband. I avert my eyes and let them have their moment.

For if you forgive men their trespasses, your heavenly Father will also forgive you.

Matthew 6:14 NKJV

Hear my cry, O God; Attend to my prayer. From the end of the earth I will cry to You. When my heart is overwhelmed; Lead me to the rock that is higher than I.

Psalm 61:1-2 NKJV

VENICE

Chapter 18

ROMANCE & DELIVERANCE

Each time we pray, we are declaring that the heavenly realm takes preeminence over the natural realm. Develop a heavenly perspective to get heavenly results.
Kynan Bridges

"Ouch!"

"You let them get too long."

"OUCH! I'm very sensitive. I'm not a policeman like my father wanted me to be."

"It's not my fault. You let these grow too long!"

This conversation drifts across the hall from the P's boudoir as I pack my bags for home.

"Dare I ask what's happening in there?"

"She's cutting my toenails. Owwww!" Mr. P groans.

"I'm sorry." Mom sounds like she *really* means it this time. "I always hurt one toe."

"That's the expectation. If there was no blood, I would be disappointed." Mr. P's sarcasm drips like his bleeding cuticle.

"When did you last cut them, P?"

"I don't know. Maybe before we left for Spain."

"No wonder!"

"Have you finished?"

"I hope so. It gets on my nerves to hear you holler. Let me get you a Band-aid."

"I'll get it, Mother. Where do you keep them?"

"Under the bathroom sink."

From the doorway I hand her a medium-sized Band-aid. Mr. P is on his back stretched across their bed, his right foot in Mom's lap as she faces him.

"I might need a damp paper towel," she sighs. "I made him bleed."

"For a change." Mr. P can't turn off the sarcasm.

Returning with a wet washcloth I assess the situation. "I was going to ask if you wanted to tell your falling-in-love story today, but it doesn't sound very lovey-dovey in here."

"I'm fine," Mr. P chuckles. "This *is* my own fault. I waited too long. And you know your mom has a hard time cutting things with her right hand."

"It's true, P. Don't ask me to do this again, please. There are a lot of things I'm good at, but pedicures are no longer my forte. Not since the accident. People look on the surface and don't realize when you've been in an accident you might have a crooked arm or a pushed-in shoulder or a delicate brain."

"I realize, Princess P. I'm sorry." He brushes her cheek with the back of his hand.

"So you two *do* want to tell stories?" I ask again to be sure.

"Yes!" they chorus.

"Should I just come in here?"

"Might as well," Mr. P says. "Seeing as I can no longer walk."

The P's laugh like middle schoolers do when nobody else sees anything funny. Sometimes I forget how old they really are.

I sit on a low velvet chair with my laptop. They lay on top of their sheets, her hand wrapped in his. The room is unusually warm for June.

"When we were young and dating," Mrs. P says, "It was difficult to imagine the day when one P would be too old and stiff to cut his own toenails and the other P would be too crippled to help."

"You're not crippled Mrs. P," he says.

"No, but my arm acts like it sometimes. And everything hurts today. I've worked too hard in the garden after all our travel."

"I'm sorry, Mom. We don't have to do this today if you need to rest."

"This is the best part of the whole book!" Her voice is excited. "What's next? Let's go!"

"Can we tell the story of your first visit to Switzerland?"

Mom doesn't hesitate. "It was May of 1990," she begins, talking directly to Mr. P. "We were really good writing friends. I had empathized with you when your father died, and you comforted me when my Mamaw died.

My mother directs her next words to me. "My grandmother's dying words gave me the go ahead with Mr. Pennock. 'Mamaw, are you okay with Jesus?' I asked. She was. Then Mamaw said, 'You're still single and I don't want you to stay that way. I don't want you to be lonely like I've been. Don't forget that man in Switzerland.'

"That's exactly what she said. And I never did." Mom props herself up on her good elbow and looks directly into her husband's face. "Why did you invite me, P? Two weeks is a long time for a girl to go to a foreign country with a strange Englishman," she teases.

"All we did was talk about Jesus," comes his tender response. "That aroused something in me. I knew I had someone who would never condemn my past. I had strange and unusual feelings. Romantic feelings. I wanted to show my life to you."

"I'm the only one you had these feelings for?" Her tone is almost plaintive.

"Of course. I knew I would marry you, didn't I?"

"Right off?"

"We somehow knew it when we met," he states.

"I think so," she agrees.

"You don't just invite someone from America, do you? Unless you know something."

"You did absolutely everything romantic a girl could dream of. Where did you learn all this stuff? Did you get it from a movie? I have never known *anyone* so romantic."

Mr. P's eyes are closed. He is smiling. Mom dishes the details my direction.

"He greets me at Zürich airport with a huge bouquet of flowers. And a box of Swiss chocolates, of course! He stops along the way to Ticino and buys me something wonderful. Let me show you . . ."

Mrs. P forgets her aches and leaps out of bed. Gently she takes a hand carved wooden box from her dresser. "He bought me this music box," she says, her voice lilting like a happy child. "It plays *Edelweiss* from *The Sound of Music*." Mrs. P winds the key. Sweet notes fill their bedroom with nostalgia.

"It was like a movie, P. You treated me like a princess. For the first time in my life I felt like one."

He chuckles with his lips closed, like he sometimes does.

"This man with an accent who can speak all these languages buys me flowers, chocolates. *and* a music box. Then he takes me to his apartment where he runs the most fragrant bath with bubbles and soaps and smells from the South of France. He puts the flowers in a vase beside the tub and cooks me a fancy dinner."

"Fancy?" Mr. P interrupts. His voice is smiling. "I don't cook fancy."

"You fed me gnocchi with gorgonzola cream sauce. What American girl has *ever* eaten gorgonzola cream sauce?"

She lies down again beside him, their hands automatically finding one another. Mom shares her memories in real-time.

"After our meal we walk to Gandria. Remember, P? I wear that white-bibbed dress with tiny lavender flowers and tie my hair back. My favorite childhood book was *Heidi*. I think I need to look like her since I'm in Switzerland."

"Oh, dear," Mr. P groans.

"It's true," she giggles. "I skip barefoot along the lakeside where all these rich Italians are sitting out on a Sunday evening with their fancy gold jewelry. You heard them making fun of the American Heidi when I went to the loo, didn't you?"

"Yes, I was embarrassed for you. But you didn't know Lugano fashion, did you Mrs. P?"

"I was happily oblivious. I was enjoying the cherubic white angel statues and paintings in your favorite café by the lake."

Mom glances at me and expounds, "We had coffee and Gugelhupf. That became a tradition throughout our marriage. Years later, the owner even gave me the recipe."

She continues in present tense.

"When we get back to his apartment Mr. P asks, 'May I see your clothes?' My dresses hang on the back of his bedroom door. I show him everything I brought. I have several spring outfits he approves of, but when he sees my blue and white pinstriped sailor dress with the big bow on the back he says, 'Do you mind if you don't wear this one and the one you have on?'

"I really liked him. but at that moment I felt tears stinging my eyes. I wanted to go home. His words hurt my feelings and made me angry. I had much to learn about culture. In America, we wear what we want. In Europe—especially Lugano back then, clothing had to be a certain way, mostly black. People were posh. And rich. Women wore fur coats and designer high heels to shop at the grocery store."

"Not like Walmart," Mr. P says. He suffered from serious culture shock when they moved to America seventeen years ago. Still does.

"I'd never lived in a world like that," Mom continues. "Of course Mr. P knew this and was trying to protect me from being made fun of. To me though, it felt embarrassing to have this man tell me what to wear and not to wear. Part of me wanted to run away. Part of me wanted to trust him and stay."

"So you stayed in his apartment?" I raise one questioning brow.

"I *did*. He gave me his bed and politely slept in the living room. Didn't you, P?"

"Sounds like a lack of boundaries to me," I tease.

"He was very proper. He always booked separate rooms. We have a hilarious story about beds on that trip. But first we go to Portofino."

"Portofino," Mr. P sighs. "It's one of my favorite places, you know. For years I would go to some isolated village and walk all down through the olive groves to Portofino and think I was in heaven. The only thing missing was my angel."

He's talking in a certain tone, which like my Mamaw's china, is reserved only for special occasions. Going down memory lane with Mrs. P is obviously a special occasion because his voice is warm with emotion.

"On that first trip, I took her to some of my most cherished travel spots—Portofino, the Cinque Terre, and Venice. Places I went alone for years. Special places I dreamed of taking a wife to one day as I wrestled with God in the Valle Verzasca, saying like Jacob, *'I will not let You go until You bless me.'*

"Portofino," he continues, "must be one of the most beautifully situated spots on the earth with its picturesque harbor and pastel houses. It was wonderful before Rick Steves ruined everything with his travel books."

"It's true," Mom agrees. Back then, model-looking women with straight blonde hair and designer sunglasses sat out at little tables looking all posh. Now big boats dump loads of German and Brit lookalikes in their shorts and tennis shoes, the men and women undistinguishable with the same haircuts. That changes the atmosphere somehow, doesn't it, P?"

"Mhmmm. It ruins quaint places to have loads of tourists pouring in," he agrees.

"I think I was the only tourist on the day you kissed me in Portofino."

Mom has the bird face. She is also enjoying memory lane.

"Wouldn't I have been too shy to kiss you in Portofino?" he teases. "So soon after your arrival."

"You were not acting shy at all. Not. At. All. You kissed me. I remember everything. The music—everything."

Mom props herself up to look at me as she says, "Literally, a whole orchestra is on a very large boat playing this overwhelmingly beautiful music as they come to dock. It *was* like a movie set. As we cross the piazza Mr. P begins singing *When I Fall in Love.* Back then his voice was still strong . . ."

In real time, Mr. P starts crooning about moonlight kisses. Mom joins him, their voices blending as they serenade me with their first and favorite love song.

"A kind handsome man was singing to me in public. I was bowled over!" Mom continues her story. "What girl can even take all of this? A man might do *one* of these things, if you're lucky—two. You did it *all,* P. You did it all."

"And then he kissed you?" I lead.

"Not yet. We hike to the top of the cliffs, under the olive tree. *Then* he kisses me. And, Mr. P, it was a proper kiss. Not some shy peck."

"Ooooh! Mr. P." My voice is playful. "What was happening?"

"What was happening?" Mr. P sits up in bed with his back against the red wall. "No woman had ever caused me to turn my head, and say to myself, *Oh, isn't she beautiful!* But with Susan, God placed a *very, very* special attraction inside of me just for her. I've never felt that way toward any person before or since.

"She awakened boyhood dreams of the women I found attractive from films and acting. American boys may have collected baseball cards. As a child *I* collected cards of famous actresses like Deborah Kerr and Doris Day—classy women, not the trollopy kind. Susan reminded me of the me I was before I wasn't me at all. I was absolutely smitten."

"You weren't the only one," Mrs. P recalls. "But Portofino was just the beginning. Next, we go to the Cinque Terre. Right, tour guide?"

"Yes, but we stayed in Sestri Levante, remember?"

"Of course. Where the funny bed story happened.

"Between the two of us," she explains, "we had five beds in a typical Italian family-run hotel. He had three beds and I had two beds. When Geoff booked us in, the whole clan was sitting around a large table preparing to eat. He said to the proprietor in Italian, *'We need two rooms, please, because I snore.'*

"We looked at each other and I got the giggles. Then *he* got the giggles and we giggled until we were giddy. The Italian family, even the grandma, heard everything. We had to walk past them to get to the stairs. I was laughing so hard by the time we got upstairs I slid down the wall to the floor. I felt forty-one going on fourteen. We weren't *ready* to sleep together. We weren't *going* to sleep together. But we had *so* many beds to choose from."

It's Mr. P's turn.

"The next day, I took her on my favorite walk in the whole world—the path from Monterosso to Vernazza in the Cinque Terre. Once an area of unspoilt beauty, this path is high above the sea among terraced vineyards."

"It's a dangerous walk. People have died falling off the trail," Mom interjects.

"It *is* a dangerous walk. I don't know if I could do it now," he says. "But I prayerfully walked those seven miles for many years—usually in the autumn or spring before it became overrun by summer visitors. That spring, I had a visitor of my own, didn't I?" He glances at Mom.

"She skipped barefoot along the narrow path ahead as I walked and sang my usual praise songs. She was like a curious child, smelling every flower. She even peeked through the keyhole in a green door. I thought she was lovely, and funny, and unique."

"You did, P?"

"Of course I did. You still are lovely and funny and unique."

"Awww. I'm going to call you 'the *mushy* P's,' I tease. "Where did you go after Vernazza?"

"I took her to Venice. It was a surprise. She screamed out when she realized where she was."

"I couldn't help myself! There was nothing I'd ever seen in a book or a film or my own imagination that could have prepared me for Venice! I wrote the entire experience in my diary. Should I read it?"

"Sure, if you want."

My mother . . . the closet writer. She keeps journals and diaries and fills little notebooks with detailed stories of her adventures in real life and imagination. Disappearing for a moment and returning with a hardback journal, covered in marbled Venetian paper, Mrs. P props herself up on pillows and begins to read. These are her words. I've only changed the tense.

> *We are awake at 4 o'clock in the morning. We drive to Desenzano del Garda, a small resort town near Lake Garda. From there, we catch the train to Venice, but I don't know where I'm going.*
>
> *Ten minutes before we arrive, Geoff says, "Keep your eyes closed."*
>
> *I kept my eyes shut tight all the way over the long bridge leading to Stazione di Venezia Santa Lucia. I take his arm as he guides me through the station and down the stairs until we reach the Canale Grande.*
>
> *I gasp and cry out at such an unbelievable site! I'm amazed by the old-world architecture and an entire city with each edifice standing in water. Built on wooden piles, Venice was once a fortress against the enemy. A wonderful city without roads, only water canals. I stand fascinated, watching the boats carry produce and other goods up and down the canal.*
>
> *What a totally exhilarating and new experience! We walk the narrow streets, crossing over arched bridges that intersect. At one surprising moment, Geoff sends me off to the other side of the canal via gondola. He takes photos of me crossing the 'street.'*

As we walk along, I stop to buy gifts for family. The shops are an amazing exhibition of fine workmanship–leather bags, works of art, and handmade designs, all high-end, like I have never seen. The Italians take pride in fashion. I am totally fascinated with the beautiful scarves, clothes and multicolored Murano glass sparkling in shop windows. Geoff presents me with a lovely tapestry handbag. The spoiling has truly begun.

We stay overnight in the Albergo Marin, a quaint inn on a back calle. Geoff booked separate rooms, next-door to each other. Whenever he wants my attention, he taps on my window with his umbrella.

"Madame, how are you doing?" he asks.

His umbrella tap, tap, taps many times. What a very funny way to speak and get acquainted. I lean out. He leans out. We can nearly touch, but we don't.

The train is on schoporo (strike). With the shut down, we end up stranded in Venice for three days!

This English man has a great accent and crazy humor. He says, "Hi, babe," in a silly low voice in his effort to sound American. I can't help but laugh.

Day Three

We take a boat to the island of Burano. On this island, the old ladies sit outside multicolored cottages making intricate lace tablecloths. The atmosphere is one of happy people, content with their work. As we pass, one woman has all her furniture out of the cottage. The dear signora is singing and scrubbing with such joy.

We walk, shop, take pictures, and eat fabulous melanzane alla parmigiana, manicotti, and slices of pizza. I'll never forget the ensalata mista and the tiny side dishes of assorted olives.

We turn a corner, and a pianist is playing the most beautiful music. Suddenly, I feel overwhelmed—like I am in a movie. Geoff and I start laughing. Yes, falling in love.

In the evening back in Venice, I notice people are dressed up. Their children too, even though they are playing.

Geoff takes me to San Marco Square, where we have the most expensive cioccolata calda ever, like 10,000 Lire each! An orchestra is playing, and the view of the San Marco church is awesome with its grandeur! We stay out late, talking and looking at each other. Deep in my soul I know we are meant for one another.

"I'm crying." Mr. P wipes his eyes. "I'm there with my Principessa. We must hold onto these memories because Venice isn't Venice anymore. It's absolutely dead. I just read on CNN Travel that Venice is supposed to reopen next week, but who will go?"

"It's true," Mom says. "Nothing is the same after this pandemic. We love too many Italians. It hurts to see what they are going through. I will never forget the videos of them singing off their balconies during the lockdown. In Spain, we clapped. In Italy they sang opera."

"That's Italia! Who knows when tourism will ever pick up?" Mr. P sniffles softly.

"I'm so glad we had our romantic Italian moments, P. Don't you have some bits that *you* wrote during our first visit to Venice?"

"I must have, but I don't know where they are."

"I do," Mom says, vanishing again. She returns with a small stack of pages, written in Mr. P's blue ink script.

"Do you want to read anything before I give them to her?" Mom asks.

"No."

"Looks like these have been ripped out of something," I say as she hands me the papers.

"They have. I don't know why he destroyed his journal, but this is what's left."

"It was too personal," Mr. P remembers. "Some things you don't want your grandkids to read after you die. When you're as old as I am, you think of these things."

He laughs.

"That's not funny," Mom says with a pouty lip. "Don't leave me, P."

I scan his notes and find just what I'm looking for.

"Listen to this," I say. "Unless you want to read it, Mr. P."

"Go ahead."

> *The railroad workers are striking. I'm starting to have intense feelings I never had before. I have been to Venice a lot of times with a lot of different people, but this is an entirely a new emotional experience. We seemed to laugh and really enjoy being together. I know I am going to propose one day. She has a beauty on the outside for sure, but it is the beauty on the inside and a deep, deep love for Jesus that makes her different from anyone else I have ever known.*
>
> *After three days, the train strike is over, and we return to Switzerland. After just one week alone with Susan in Europe, I know one day she will become my wife.*

"I'd forgotten you wrote such lovely things, P. Venice is where we knew, that we knew, that we knew. Isn't it?"

"Yes."

"This is good stuff, P's. What else do you have?"

Mom is flipping through her journal.

"I just have the part about when I called him, 'Honey.' That sure opened a can of worms, didn't it, Mr. Pennock?"

"It did. Do you have that all written down?" he asks.

"Every word."

"Oh, dear! That's quite a dramatic story, isn't it?"

"Can I hear?" I ask. "Do I know this story?"

"I don't think you do. It's not one we usually tell over dinner."

"Is it important for the book?" I ask.

"Yes," both P's agree.

"Please do share."

"Okay, but let's explain a few things first," Mom says. "This is our last adventure before I return to America. He takes me to Wengen in the Swiss Alps." Like P's father, I also became emotional riding the cog train straight up the mountain. It's hair-raising and breathtaking with the Jungfrau stark above us and the valley dropping steep below."

"I think my dad rode the cable car on the *other* side, not the cog train," Mr. P recalls. "Both views are incredible!"

"And that crisp clean air! It was all so romantic," Mom sighs. "You took me to that little inn where I ate fresh, creamy fondue for the first time."

"With the band playing!" Mr. P remembers.

"Oh the music! *Everywhere* we went that trip, music filled the air like he'd planned every detail."

"I think God planned the details," Mr. P says. "I've gone to all those places for years and never heard such beautiful music—playing as if on cue. Didn't we stay at the Hotel Eden?"

"Yes. My room was lovely with lace curtains like I have downstairs, and large pink roses on my duvet. There were two heart-shaped chocolates on my pillow. Since you had your own room, I got to eat both! Everything seemed too perfect."

"But that's Switzerland. Everything *is* perfect," Mr. P says. "Except for the prices."

"I even remember the window box filled with violets. I could see their purple heads from my bed. The grand finale was a giant fireworks display with the echoes reverberating off the Alps on each side of the valley!"

Mom pauses and again leafs through her journal.

"There was another fireworks display," she says cautiously. "Everything was perfect for the whole two weeks except for two things that caused tension between us. I moved on from the Heidi-dress-thing quite quickly. Now it's the end of the trip and something happens that really upset me. I wrote everything down. And I think you are holding P's version in that stack of papers in your hand."

"Read yours first," Mom.

"I'll start with the part just after Venice."

> *Romantic and intimate moments brought us closer together than ever. Dizzy as teenagers in love, yet adult enough to know we are on the same spiritual page.*
>
> *We went to the Lauterbrunnen Valley. The air smells clear and invigorating. We walk hand in hand along the narrow path. "Honey!" I exclaim, "This is the most beautiful view I have ever seen!"*
>
> *He releases my hand and turns his hands upward in an effeminate gesture saying, "No one ever calls me, 'Honey.'"*
>
> *I stop and turn to face him, confused. "I am from the South! Everybody is 'Honey'. For me not to say 'Honey' would be like cutting my tongue out."*
>
> *We retreat from one another. I to pick flowers in the meadow, and he to continue walking.*
>
> *I walk alone by a giant crashing waterfall, picking alpine flowers in the glistening green meadow. God, of course, can hear my prayers above the noise of the water. I always feel nearer to God up high, surrounded remarkable beauty.*
>
> *I walk back to sit on a bench beside a quaint old church.*
>
> *I'm thinking about Geoff's reaction to me calling him Honey, realizing there is a bad spirit in operation—possibly from an ungodly soul tie with another person. Immediately, righteous indignation wells up inside me.*
>
> *"God," I pray, "I know this man loves me, but there's something not right here. I sense a strange spirit.*

I am falling in love with him. But, before we can go one step further down the path toward marriage, he needs to be set free from the soul-destroying force that manifested itself a few minutes ago.

'What I saw was nothing like the man I've recently spent three days with in Venice. It was as if something else came over him the moment the word 'Honey' slipped from my lips. Please reveal to me what is going on here."

The Holy Spirit impresses my mind that because of relationships Geoff had in the past, the enemy entered his life through ungodly doorways. I know he loves God and wants to be free of all bondage from the past. Because I love him, I fight for his soul. In my heart, I realize whether or not anything further becomes of our relationship, I know enough about spiritual warfare and care enough about this man I will fight for him in the spiritual realm.

Looking around, I notice I am alone. I begin to speak aloud, "In the name of Jesus I rebuke all evil spirits harassing and afflicting Geoff in any way. I rebuke in the name of Jesus all spirits of homosexuality, and all who came because of soul ties formed through ungodly relationships. I break these ties in the name of Jesus."

Mom stops reading. "That's all I have."

"That's a lot. Thank you. Very, very powerful. And you were right. Mr. P's version *is* here. I think he should read it."

I hand Mr. P's journal pages back to him. He reaches for his glasses and reads.

I walked with God along that familiar path, feeling unfamiliar feelings and processing my reaction to Susan calling me 'Honey.'

Jesus, there is a story behind that word! There is a five-year bondage behind that word! His name is

Asger. I want to be completely free from any reaction that has anything to do with Asger or anyone else I have had feelings for, or unholy relationships with.

Walking and praying in all that beauty, I realized I had another beauty coming into my life. For the first time in my life, I realized I was falling in love with a woman who radiated beauty inside and out. God was always with me in the mountains when I was alone with him. Now, instead of the sick codependent feelings I had before, I was here with someone who related to God and to me in a true and wonderful way.

I sang out loud like always, "Praise, my soul, the King of heaven . . . ransomed, healed, restored, forgiven." The verses were my prayer. I walked and praised Jesus' name that my years of longing for death were over and new life—with death-to-self was starting to happen.

As I turned to walk back toward the woman who would become my wife, the oppression physically left me. I immediately felt lighter, freer. My feet moved faster and faster until I was almost running back to the bench where she sat. Praising God, I sank down beside her trying to catch my breath.

"Something has just happened," I puffed. "I felt something leave me!"

There, in what must be the most beautiful scenery in the world, God set me free!

And I will give you the keys of the kingdom of heaven, and whatever you bind on earth will be bound in heaven, and whatever you loose on earth will be loosed in heaven.

Matthew 16:19 NKJV

MR. AND MRS. P, 2020 SPAIN

VERNAZZA, CINQUE TERRE

Chapter 19

AFFAIRS TO FORGET & REMEMBER

In no way does scripture ever speak of healthy people to stop working. Nowhere do we see that in God's design for productive minds and bodies to perpetually lie on a beach, ride on a golf cart or sit on a fishing boat. The entire concept of saving money so we can live a life of ease and self-indulgence has no Biblical concept whatsoever.
David Platt

Let my heart be broken by the things that break the heart of God.
Bob Pierce, Founder of World Vision International

"It's your son. He's calling to wish you a happy Father's Day."

Mrs. P hands the phone to her husband. His face lights up as he puts it to his good ear. "Come stai figliolo?"

"Now *that's* a story," Mom says as Mr. P disappears into the other room, his free arm gesturing like a mafioso at a family reunion.

"It is. Who could understand why an old white Brit and a young black Eritrean would always communicate in Italian?"

We are just finishing dinner. It's been a quiet Father's Day—just me and the P's. Self-quarantine is over. Nobody here has COVID. *Thank You, God!* In a few days I'll rent a car and drive home to My

Honey. But first we need to get these P's married in the manuscript. Two exciting chapters to go!

Mom and I clear the dishes. She puts the kettle on for tea.

"Did you hear the story about Black Lives Mattering?" Mr. P asks after ending his phone call.

Mom sets his tea and a raisin scone in front of him. "Which story? That's all the news talks about lately. Makes me worry about our Moses. Is he alright?"

"He's fine. All *he* talks about lately is the Bible. He believes Jesus is on His way."

"What's your story Mr. P?" I implore.

"Black lives matter to *me*," he says between bites of scone. "I have a black son."

"You have two black sons," Mom reminds him. "One Eritrean, and one Ethiopian."

"How did *that* happen, Mrs. P?" His eyes dance with mischief. "My wife's skin is so fair." He finishes his tea before telling us the story.

"In all the years I traveled to Italy I never saw one black person, not one. When we went to Bari to share the gospel in 2006, refugees from northern Africa were just starting to pour in."

"They came by the thousands on boats from Libya," Mom states.

"I remember. The most haunting photo showed drowned refugees' clothing strewn along the shores of Lampedusa after an overfilled boat fell apart."

"Italy didn't know what to do with them," Mr. P continues. "I phoned every embassy trying get them some help. The boys left the refugee camps with nothing. Your mother and I had compassion on the ones sleeping in Bari Park. She started conversations with them. We got to know their stories."

"It was cold. They were sleeping on park benches, cold and hungry," Mom adds. "We couldn't stand it. We had to do something. We helped them as best we could. Mr. P gave his own shoes to one boy."

"I'd go to the park before church and get them," he says. "Sixteen black boys crossing the street to the coffee bar. It was very unusual. They would normally be ignored. But I shouted loudly in Italian, 'I want sixteen cappuccinos and sixteen brioche for the refugees who sleep in *your* park!"

He chuckles with the memory.

"I took them to church. People stared. People acted strange. The church was not warm and friendly toward them. One night it was freezing—freezing outside! These guys were sleeping on the ground or on benches in the park. I couldn't stand it. Couldn't sleep knowing about it. I left your mother and went to the park and got them all. I sneaked them into the basement of the church where it was warm, and I slept there with them."

Mom's eyes spark. "Mr. P got in big trouble with the church. Oh, they were nasty! It's a long story. We could write a whole book just about our work with refugees."

"Two of them adopted us as parents. That's why I have a black son who wishes me Happy Father's Day in Italian.

"Black lives mattered to *us*. Just not to the church people. I can hate religion and have no respect for religious people because a lot of it is just a load of crap. Religion and legalism could have destroyed me completely."

He's getting worked up now. I feel a rare Mr. P rant coming on.

"You go to a new city, you go to church, and get nothing but 'hello' and 'goodbye,' and 'Have a good week.' You leave as empty and lonely as you came. But you hear there's a gay bar in town . . ."

He pauses. Shrugs both shoulders. Fights tears.

". . . Christians *love* to condemn homosexuality, but the worst sin may very well be religiosity. I could be dead from AIDS and gone to hell if it were up to pastors or religion to help me. I felt the same about those boys. They could have frozen or starved to death and nobody cared. The so-called Christians just passed by the park on their way to church and sang the same old hymns, prayed perfunctory prayers, and did nothing to help their brothers in need. It brings out anger in me!"

"I see that, P. You have tapped the old suffering," Mom empathizes.

"This is why people give up and lose it when they don't understand the Gospel or have their own deep relationship with Jesus. They expect church to be this warm, loving, safe, healing place. It's not. Only Jesus can be all of that. Our job is to introduce people to Him and to love them. We can expect nothing from 'the church.' We must *be* the church.

"My adventurous traveler's spirit *has* been used for God," he continues. "I only feel powerful when I'm 'out there' doing something for Him. Jesus commanded us—not to sit in church pews, but to "*Go!* and make disciples." When we are on fire for Him and making disciples, we become less selfish and more like our Savior. I cannot just sit around and grow old in my rocking chair. Every day my prayer is the same as John Wesley's on his eightieth birthday, *God don't let me live to be useless.*"

"Mr. P," I declare. "You are *not* useless. Your life is a testimony and an inspiration. Your willingness to go to foreign places and share Christ with individuals is amazing. I mean, you spent your 79th birthday on *lockdown* overseas, waiting for the borders to open in a country where it is forbidden to proselytize."

"The irony is," he responds, "there are two things a person can do to risk immediate imprisonment in that country: act out homosexuality and share the Gospel."

Insert dramatic pause.

"In my life before, when I was a different kind of 'fisher of men' I took great risks to act out my own selfish desires. Why would I not take a great risk now to share the good news about Jesus with someone who is lost? How can I ignore statistics in a place where one person in 10,000 is a Christian?" he questions. "Do I take no notice? Just sit here in America where nearly forty people in a hundred are already churchgoing believers and everyone else has a praying grandmother? I'm still upset we were blocked from reaching an unreached people group because of this pandemic."

"Mr. P," I reiterate, "what I want you to understand is *even* if you aren't in a remote village somewhere, you are *still* sharing the Gospel. You sacrificing your privacy to write this book is huge. If you never leave your chair again, I am sure there will be people in Heaven because of the way God will use your testimony."

He removes his glasses. Wiping his eyes he says, "I hope so. I really hope so, because I have *suffered.* So much. But it will be worth it if just *one* person doesn't have to go through all the valleys I've been through."

Mrs. P wraps her arms around her husband, comforting him with quiet compassion. After a few moments he returns his glasses to their place on his face. She takes her seat at the table.

"Speaking of going through valleys, are you two up for talking about what happened after the Lauterbrunnen Valley deliverance session?"

They look at one another.

Silence.

"What?" I ask.

"We spoke about this last night in bed," Mom says.

"Something evil *did* leave me that day," Mr. P reiterates. "There is no question."

Mom nods. "Absolutely. But that wasn't the end of the story because there are some things we learned later that could have been helpful—deeper things about ungodly soul connections."

"And boundaries," he adds.

"Yes! Boundaries. Or a complete lack thereof," Mom declares.

They chuckle.

"So, what's the secret P's? I can tell you're hiding something."

"We were planning to hide something. No, that's not right," Mom corrects herself. "We have nothing to hide. We were just not planning to share this next part with the readers. It's very personal for Mr. P. And quite frankly, I'm tired of talking about Asger."

"So . . . ?"

"So, we discussed it last night and decided to tell the *whole* story," she says. "I even found a bunch of letters and cards that might be helpful."

"It might help *somebody,*" Mr. P affirms.

"I'm proud of you, P's. Let's go for it."

"You don't just wake up one day healed one hundred percent. At least that wasn't my experience. This whole thing about coming out of these kinds of sins is like overcoming anything. In your relationship with God you grow, you mature—you leave it behind. I had come out of something, but I had no idea what I was going into. And no idea how the devil was going to try to ruin everything.

"After Susan left Switzerland," he pauses. "I never call you 'Susan' do I?"

"No."

"That sounded strange."

"And after all that palaver about calling you 'Honey,' I never call you 'Honey,' either, do I?"

"No."

"Ever since we became 'The P's,' we only call each other 'P,' although *sometimes* I am 'Mrs. P' or 'Principessa.'

Mr. P tries again, "After Susan left Switzerland, she wrote me a card. I kept it in my Bible for years."

He goes to the desk and shuffles through some papers.

"Here it is."

"*Sir,*" he reads. "*I've enjoyed acting in this movie of life with you. I know the heavenly audience has enjoyed it as well. I will repeat—you are the most romantic man I have ever known. A super classy guy! I won't ever be the same after my adventures with an Englishman. I will carry the good times in my heart. I will praise God for the victories won and always keep you in my heart and prayers.*"

"That's really sweet P," Mom says. "I didn't know you hung on to that. Guess what I found upstairs?"

"What?"

She unfolds a three-page front and back handwritten letter.

"You wrote this just after I left Switzerland. It's dated May 14, 1990."

Mrs. P proceeds to read the whole letter aloud. I'll include a few paragraphs here:

> *Madam,*
>
> *How ya doin,' babe? This macho man is jus a doin' fine!*

"That's how he talked to me when he wanted to sound 'American,'" Mom laughs.

> *I'm on my way back from Geneva from staying with Massimo (the friend who helped me spiritually early on) and his wife. He was crying with laughing at our five-bed story. I smile often to myself during the day thinking about it all. God was certainly with us in a very big way.*
>
> *Months ago, when I last saw them it was all about Asger. Now it was all about Susan. You are all I talked about! I had to ask myself often, 'Is this really me?' My friends are in such shock they may have to go to the psychiatrist. They ask me so many questions. I'm enjoying it!*
>
> *I'm on the train. It's six hours journey, then I have the psychologist and art class. Last week I did ink for the first time. I have drawn a picture of "My Valley" from one of my photos in pencil and I will do it in ink tonight. I have no idea how to do trees and the leaves falling on the ground. I was really into it last Monday, like someone who was in love!*
>
> *How are you feeling at this moment, madam?*
>
> *I have studied about and read every book I could get my hands on for years—about healing. I am 100% sure in my mind that healing is included in the atonement and that it is in the nature of God*

that all should be healed (even though for some reason, all aren't). There are two things I can argue on until the cows come home and not budge an inch. One is justification and the other is healing. (I am on a spiritual and emotional high at the moment. Can you tell?)

I am claiming God's full healing and I will not take 'no' for an answer. This, I believe, is Biblical.

After I left you at the Zurich Airport, I had the nicest salad, chicken curry sandwich and rhubarb tart.

I'll close. I miss you, madam.

God bless.

Much love, Geoff

P.S. When the maple leaves do fall, I will give to her my all!

(Oh, dear! What am I saying?)

"It was difficult to be alone again after she was gone," Mr. P recalls. "I missed her laughter and her prayers and waiting for her to titivate before we could go out. I missed her dresses hanging on the back of my door and the way she noticed all the beautiful details in everything I took for granted. I filled my time with work and with planning an autumn proposal in America. All my friends who met Susan approved and encouraged me about moving forward with plans to marry her.

"I still sent spiritual postcards to Asger, wanting him to have the same experience with Jesus and the same freedom I was finding, but I didn't wait by the post for his responses as eagerly as I used to.

"When I told Asger I planned to propose in October, I felt he seemed envious. He came to see me in September and wanted to go to the Cinque Terre."

"Here's where a boundary was necessary, but nonexistent," Mom interjects.

"I didn't think anything of him coming to visit. Ever since I moved to Switzerland, I had visitors come and stay with me. I'd take them around. Two good gay friends from my Bournemouth hospital days often came on holiday through the years. So when Asger wanted to come over, it felt normal. He'd come to Lugano at least twice a year for a long time. I really believed we were friends. After all my struggles, I thought he would be happy for me to have found a woman I loved and wanted to marry.

"I realized though, each time I talked about Susan, Asger would get jealous and act strange. By this time he had left the road of believing there was a way out and had a boyfriend. We still had *what I thought* was a close friendship and deep spiritual conversations.

"I had fought for years to get Asger emotionally out of my system and I'd experienced something leave me when Susan and I were praying in Lauterbrunnen. But I hadn't been around him since that happened. And I wasn't in the habit of practicing good boundaries.

"We went to the Cinque Terre and spent one night in Vernazza. The place we stayed overlooked my favorite footpath through the vineyard to Monterosso.

"Unlike when Susan visited, I hadn't booked two rooms with five beds between us. To save money, I'd booked one room, thinking it didn't matter that we stayed together. We weren't lovers. And we'd often shared a room when he visited. When we arrived, there was *one* bed between us.

"We shared the bed. Asger always slept in pajamas. That night he slept nude. When I realized he was trying to seduce me I felt small, like David facing the taunting Goliath. I knew what Asger and Satan wanted. After years of walking the straight and narrow, I was not interested in going backward. I prayed, *Thank You God I am heterosexual and whole.*

"I turned my back to Asger. Through the window in the moonlight I could see the footpath. This makes me cry . . . I saw a vision of my Principessa skipping up the hillside in her bare feet like she had in the spring.

"My emotions were with her."

His voice breaks. Tears flow.

". . . and not with the person beside me, upon whom I'd been emotionally dependent for years. In that moment I *knew* my giant was slain.

"Early the next morning I swam in the Vernazza harbor, praying, and praising God for the proof my love for Susan was stronger than my codependent relationship with Asger.

"Goliath died in the Valley of Elah. My giant died in Vernazza. I wrote the date in my Bible. See those two photographs on the wall? Valle Verzasca and Vernazza. Now you know the story behind the pictures. Once you win that first victory, with temptation in your face, the next, and the next are easier."

"After that you clung to God with an even stronger kind of faith, didn't you?" Mom asks.

"Yes. That victory strengthened me."

Her head bobs in agreement. "Would you believe I found a Vernazza postcard in our box of cards upstairs?"

"I didn't know you kept all of these cards and things for three decades and a hundred moves!"

Mrs. P hands him a postcard with an aerial photograph of the sun shining on Vernazza Harbor. On a tiny lavender sticky note, in Mom's cryptic cursive are the words, *emotional and psychological shift.*

Mr. P is overcome with emotion as he reads aloud his own words from thirty years ago.

> *The Giant Died on Sabbath, September 15,1990.*
>
> *In this harbor as I was swimming, I felt the presence of God at that moment as, "He reached down from on high and took hold of me; he drew me*

out of deep waters. He rescued me from my powerful enemy, from my foes, who were too strong for me. They confronted me in the day of my disaster, but the Lord was my support. He brought me out into a spacious place; he rescued me because he delighted in me. Psalm 18:16-19 NIV

He used the place I loved the most to do the thing I needed the most. He is beautiful.

"The hairs on my arms are literally standing up and I have goose bumps. I felt God's power and presence again as you read that," I say.

"He *is* beautiful," Mr. P repeats once he composes himself. "I'm so glad you found this, Mrs. P."

"I have another card you wrote to me dated 9-30-90, just two weeks later. You must have mailed it right before you got on the plane to come over and propose because I found a receipt for our wedding rings, purchased in America on October 2."

"What does it say?" he asks.

She reads:

Hi. (No Englishman ever says 'Hi.')

It's 2:30 AM and I can't sleep. (As you know.) I have now taken another pill. I shall be like a zombie at work.

My workmates are used to my psychological disturbances, but they have never been caused by a WOMAN before!

I can't believe I'm coming to America! I always take a sleeping pill on the plane—otherwise one is too excited and it's impossible to sleep."

"You were so excited you couldn't sleep. And neither could I. I cleaned my little house from top to bottom, especially the basement bedroom where you would stay. This would be the first time I allowed you into my world. I was absolutely over the top proud of my 'secret Englishman' and I wanted my girls to meet you. I felt anxious about what they would think about you."

"I didn't know you had those feelings. I thought your girls were lovely."

"Why thank you, Mr. P," I say. "We thought you were a hottie, even if you *were* old. Funny how I'm a year older than you were then, and I don't think I'm old at all. I actually texted my sister today and asked her what she remembers about you from that visit. She was only sixteen, you know."

I scroll through my texts to find what Sis sent. "*I thought he was witty, sharp and comical. He had good taste in shoes and locales. He was fashionable and kind.*"

"I was twenty. I drove home from college to meet the man my mother was giddy over. I remember you telling something about your past over dinner at a restaurant one evening. After seeing the way you two were insane about each other, I wasn't worried. Besides, who wouldn't want a stepdad with a handbag fetish? After seeing the awesome bags you gave Mom, I thought you were a pretty cool guy."

Mr. P laughs.

"He always does buy the greatest bags. Even his sister will say that," Mom agrees. "I still have the one he bought in Venice. Too bad the miniature travel case with metal handles died in the accident. It was the handbag of all handbags."

"You definitely have an eye for unique designs, Mr. P."

"Not anymore," he groans. "Where can I go for unique bags in our town? The Dollar Store? The Goodwill? Walmart? Please.

"I knew I was taking a risk with proposing to my wife," he smirks at my mother, but he's talking to me. "She lived in America where there were no quaint villages, castles, or cathedrals. I wasn't at all interested in America. She was the only attraction. I knew if I married an American, someday I might end up in America."

"And here you are. Be glad you don't play the lottery," I tease.

"What?"

"Just a joke. Tell about your proposal."

"I wanted to do something romantic and memorable. I'm sure you've heard of an old movie starring Cary Grant and Deborah Kerr—*An Affair to Remember?"*

"Of course. And I like it much better than the remake with Warren Beatty and Annette Bening. I love the movie and I hate it. I've seen it twice and bawled like a baby both times."

"Exactly," agrees Mom. "We've watched it a few times over the years. The really sad thing is, in a way we live it, don't we P?"

Mom's eyes immediately pool with tears.

My mother rarely weeps, but I understand her pain as I remember the tragedy that keeps the lovers apart in the movie. It's all too familiar for comfort when you know the P's whole story.

"It's true," Mr. P reaches for his wife. "But how could I have known about the accident when I got the idea to propose at the top of the Empire State Building?"

His voice is tender.

"At least we had one fantastic year together before I was ruined."

"You weren't ruined, Mrs. P. Just look at you, running circles around me in the garden today. You are incredible."

"I'm old and I feel shattered with all of these memories and things. I dreamed our life together would be so different than it was after the accident. Thinking about how excited we were when our love story began and reading our cards and letters . . ."

My mother actually breaks down and sobs. When she stands to get a tissue, Mr. P stands, too. His shirt *becomes* the tissue as she cries into his chest.

Writing this book is this couple's sacrifice of praise to a God who died to redeem all of our lives from the pit. No sacrifice is without pain. Romans 5:3-5 says it best: ". . . *We also glory in our sufferings, because we know that suffering produces perseverance; perseverance, character; and character, hope. And hope does not put us to shame, because God's love has been poured out into our hearts through the Holy Spirit, who has been given to us."*

While I give the P's a moment to regroup, I leaf through the well-worn stationery Mom has placed on the table for me to use if I need details for this part of their story.

I pick up a small foreign-looking card with the Matterhorn in watercolor on the front. It's from Mr. P to his 'Principessa P' on their first anniversary. Dated August 18, 1992. Exactly thirty days before the morning he screamed, "Aiuto!" until he was hoarse because his capsized Renault kept his princess bride upside down and captive in her seatbelt.

To my dear wife of a year today,

I'm not what I ought to be.
I'm not what I will be.
But I'm not what I was.
Thank you for all your love and the happiest year of my life.
May He help me to be all you need from me.

With much love, Mr. P

"Your first year of marriage was the happiest year of your life?" I ask after they sit again, this time with cobalt blue glasses of pink lemonade and plenty of tissues.

"Yes." They respond in unison.

"Who had as much fun as we did that first year?" Mom adds. "We packed it in, didn't we? It was like living a movie."

"Shall I tell about the proposal?" Mr. P inquires.

"Sure."

"I waited until the last day."

"We'd gone all around New England visiting the quaintest places America has to offer," Mom adds.

"I liked Vermont the best," he remembers. "The red leaves that autumn were incredible!"

"As the days went by, we talked often about marriage. I wondered when he would propose."

"I wanted to surprise you in a really, really big way. On the way to JFK Airport I asked our driver friend to take a detour through Manhattan. For the second time in my life I took the lift to the top of the Empire State Building. Only this time I wasn't alone with demons of shame and guilt and self-loathing telling me my life wasn't worth living. I was holding hands with a woman who loved God and loved me despite all my faults and failures. Someone who understood the unmerited favor of a God who pursued me even though I told Him to go to hell.

"In the very observatory where I once wanted to end it all, I touched the face of an angel and asked in the world's most romantic language, 'Veux-tu m'épouser?'"

"She said, 'Yes.'"

*Is not this the kind of fasting I have chosen: to lose
the chains of injustice and untie the cords of the yoke,
to set the oppressed free and break every yoke?
Is it not to share your food with the hungry and to provide the
poor wanderer with shelter—when you see the naked, to clothe
them, and not to turn away from your own flesh and blood?
Then your light will break forth like the dawn, and your
healing will quickly appear; then your righteousness will go
before you, and the glory of the Lord will be your rear guard.
Then you will call, and the Lord will answer; you
will cry for help, and he will say: Here am I.*

Isaiah 58:8 NKJV

CHILLON CASTLE, LAKE GENEVA

Chapter 20

YOU WERE MY FRIEND & WE WALKED TOGETHER

People experience the life-changing force of healing relationships when something powerful comes out of one and touches something good in another.
Larry Crabb

I'm completely dominated by God's Word. And I'm not controlled by my emotions or the emotions of others.
Kynan Bridges

"I'm going to turn off the sprinkler before it gets dark and I fall down the steps."

Mr. P sets his mug on the coaster next to his chair and stands up.

"Ouch!"

"What is it?" Mom asks from the kitchen.

"My back. I hurt it planting those cypress trees."

He gingerly walks toward the door, his right hand pressed into his lower back.

"I told him seven trees was too many to plant by himself. He doesn't listen. He won't quit until the job is done," Mom frets, watching him through the window.

"While he's out there, I want to tell you something about Asger," she says joining me at the table where I'm editing my draft of last night's chapter.

"Yes?"

"There are layers in human relationships. Some have more depth because of time, spirituality, sexuality, or codependency. We can open doorways to the enemy through ignorance or a lack of boundaries. One mistake Mr. P made was allowing Asger to come over one last time before we got engaged. That situation in Vernazza should not have happened.

"He thought Asger was on the same spiritual journey he was, but that wasn't true. Mr. P wasn't acting out. Asger didn't want restoration. He wanted to play. He had a boyfriend again and had opened himself up to be used by the devil.

"Geoff and I have both made the mistake of thinking we are being Christians by letting people into our personal space. It took some time for us to figure out how to minister to people yet maintain our emotional distance. Not keeping good boundaries has caused us some problems.

"Even after we were married, there were no boundaries set against Asger. Somehow, we thought cutting him off would be cruel because his lover had burned to death in front of him. We felt sorry for him. We were kind to him. He came to our home.

"But Asger was contemptuous towards me. Once, he and a female doctor friend visited our apartment not long after P and I married. Asger made the comment, 'It does not matter that Geoff is married to you or whether you have sex or not. He *still* prefers a man to a woman.'

"I have never been so mad in my life. Asger was cruel. How he talked to me was cruel."

Mr. P opens the door. His glasses look like a windshield in a thunderstorm and his shirt is soaked.

"What happened to you?" I say before he gets into Mom's line of sight.

"I really shouldn't buy those cheap Chinese garden hoses."

He removes his glasses, searching for something dry to wipe them with. Mom hands him a napkin.

"The threads always strip, and they leak at the connection. Never mind. I'm okay."

He sinks into his chair and picks up his tea where he left off.

"What are you two talking about?"

I say, "Boundaries."

Mom says, "Asger."

Mr. P says, "Oh, dear!"

"He was out of control, wasn't he, P?"

"He was disrespectful to my wife," Mr. P responds.

"*And* to you," Mom adds. "I was telling Julie about him saying you would always prefer the anatomy of a man to the anatomy of a woman."

"*That's* a lie of the devil!" Mr. P adamantly declares. "I am not tempted by men. I haven't been for eons. But if I were, I have learned how to resist the devil's lies. Temptations toward certain kinds of sin lessen as we walk in obedience to the truth of who we are in Christ. If God's truth is 'I am heterosexual and whole,' denying who I am can kill me. However homosexual a person feels, the truth of their heterosexual DNA is deeper still.

"We are never promised exemption from temptation. If Jesus was tempted in *all* points, why can't we be tempted? The focus of the Bible is how to conduct one's life. God says a lot about how to relate to your wife, but he never says how to relate to your same-sex partner. I feel this is more convincing than all the verses *against* homosexuality.

"People make it all about sex," he goes on. "Everything these days is all about sex. Even the BBC is all about sex!"

"Sex—and stabbings in England," Mom adds. "That's all the BBC News talks about."

"Those homosexual-cure places stressed sex too much. Because really, it's much deeper than sex. It's about a relationship with Jesus. We are not called to be a happy people, but a holy people. The more we become like Jesus, the less we desire the things that turn our thoughts from Him. Jesus said, 'Deny yourself,' even though you want it. You can't have everything you think you want in life. It will destroy you. That's what happened to Asger."

"Sadly, when you destroy yourself, you try to take others down with you," I observe.

"That's what Asger was doing—trying to hurt us both. He even mailed a letter to our house saying those untrue things about me fancying men over my wife."

"A letter to both of you?" I ask.

"*Yes*," Mom affirms. "As a woman, you don't want to go through everything I went through to marry someone with Mr. P's history and have some cheeky gay guy acting like that. It really, really made me angry."

"We stopped communicating with him," Mr. P says. "I couldn't risk him trying to sabotage my marriage. We cared for his soul, but we had to protect ourselves. I learned that lesson too late, didn't I?"

He looks at his wife. She does *not* have the bird face. Some memories still trigger anger.

"I'm sorry, wife."

"I'm sorry for *you*, Peedy. You really suffered because of Asger's animosity. We must pray for people—for God to unbind their will. But we cannot allow them into our personal arenas. Healthy boundaries help limit the evil people commit against us," she reiterates.

"After the Giant was killed, maybe I should have just killed the relationship completely," Mr. P says.

"Why didn't you?" I ask, moving from the table to Mamaw's antique green chair, (the one piece of furniture in my mother's living room I hope to inherit one day). Mom moves, too. She sits in a tiny red rocking chair across from Mr. P. Now we will be able to hear one another without straining.

"Why didn't I kill the relationship?" Mr. P repeats the question. "Two reasons, I guess. Number one, I cared about his soul. I ought I could continue to influence him in a positive way."

ng pause.

"And number two?" I prompt.

"I did what my psychologist told me to do. Remember, I'd been seeing a psychologist about my codependency? The closer I got to Susan, the more I prayed about what to do regarding my friendship with Asger. After she came over on holiday the first time, I felt the relationship with Asger needed to come to some kind of end."

Mom pipes up. "Codependency is psychological demonic bondage. The nearer I came to P, the harder the devil hung on. I started fighting for Mr. P in the spiritual realm. It was pretty intense. Sometimes these psych people make things all about will power or decisions in the natural realm. They ignore the demonic forces at play."

Certain close friends advised me to drop Asger completely," Mr. P continues. "'Don't write him anymore. Just forget him,' they said.

I said to God, 'I need to know what to do. I will take it as a sign from You if I receive the same counsel from my secular psychologist and my Christian counselor. They have got to both tell me the exact same thing and I will do it.' That's what I prayed."

"Sounds like a good Gideon prayer to me," I affirm.

"They both thought it best to continue the relationship until it faded out naturally with no codependent feelings. They said if I just cut Asger off, he would remain there in my mind as something unresolved or even desirable. Can you understand that? They thought it best to play it out until it was dead.

"I agreed and believed it should get to such a point that I could invite him to our wedding without feeling *any* emotional thing about him at all, except that he would just be like any other friend who attended. That's what happened. I must have forgiven him for everything, because he *was* there, and I felt absolutely *nothing*. All I could think about was my beautiful bride.

"Ever since Vernazza I knew for certain the emotional hold with Asger was broken."

"But that didn't prevent you from being hurt when he got his last digs in," Mom says.

"No, it didn't."

"What happened?"

"You don't have this saying in America, but when people used to ask me in Italian, "How are you today?" Quite often I would say, "Sono psicologicamente disturbato." That meant, "I'm a bit psychologically disturbed." It was a joke—until it wasn't.

"Two months after Susan and I were engaged, Asger phoned me at work. Something he had never done before. He said, 'I want you to know I've had you on a string for all these years on purpose. I knew you were dependent on me and I profited from it.'

"His words really, really hurt me. I broke down, right in the nurse's station because I thought I had a close spiritual friend for all those years, but all at once I realized it was false. Our friendship was a joke. A betrayal. He kept me emotionally engaged on purpose to boost his own ego and to use me for a free place to go on holiday in Switzerland. He wasn't a real friend after all."

"When the lie is exposed," says Mom, "the devil becomes angry. Poor Mr. P."

"As I processed Asger's phone call, I kept breaking down and crying at work. I felt like I'd been made a fool of. My brain was trying to figure out what was real and what wasn't. I thought of all the hours of talking and praying together, and of the time I spent sharing meaningful spiritual thoughts and verses with him. Especially before he gave up on God's ability to keep him from falling. For him to tell me it was *all* fake just broke something in me. I ended up two weeks in the psychiatric clinic and five weeks off of work. Susan came over during that time."

"You did, Mom? I don't remember this at all."

"You were away at college. We never talked much about it. That was a very difficult season just six months before our wedding date.

"Even now I don't like to talk about it," Mr. P says. "Although I have had no romantic feelings or any feelings for Asger or any guy for decades, talking about him is a painful memory. How would you feel if a close friend who you prayed with and shared the Bible with for years told you they had you on a string the whole time? That would hurt, whether it was Walter, or Heinz, or anybody else, wouldn't it?"

"Of course," Mom agrees. "It's betrayal. It's rejection."

"It's emotional abuse," I add.

"There is a verse in Psalms where David wrote about being betrayed by his friend who walked together with him. That gave me comfort."

"I know which one you are talking about. It's Psalms 55," I recall.

Mr. P picks up his Bible from the little table next to his chair and reads, *"If an enemy were insulting me, I could endure it; if a foe were rising against me, I could hide. But it is you, a man like myself, my companion, my close friend, with whom I once enjoyed sweet fellowship at the house of God, as we walked about among the worshipers."* Psalm 55:12-14 NIV

"It isn't that I was still emotionally involved with the Giant, it is that in *my* mind I had compartmentalized all the negative red flags and I really thought he was my good friend. When the relationship played all the way to the end, Asger showed his true colors. Like both my psychologist and counselor predicted—after that, it would have been impossible to have any feelings for him anymore."

After five seconds of silence, Mr. P continues, "He must have been jealous. He didn't believe my reality. I had fought—literally screamed out to God in the Valle Verzasca. When it was done, it was done. I loved my wife. I've never looked at anyone else in a sexual way after I married my wife. We have a spiritual bond that goes over the top of everything else."

The P's lock eyes for a long moment.

"That's true, P. That's deep," Mom finally says. "Asger *was* jealous. He minimized your healing and tried to cast doubt on what God did in your life. You didn't need a friend like that."

"No. I didn't. God had already given me some of the best friends a person could ask for, but after I suffered the nervous breakdown I went into a deep darkness and ignored everyone."

"I've certainly been there," I say. "Those deep, dark seasons are silent invitations for our friends to help dig us out of the hole. It's the, 'I was sick, and you visited me,' part of what Jesus says in Matthew 25. Depression *is* a sickness. Unfortunately, I've discovered most people are afraid of me when I am in the pits. They steer clear. Did anyone show up for *you*, Mr. P?"

"Yes."

"Who?"

"Heinz."

"Oh!" exclaims Mom. "We just asked Heinz about this the other day. He sent a note on WhatsApp this morning with all the details he can remember."

Mr. P's eyes brighten. "You didn't tell me, Mrs. P."

"I didn't have a chance. Shall I read what he wrote?" Mom doesn't wait for a reply as she reaches for her phone and her glasses.

"This should be interesting," notes Mr. P.

> *Geoff did not answer the phone for weeks. Walter, Connie, and I were worried and suspected he went into depression. One day I went to see him, but he did not even answer the door. I was not sure if he was at home because he often went into the mountains alone to fight with God. After I discovered he did not even go to work anymore, I insisted on ringing and knocking until he opened the door.*
>
> *When I stepped into his apartment, I learned what it means to go into depression. The whole floor of the apartment was covered with clothes. In the kitchen cabinets there was nothin' left. Everything was in the sink to be washed. I never had to confront a situation like that and didn't know what to do. But I loved my friend, so I started washing everything. Some dishes had been there for weeks and it was*

> *hard to clean them. After I picked up the clothes, I took Geoff home to stay with us for a while.*

"I remember!" interrupts a misty-eyed Mr. P. "When I came out of the psych hospital, I stayed with Heinz and Connie for quite some time. They fed me and prayed with me. I went with Heinz each day to the 'per corso vita' and did exercises in the woods. The fresh air and friendship really helped."

"Wait! I'm not done!" Now Mom interrupts. "Let me finish reading what he said."

> *Every day we went out to walk in the woods and in the beginning, Geoff had a hard time. He would not walk a lot. But each day, he walked better and more, so he managed to walk out of depression. Often, we helped each other and prayed a lot together. He always told us we were his family and I liked that. These are some things I remember about that hard and beautiful time. From, Heinz*

"Dina and Gusti also invited you for meals, remember? They were so understanding and kind. What I've always loved about your friends (who became my friends), is they never pretended to be better than you or anyone else. You could be your authentic self and be loved. And so could I."

Mr. P's head nods in confirmation. "Through all my pain and confusion my true friends were there. I marvel at their love and patience. I used to always say I had the most wonderful friends in all the world. I've never had better ones since, nor will I until I reach the kingdom."

"I just thought of something." Mom turns toward to me. "Do you know what all the friends did for us after the accident? When my brain was so injured I had no emotions?

"What?"

"They got together," she chokes up, "and recreated our wedding reception in Walter's garden. They cooked all the exact foods and everything. To help me remember I was married. I was so damaged."

The P's are both crying now.

"Having beautiful people . . . in your life . . . is like having a treasure," Mr. P says between blows of his nose.

"That accident almost made Mr. P lose his faith," Mom says. "Again, God used these wonderful friends to minister to us.

"I don't think we've mentioned Yogi yet," she continues, "but he was another true friend. He came faithfully to the house week after week to re-study the Bible with me because with my head injury, I'd forgotten what I believed. We studied at the table and Mr. P was also able to hear God's word read aloud. Like God promises, His Word does not return unto Him void. Those scriptures helped Mr. P as much as they did me."

"I didn't know these stories, Mom. And I'd forgotten how damaged your brain was."

"I didn't know who I was. I didn't know who P was. I didn't know anything on an emotional level. You know how God says He keeps our tears in bottles in heaven? When I tried talking to Him after the accident I couldn't even speak because I was crying. My tears were liquid prayers."

"I hate what happened to my wife. And to you," Mr. P's voice trembles with empathy.

"We have suffered, haven't we, P? But we have also healed. God healed my brain and He healed yours after you came out of the psych ward. My charcoal detox didn't hurt any either," she chuckles.

"Your what?"

"Remember when I arrived you were still shaking inside from all the medication the hospital had given you? It was really too much, just like last summer when you came out of surgery. I don't know why they overmedicate people. And then they want to give you more medication because you shake. Well who wouldn't?

"Anyway, I went down to Lugano by myself and bought activated charcoal powder from the 'erbalista.' It helped to clear your system of the poison they kept poking down you. After a couple of days you weren't completely well yet, but you took me sleigh riding in ritzy St. Moritz. We talked and prayed about everything."

"I was not in good shape. I thought you had a lot of faith to want to marry me," he says.

"I wasn't worried. I think I understood you because of some of my own experiences with codependency and friendships gone sour. I had learned some points that helped me have compassion."

"Our life experiences *do* give us compassion for others, don't they?" he asks. "Compassion precedes healing. Jesus was moved with compassion then He healed people. I believe in healing on all levels."

"I know you do. You always have. That's why you clung so hard to God through all of these hard stories," Mom affirms him. "You even clung to Him for me when I couldn't do it for myself."

"Looking back," he says, "I think one of the main points I hope to get across to anyone reading this book is that my tormented mind *was* healed. For most of my life I was tormented like a nutcase. Through each experience I grew closer to God. Through His power and deliverance, that pain I always had inside went away and *never* came back. My physical torture and constant headaches are gone. My emotional torment and guilt is gone. I am assured of everlasting life because I know who Jesus is. I am renewed daily in the spirit of my mind. A person needs to know this is possible.

"I feel like my whole life can be summed up in this one verse:" He picks up his Amplified Bible. *"Psalm 118:5. 'Out of my distress I called upon the Lord and the Lord answered and set me free.'* You can put that on my tomb, Mrs. P."

"Don't leave me, P."

"I hope I don't."

"I do love you, Peedy."

"And I love *you*."

"We will stand on the sea of glass together one day," she prophesies.

"I hope it doesn't cut my feet," he teases.

"We will be there, Mr. P."

"We will make it, Mrs. P."

. . . Regarding your previous way of life, you put off your old self [completely discard your former nature], which is being corrupted through deceitful desires, and be continually renewed in the spirit of your mind [having a fresh, untarnished mental and spiritual attitude], and put on the new self [the regenerated and renewed nature], created in God's image, [godlike] in the righteousness and holiness of the truth [living in a way that expresses to God your gratitude for your salvation].

Ephesians 4:22-25 AMP

NEWLYWED MR. AND MRS. P

SANTA MARIA ASSUNTA, TORELLO

Chapter 21

NOW & THEN

The world says, "Love yourself, grab all you can and follow your heart." Jesus said, "Deny yourself, grab your cross and follow me."
Francis Chan

"People who haven't traveled haven't lived. People who grew up here, they may have been to Pittsburgh or Disney or somewhere. But really . . . many people have no idea about the world because they haven't had a chance to explore it."

The P's are chatting in bed, like they do every night. They've each given me handwritten versions of their wedding story from long-ago journals. I'm propped with my laptop in the room across the hall, deciphering and combining their notes for this final chapter. Both doors are open between us.

"Then I guess I've *really* lived," Mrs. P responds, "because, thanks to you, I've certainly traveled."

"You've even traveled without me."

"That's true."

"Something I really admire about you . . ."

"Yes?"

". . . is how you took your settlement money from the accident to build that church in Romania. That was incredible!"

"I'm so happy the church is now an orphan school and safe haven for abused and trafficked children. Helping others helped *me* heal. It gave me a renewed sense of purpose, despite my broken brain."

"I will always remember when one of our nurses at work asked, 'What has your wife been doing this week in Romania?'

"'Well,' I said, 'She bought a man some false teeth, paid for someone a divorce, and got a prostitute a baby carriage. Oh, and she bought a cow. All on the Visa card.'"

The P's laughter fills the whole upstairs.

"This is the wife God has given me," he says. "Of course my colleague didn't know what to say. But it was all true. Apart from the Visa card."

"I wish I *could* have used the Visa card. What risks I took carrying all that cash across the borders. We wouldn't be able to do that now."

"That's true," he says. "We can't do *anything* now with this coronavirus spiking again. Did you know the EU may bar Americans from travel when they open for tourism in July? I just read that today. I'm glad we did our work when we had the chance. I love how God used my travel addiction to do mission things. And how He gave me a wife with the same spirit of adventure and compassion."

"Me, too, P. It kept us young for a long time. Remember when we helped after the earthquake in L'Aquilla? You and me in our official yellow caps, serving food to those poor dazed Italian ladies."

"That earthquake thing drew out more compassion in me than any other ministry in my life. My heart broke."

"Mine, too."

"You know one of my favorite verses is, '*When He saw the crowds, He had compassion on them, because they were like a sheep without a shepherd.*' I want to have the same compassion as Jesus. Of all my bad traits and good traits, I praise God for giving me compassion. It really touched me when I retired from the Ospedale Civico, and the head surgeon wrote on my report, '*Geoff's best trait is compassion.*'"

"I know this firsthand, as your wife. I don't know where I would be if you hadn't been so compassionate through my years of suffering after the accident."

"My compassion certainly did not come about in theological college, but through accepting the compassion of Jesus for *me.* '*While I was yet a sinner Christ died for me.*'"

"People talk about the Gospel, P. But you have *experienced* the gospel. Your life shows how it plays out. That girl across the hall has written it all down."

"I can hear you," I say.

"Hear this," Mr. P responds. "The *only* way to break sin and addiction is to believe and fight with faith that Jesus loves you and accepts you even while you're still sinning. When you feel guilty, you are under law and law will stimulate you to sin. That's Romans 7:5. Write this down."

"Okay."

"And this," he adds. "Two favorite texts which helped me were, '*There is therefore now no condemnation to those who are in Christ Jesus, who walk after the spirit not after the flesh.*' If a person can just believe that truth and come out from under the weight of condemnation . . ."

He is silent for so long I wonder if he's fallen asleep.

"What's the other favorite text?"

"Oh, and John 17:23, the most incredible verse in the Bible. '*God loves you and me just as much as He loves Jesus.*' Can you let them know this truth?"

"Yes."

To Mrs. P he says, "If people could just realize how much they are loved, I think they would not be so selfish and always thinking about porn or finding a sexual partner. They might even go out and do something for Christ."

"You're probably right. That's what kept us going through all the years. We even handed out papers on our honeymoon, remember?"

"You handed out papers on your honeymoon?" I shout into their bedroom.

"Yes!" they chorus.

"That's crazy, P's. One would think you would be doing other stuff on your honeymoon."

"Oh, we did plenty of other stuff," Mom laughs.

"The first time we made love was on our way to Monte Carlo," Mr. P stage whispers to Mom. "That sounds posh."

"Wasn't it in Monaco? That's posh, too."

"It's the same place!" he laughs.

"I remember waiting until the next day because we were too exhausted after fourteen hours of wedding and reception."

"Well, I'd waited fifty years to make love to a woman. What was one more day?"

They twitter like teenagers.

"I was a bit nervous," he admits. "Maybe more than a bit."

"I asked you if your friends had explained anything to you," Mom laughs. "I guess they didn't need to, did they?"

"They gave me a book, *Becoming a Friend and Lover,* " he chortles. "I read it cover to cover."

"What *I* remember didn't seem like book knowledge," she muses. "Our entire trip was a dream. Walking by the sea in Menton, swimming under the bougainvillea in Villefranche, window shopping in Capri . . . But the *best* sex of our honeymoon was on the island of Procida, don't you agree?"

I'm straining to hear the P's pillow talk because I know this is what we *all* want to know after wading through this entire saga. The begging question you never want to ask your parents, *"How was the sex?"*

I hear Mr. P's voice. Something about, ". . . a lot to learn and a lot of growth." Then, "It was strange and beautiful to make love with someone and not to feel guilty about it. A terror used to fill my heart when, years ago I read I Corinthians 6:9, where it says,

'Do you not know that homosexual offenders will not enter the kingdom of heaven?'"

"There are a lot of other sins listed in that same verse," Mom reminds him. "People always forget about the greedy, drunks, and cheaters, but they drive the homosexuals straight to hell."

"It's true," he agrees. "I only noticed the one word I knew was me. I praise the Lord for His wonderful grace and compassion that now I can say verse eleven, '. . . *and that is what some of you were. But you were washed, you were sanctified, you were justified in the name of our Lord Jesus Christ and by the Spirit of our God.'* According to the blood of the Lamb, it's as if none of my past ever existed.

"I was thinking about something else," he continues.

"What?"

"I was absolutely miserable in my sin. I was never going to be one of those people happily marching in the Gay Pride parades or anything. But we know some gay people who have been together for longer than we have, and they love each other and appear to be very happy. I wonder what they would think of my book, if they read it."

"Well, your story is *your* story," Mom says. "Everyone's experience is different."

"I guess what gives me the most peace is I'm absolutely sure of eternal life because Christ *is* my life. That's somewhere in Colossians, chapter 3. And that's all I could hope for anyone to be able to say with certainty."

At this moment the neighbor next door decides to play AC/DC at top volume and I'm really straining to get what the P's are saying. I hear Mom's voice now.

". . . maturity is to have the capacity to please God and bless God. That's what it means to really love God. Do we love Him enough to allow Jesus to keep God's commandments through us?"

"My wife is such a theologian," he teases. "That is what attracted me to you from the beginning, your knowledge of the Bible and your love for Jesus. Thank you for becoming Mrs. P. On our wedding day I loved you more than I have ever loved anyone."

"I hope that's still the case," Mom teases.

"Of course it is!" he says in a voice loud enough I don't have to strain.

"You've put up with a lot," Mom says.

"And so have you."

AC/DC is gone. Someone must have complained. Now I can hear *every* word.

"Some of my friends and clients in America were terrified for me to marry you. They said, "Don't marry someone at his age who has never been married before! And they didn't even *know* the whole story," she giggles and continues. "My father was also concerned. He knew a bit of your story. I'll never forget *his* philosophy."

"Oh, dear. What did he say?"

"He said, 'If a person is going to sin, they need to sin *normal* sin.'"

"What does *that* mean?"

"It means he thought your sin was worse than his sin and I probably should marry someone with a history of 'normal' sin."

"How ridiculous!" Mr. P exclaims.

"He *was* ridiculous. Sin is sin. Christ's blood covers it all. Not just the 'normal' kind."

"I think I've done alright as a husband for the past twenty-nine years," Mr. P says.

"Except for not putting your towel in the wash."

"And cutting my toenails," he laughs.

"Yes. And the toenails."

"Maybe I should pray about that."

"What?"

"The towel and the toenails. "If God can answer one prayer, He can answer two or three, don't you agree?"

Their muffled laughter mingles with the squeak of bedsprings as they turn and settle in.

"Goodnight, P," she says.

"Goodnight, Principessa."

I should have written "spoiler alert" before their bedtime chatter. But, since they already revealed honeymoon details, I'm sure they won't mind if I include this piece I just found in Mom's handwriting:

> *. . . The next place, a remote volcanic island called Procida is a dream. Through the gate of our Italian Villa, we walked beneath a giant vine-covered archway extending the full length of the property to the clear blue sea. On each side were trees loaded with juicy yellow lemons. Various flowering plants lined the pathway. The air and the fragrances were invigorating. One corner of the garden holds a huge cage filled with nearly 300 singing birds. We sat on a long, smooth marble bench to soak in all that beauty.*
>
> *Rose petals were strewn along the entry to our hotel room. My husband didn't leave out any details in planning this surprise honeymoon. A tall statue stood on each side of the wide double doors to our room. There were several statues along the walkway. One in particular caught my attention, as it was of Moses holding the Ten Commandments. I felt pleased we had honored God's plan to wait.*
>
> *Upon entering our room, we were astounded by the eighteen-foot ceiling. Later, as my husband loved me, I noticed the mural on our ceiling was of angels holding hand-painted passion flowers gathered together with huge blue bows, holding each cluster. One of my favorite memories happened on this island. Amazing!*

I'm smiling and feeling false guilt as I read my mother's diary from nearly thirty years ago. I have permission, but it still feels strange. She must have written all this on their honeymoon. The details are fresh, but the penciled words have faded.

I think it's fitting to close this book with Mr. and Mrs. P's fairytale wedding memories, snippets from journals written in their very own words. His first:

> *I stood with my friend Walter under the stone archway of a 1200-year-old church. Waiting. Experiencing emotions I had never in my life felt before. There I was, fifty years old, surrounded by friends who had been like father and mother to me for years—earthly friends who had also been like Jesus, my best and most faithful Friend ever.*
>
> *How can I describe all the emotions I felt as Heinz's car arrived with my bride? Out she stepped, "la mia gioia"—with her smiling face and blonde hair glistening in the sunlight. My princess! My angel! So lovely. So refined, above all others. She had not yet seen the perfect place God and I chose for our wedding. I wanted it to be the ultimate surprise!*

And now we sneak a peak inside Principessa's heart on her wedding day:

> *While packing a few extra things for the honeymoon, I thought about how all this romance began. We had, many years before, met at a Christian seminar. I remember I had on a red hat and my groom-to-be really liked my hat. He greeted me for the first time by kissing me right on the mouth! Well then, that was special . . . and he was interesting. I asked a lot of questions about Switzerland that day. Now I have had a fairytale wedding in Switzerland!*
>
> *Standing together in the perfectly ancient church was beyond a dream. Absolutely everything surrounding the moment was made of dreams that little girls think up or see in movies. I was the American bride and had never been in this area of Ticino, Switzerland or seen the stone fairytale-looking church before.*

The ride up the mountains was exhilarating! The driver, Heinz, was one of my groom's dear friends. We sang the most appropriate song while driving in the Swiss Alps: 'Going to the Chapel of Love.' Singing kept my nerves calm. We didn't miss a beat while I watched the ever-changing scenery. The deep azure blue sky covered us with its glory as we climbed higher and higher, my excitement mounting with every turn through ancient villages, past old-world churches and through green meadows lined with stone walls and perfectly placed chestnut trees.

As we passed the last village church and entered a very rough and rocky lane, I cried out, "Where on earth are we going?" Light could barely pass through the dense forest. The long limbs of trees were ragged arms reaching out to us. Gnarled tree roots reached over the road connecting to the other side. It was the roots that caused Heinz' gorgeous red Mercedes to rock side to side, jostling us up and down. This was a remote place like I'd never seen in my life.

At long last, we came to a clearing with a natural-colored wood fence surrounding a lovely green meadow. Golden light brightly danced through the grass as the soft breeze blew through its ever-moving blades. A white horse grazed at the far edge of the meadow. I wondered to myself, 'Should I mount the horse and ride up to the church door? After all, isn't this is the perfect setting for a princess bride?'

Below the meadow was Lake Lugano, surrounded by lush green forests full of chestnut trees. I took a deep breath as I stepped out of the car, looking up at the brave old bell tower perched atop the church where I would say, "I do." I straightened my icy blue satin dress with its lovely beaded white lace bodice. When I purchased it in an American boutique, I had no idea how perfect it would be for the weather, culture, and mysterious setting of my wedding day. I took Heinz's arm and started our walk along the side of the church toward the arched door where my 'Il bello' groom was waiting.

My white satin shoes got a workout as I walked over the rough, stony path. I was laughing and tripping my way along, at times looking up at the ancient edifice. Really, I couldn't believe my eyes. I was lightheaded and almost intoxicated with the romantic beauty of it all.

Geoff really outdid himself finding this place! The arched entryway was decorated in fresco. I noticed a huge bouquet of various flowers in shades of blue with lots of white baby's breath gently draping in different directions from the typical Italian terra-cotta vase. For my bouquet, together we chose flowers on the market, flowers special to us—blue hydrangeas and red roses, arranged by his favorite Spanish 'fioraia.' Simple, but lovely.

My groom and I wore the joy of God-given love on our faces. Our eyes met as we entered the softly candlelit church, full of foreign guests and family, both American and British, including my two daughters, Geoff's mum, sister, brother-in-law, and two nephews. Our guestbook holds names of friends from Germany, Italy, Finland, England, Sweden, the French part of Switzerland, and America.

Our wedding music even drew a few tourists, who happened to be out walking the trails. Some actually came inside to watch our ceremony.

Geoffrey Pennock looked tall and very suave standing in the front of the church, as if he belonged there. In our photos, the American bride and her two daughters appear a bit overwhelmed. I felt I was in the middle of a dream! I was—the groom's lifelong dream. For how many years did he pray this day would arrive?

Seated on antique chairs decorated with traditional ribbons and flowers, we were serenaded by our dearest friends. As we lit our unity candle in its antique holder, the light reflected on our faces and our joy spilled over into every dark corner of the room. We said our vows then we kissed a forever kiss. The pastor kept saying, "Geoff! Geoff . . . Geoff!" But my groom did not hear. It was his day, and the kiss would end when he was ready. Wow! As the bride, my knees were going weak with so much excitement in a foreign land! With tears in our eyes and hope in our hearts, we each took a microphone and sang our special song, 'Father Make Us One.' Our adventure had begun.

I close my mother's marbled Venetian paper journal and pick up Mr. P's. Toward the end, neatly penned in blue ink are his final reflections on their beautiful day.

This was my moment, the result of so many tears, so much prayer and searching—sometimes in the wrong direction and wrong places. I was truly my authentic self. God had finally answered my "I will not let you go unless you bless me" prayer.

The mountains, lake, sunshine, church and beautiful Susanna, my "Principessa P!" Everything was all I had ever dreamed of for my wedding day! It was a day filled with the blessing of all blessings, a piece of heaven! I experienced a glimpse of the way Jesus will feel about all of us on the day we meet our Bridegroom face to face.

Let us rejoice and shout for joy! Let us give Him glory and honor, for the marriage of the Lamb has come [at last] and His bride (the redeemed) has prepared herself.

Revelation 19:7 AMP

Behold, He is coming with the clouds, and every eye will see Him...

Revelation 1:7 AMP

I waited patiently and expectantly for the Lord; And He inclined to me and heard my cry. He brought me up out of a horrible pit [of tumult and of destruction], out of the miry clay, And He set my feet upon a rock, steadying my footsteps and establishing my path. He put a new song in my mouth, a song of praise to our God; Many will see and fear [with great reverence] And will trust confidently in the Lord.

Psalm 40:1-3 AMP

RESOURCES

Beyond Boundaries, Henry Cloud
Andrew Murray on Prayer, Andrew Murray
Embracing the Journey, Greg and Lynn McDonald
Healing Miracles for Your Family, Art Thomas
Humility: The Path to Holiness, Andrew Murray
Kingdom Authority, Kynan Bridges
Letters to the Church, Francis Chan
Paid in Full, Art Thomas, James Loruss, & Jonathan Ammon
Predators: Pedophiles, Rapists, & Other Sex Offenders, Anna Salter
Radical, David Platt
Safe People, Dr. Henry Cloud & Dr. John Townsend
The Autobiography of George Muller, George Muller
The Papa Prayer, Larry Crabb
The Relentless Tenderness of Jesus, Brennan Manning
The Search for Significance, Robert S. McGee
The Wounded Heart, Dan B. Allender
There's Dynamite in Praise, Don Gossett
Total Forgiveness, R.T. Kendall

JULIET VAN HEERDEN

Juliet Van Heerden was blessed by God in writing the book you are holding in your hand. It testifies to the reality of the power of the Gospel of Christ to transform a life regardless of challenging circumstances.

As I Walked clearly conveys the idea that God is real, for what is impossible to finite human beings is possible to our infinite Heavenly Father. This work is easy to read and practical as it shows to everyone the love of Christ with all His sympathy, empathy, and compassion.

Juliet, in her authentic and personal style, tells a story that touches the heart and stimulates the mind as it identifies with struggling people in order to allow Christ to bring about their transformation.

Dr. Philip G. Samaan
Former Missionary, Editor, Professor of Theology,
Public Speaker, and Author of a dozen books on Christ

JULIET VAN HEERDEN is an author, educator, and itinerant speaker. She holds a Master of Science in Literacy Education and joyfully shares inspirational stories of hope through the written and spoken word. She published her first book, *Same Dress, Different Day,* in 2015. For more information about her ministry, please visit julietvanheerden.com.